T0374561

DIGITIZE AND PUNISH

DIGITIZE AND PUNISH

RACIAL CRIMINALIZATION
IN THE DIGITAL AGE

BRIAN JEFFERSON

UNIVERSITY OF MINNESOTA PRESS
Minneapolis
London

Every effort was made to obtain permission to reproduce material in this book. If any proper acknowledgment has not been included here, we encourage copyright holders to notify the publisher.

Copyright 2020 by the Regents of the University of Minnesota

All rights reserved. No part of this publication may be reproduced, stored in a retrieval system, or transmitted, in any form or by any means, electronic, mechanical, photocopying, recording, or otherwise, without the prior written permission of the publisher.

Published by the University of Minnesota Press
111 Third Avenue South, Suite 290
Minneapolis, MN 55401-2520
http://www.upress.umn.edu

ISBN 978-1-5179-0922-2 (hc)
ISBN 978-1-5179-0923-9 (pb)

A Cataloging-in-Publication record for this book is available from the Library of Congress.

The University of Minnesota is an equal-opportunity educator and employer.

For my mother and Brandie

The obscurantist language that veils or normalizes oppressive policies is called into question.

—JOY JAMES, *Erasing the Spectacle of Racialized State Violence*

You must always remember that the sociology, the history, the economics, the graphs, the charts, the regressions all land, with great violence, upon the body.

—TA-NEHISI COATES, *Between the World and Me*

CONTENTS

ABBREVIATIONS

ACLU	American Civil Liberties Union
AFDC	American Families with Dependent Children
AFIS	Automated Fingerprint Identification System
AIRA	Automated Incidence Reporting Application
ARPA	Advanced Research Projects Agency
AT&T	American Telephone and Telegraph Company
AWS	Amazon Web Services
BPP	Black Panther Party
CAD	computer-aided dispatch
CAPS	community alternative policing strategy
CCCJ	California Council of Criminal Justice
CCH	computerized crime history
CCTV	closed-circuit television
CDO	chief data officer
CDCR	California Department of Corrections and Rehabilitation
CGT	crime geographic targeting
CHRI	criminal history records information
CHRIS	Criminal History Records Information System
CIMIS	Correctional Institution Management Information System
CIO	chief information officer
CJA	Criminal Justice Agency
CJIS	Criminal Justice Information Services
CLEAR	Citizen and Law Enforcement Analysis and Reporting
CMRC	Crime Mapping Research Center
COINTELPRO	Counterintelligence Program
CORE	Conference on Racial Equality
COTAS	Correctional Operations Trend Analysis System
CPD	Chicago Police Department
CPIC	Crime Prevention Information Center
CPOP	Community Patrol Officer Program
CTA	Chicago Transit Authority
CTO	chief technology officer
CuPR	Communities united for Police Reform

DART	Data Analytics Recidivism Tool
DAS	Domain Awareness System
DHS	Department of Homeland Security
DOC	Deployment Operations Center
DOJ	Department of Justice
ESRI	Environmental Systems Research Institute
FBI	Federal Bureau of Investigations
GIS	Geographic Information System
GJXDM	Global Justice XML Data Model
GPS	Global Positioning System
HTTP	Hypertext Transfer Protocol
IACP	International Association of Chiefs of Police
IBM	International Business Machines
ICAD	Integrated Computer-Aided Detection System
ICAM	Information Collection for Automated Mapping
ICE	Immigration and Customs Enforcement
I-CLEAR	Illinois Citizen and Law Enforcement Analysis and Reporting
ICT	information communication technology
IDOC	Illinois Department of Corrections
IoT	Internet of Things
IP	Internet Protocol
ISP	Illinois State Police
IT	information technology
ITB	Information Technology Bureau
LAPD	Los Angeles Police Department
LASER	Los Angeles Strategic Extraction and Restoration
LEAA	Law Enforcement Assistance Administration
LEMAS	Law Enforcement Management and Administrative Statistics
LEO	Law Enforcement Online
LTE	long-term evolution
MAPADS	Microcomputer-Assisted Police Analysis and Deployment System
MAPS	Mapping and Analysis for Public Safety
MHD	Manhattan House of Detention
MISD	Management Information Systems Division
MTA	Mass Transit Authority
MXG	Malcolm X Grassroots Movement
NCHIP	National Criminal History Improvement Program
NCIC	National Crime Information Center
NCVS	National Crime Victimization Survey
NICS	National Instant Criminal Background Check System
NIEM	National Information Exchange Model

NIJ	National Institute of Justice
NIST	National Institute of Standards and Technology
NPSBN	Nationwide Public Safety Broadband Network
NYCDOP	New York City Department of Probation
NYCHA	New York City Housing Authority
NYCLU	New York Civil Liberties Union
NYPD	New York City Police Department
OIT	Office of Information Technology
OLEA	Office of Law Enforcement Assistance
PACER	Public Access to Court Electronic Records
PIM	Pattern Identification Module
PIMS	Police Information Management System
PPO	parole/probation officer
PROMIS	Prosecutor Management Information System
RTTC	Real-Time Crime Center
SCADA	Supervisory Control and Data Acquisition
SEARCH	System for Electronic Analysis and Retrieval of Criminal Histories
SNCC	Student Non-Violent Coordinating Committee
SPRINT	Special Police Radio Inquiry Network
SQL	Structured Query Language
SSL	Strategic Subjects List
STAC	spatial and temporal analysis of crime
TCP	Transmission Control Protocol
UCR	Uniform Crime Reporting

INTRODUCTION
NextGen Nightmare

Digital databases, not detention centers, jails, or prisons, are becoming the leading edge of criminal justice in the United States. While more than 2 million people are incarcerated and more than 5 million are under some form of correctional supervision, the Bureau of Justice Statistics estimates that 100,596,300 names are stored in criminal history databases.[1] In some cities, 80 percent of the black male population is registered in these databases.[2] Whereas the Chicago Police Department is beset with "literally hundreds of millions of rows of data," the New York Police Department has access to more than 33 billion public records.[3] The National Crime Information Center in West Virginia processes data on almost 13 million transactions per day.[4] This book traces the history of these data and the machines that produce, analyze, and circulate them.

With the advent of big data, database systems have slowly emerged as logistical tools for constantly patrolling criminalized urban populations. An incomprehensibly extensive field of state-managed databases stores information on at-risk youth, "black identity extremists," crime hot spots, gang suspects, illegal "aliens," potential crime hot spots, potential criminal offenders, inmates, parolees, probationers, quality-of-life offenders, sexual deviants, and terror suspects. The information technology (IT) sector has played no small part in this development. The International Data Corporation claims that it can cut crime by 20 percent through citywide data infrastructures. Security technology firms such as Palantir have employed "civil liberties engineers" to ensure that their software will shield public agencies from civil litigation. Opportunistic law enforcement officials, research institutes, and scholars have espoused the miraculous abilities of data-driven crime control. A division in the Los Angeles Police Department once credited its predictive crime analytics initiative with a zero-crime day. Public–private organizations like the World Economic Forum estimated that digital crime pattern mapping, gunshot detection, and video analytics could reduce the incidence of crime by 40 percent. At the same time, they argued, the technologies could increase quality-of-life indicators by anywhere from 10 to 30 percent. Cutting-edge technology looks to have a bright future in criminal justice; in fact, futuristics is now taught at law enforcement academies.

But this future is actually old. Much of the criminal justice system's digital repertoire was first envisioned by technocrats and tech corporations in the late 1960s, during the onset of Lyndon Johnson's War on Crime (see chapter 1). Many of the core technologies were initially rolled out in the late 1980s, in the thick of the War on Drugs. Such was a time when the state's solution to social problems in the so-called inner city was communicated in brutally simple terms: round up and manage problematic populations with state-authorized violence. The subsequent explosion of digital criminal justice technology was therefore not merely the product of technical advancements in computing. If cities were not already committed to criminalizing and quarantining economically devalued populations, they would not dedicate obscene amounts of resources to building digitized architectures of policing and punishment.[5]

Digitize and Punish traces the late twentieth and early twenty-first-century rise of digital computing technology in criminal justice through four core arguments. The first and central argument is that digital technology and its related sciences have helped extend the Wars on Crime and Drugs. The book shows how correctional supervision, detainment, and racial profiling quietly expanded through database systems, mobile devices, and wireless networks. It also shows how authorities have appealed to data science to justify the continuation of crime and drug war policies. The second argument is that IT corporations have become primary drivers of criminal justice digitization. The book emphasizes that this understudied fraction of capital, *information capital*, has turned criminal justice technoscience into a thriving industry.[6] The eruption of criminal justice technology is not the result of the IT sector operating in a vacuum but rather the contingent outcome of information capital working in concert and sometimes at odds with state officials, university researchers, and civic organizations. The third argument is that the convergence of mass criminalization and smart cities is transforming geographies of carceral power. The book contends that smart city infrastructure, which is made up of cellular towers, cooling equipment, environmental sensors, fiber-optic cables, local area networks, mobile devices, server rooms, and smart cameras, is designed such that it allows cities to administer entire communities in ways that increasingly resemble correctional supervision. But this does not constitute a totalizing and inescapable reality for criminalized populations. It is, rather, a tendency in carceral management that warrants systematic attention. Finally, the book insists that a thorough critique of racialized governance must confront its sociotechnical dimension. On one hand, it places heavy emphasis on how the digitization of criminal justice reproduces social conditions where subjugation is rendered banal, fences and bars are made invisible, and racialized surveillance and punishment have found their way into our personal electronic devices. On the other hand, the book also draws attention to how contradictions immanent to the digitized carceral state open up new horizons for abolitionist revolt.

RACIAL CAPITALISM MEETS INFORMATION CAPITALISM

The architects of today's digitized infrastructures of criminalization and carceral management did not arrive in the dystopian form of *Neuromancer*'s Tessier-Ashpool or *Blade Runner*'s Tyrell Corporation.[7] Instead, they came in the guise of public relations–friendly companies like International Business Machines (IBM) and Motorola Solutions and little known ones like Tyler Technologies and Fulcrum Biometrics. At the start of the millennium, Oracle Corporation supplied nearly three-quarters of the federal government's database management systems. Shortly thereafter, Microsoft Corporation began to collaborate with cities to design and sell software for computer-operated surveillance, the profits of which it split with city governments. In addition to becoming fertile growth sectors for the IT industry, the prototyping of criminal justice technology has been largely subsidized by tax dollars. IT firms have siphoned billions in public grants through the Community Oriented Policing Services Office and the Office of Justice Programs to research and design products for the Wars on Crime and Drugs. In addition, public policy actively fuels the mass production of criminal justice technology. Taser International's revenue grew nearly 75 percent less than a fiscal quarter following the launch of the Body-Worn Camera Policy and Implementation Program.[8] More recently, the Department of Homeland Security's Science and Technology Directorate unveiled its Silicon Valley Innovation Program, which has funneled millions of dollars to dozens of small tech companies. Professional associations of tech executives have awarded criminal justice agencies with millions of dollars through competitions such as the International Data Group's Grand CIO Enterprise Value Award and the International Association of Chiefs of Police/Motorola Webber Seavey Award in Law Enforcement. Moreover, an ever-expanding circuit of criminal justice technology conventions reinforce the connective tissue that binds the IT sector to mass criminalization.

While IT and social management are focal points of this study, prominent studies on power in the digital age offer only so much to the project.[9] In these works, the negatively racialized poor are discussed in passing with reference to the "informational black holes" populated by "homeless, incarcerated, prostituted, criminalized, brutalized, stigmatized, sick, and illiterate persons" in the Global South and marginalized sectors of Global North cities. Preeminent sociologists maintain that these excluded areas are cut adrift from circuitries of information processing and hence are external to information economies.[10] But this couldn't be further from the truth in the impoverished sectors of U.S. cities. On the contrary, these areas find themselves increasingly immersed in networked infrastructures made up of audio sensors, datacenters, drones, electronic ankle monitors, geographic information systems, mobile digital terminals, server rooms, and smart surveillance cameras. They are constantly assessed through actuarial risk instruments, appraised through predictive analytics, digitally mapped and modeled, and monitored by smart cameras. And so long as the profit of technology corporations drives the proliferation of such technologies, criminalized populations present lucrative opportunities for IT capitalization.

A growing number of public critics offer a wealth of descriptive analysis on recent forms of computerized racism.[11] These commentators show how discriminatory designs, human fallibility, and methodological inadequacies in criminal justice software effectuate racial inequalities. But while they illuminate negative effects of digitized racism, we are only beginning to grasp its positive functions in the wider social field. Criminal justice technoscience is a productive source for all manner of knowledge, privileges, strategies, subjectivities, tactics, technical innovations, and, not to be overlooked, profits. The lens of racial capitalism helps discern how interactions between racial subordination, technological advancement, and capital have come to constitute such a generative combination. This framework harkens back at least to the work of W. E. B. Du Bois, who showed the extraordinarily productive role of racialization in early phases of industrial capitalism.[12] Du Bois discovered how the production of nonwhiteness reinforced rationales for the abduction and hyperexploitation of Africans and their descendants. He also uncovered how wealthy European Americans produced notions of whiteness to lure poor European Americans into blaming the calamities of capitalism on nonwhites. It was also Du Bois who revealed the lethal combinations of agricultural capitalism, industrial capitalism, and racial criminalization. Cedric Robinson demonstrated how racial differentiation played a constitutive role in constructing European capitalism.[13] Robinson provided a vivid account of how mercantilist capitalists exploited entrenched racial, tribal, linguistic, and regional antagonisms to peg certain groups as cheap labor sources. These thinkers, along with a host of contemporary theorists of racial capitalism, provide a solid foundation to understand how information capitalists exploit the racialized antagonisms that define our new millennium.[14]

By revisiting the history of mass criminalization from the standpoints of the IT companies, computer scientists, and technocrats, *Digitize and Punish* seeks to problematize some of the more prominent theories of social control in the digital age.[15] The book contradicts Baudrillard's theory of a simulated society where social reality is fully subordinated to or even replaced by code. It also problematizes Deleuze's theory of a computerized control society where disciplinary enclosures (cubicles, factories, prisons) and modernity's old social categories have lost their utility. This book is not about a new society of control; rather, it is about an ongoing form of racialized social management that is slowly mutating through digital technology. It is about how the carceral state uses technology in ways that do not supplant sovereign violence, discipline, or long-standing social differences but rather synthesizes them with the affordances of modern technology. It emphasizes how criminalization in the age of digital computation does not signify a new cultural logic so much as it performs an upgrade of entrenched modes of social differentiation and dominance. Modernity's racial taxonomies are not vanishing through computerization; they have just been imported into data arrays. The digitization of criminal records allows authorities to essentialize individuals using well-worn ethnoracial categories. For example, the Association of State Correctional Administrators, Corrections Program Office, and Bureau of Justice Statistics have each stressed the importance of including demographic categories like race, Hispanic origin, religious affiliation, citizenship, and country of birth into offender database systems.[16] Some criminal justice risk assessment software codes attributes like race, country of origin, and English proficiency as casual variables of criminal behavior (see chapter 2). In such instances, racial identities are not anachronisms but logic elements.

This book aims to disrupt the view that digitized social power signifies the decline of enclosures and sovereign violence. While electronic ankle bracelets might seem to represent the networked dispersion of the carceral apparatus, the bracelets are used to establish house arrest—most often in public housing. What appears dispersed at the level of individuals turns out to be clustered at the level of social groups. To compound things, the combination of criminal justice databases and the internet has made the stigma of criminal records indelible and virtually impossible to conceal. This establishes a punitive force field around formerly convicted subjects that restricts their access to capital, education, employment, housing, and welfare. In such instances, computer code is enrolled by authorities to continue the work of the Black Codes.[17] Such power therefore can be understood not as the biopolitical control of dividuals but as the necropolitical management of social groups.

RACIAL STATE 2.0

While the eruption of digital technologies in the state has captivated social theorists of all types, its implications for the racial state are seldom scrutinized. This gap is significant, as the state plays a central role in classifying populations and articulating relations between them.[18] One of the key functions of the modern nation-state is assigning racial classifications to groups of people in census tabulations, cartographies, and now database systems. In the United States, racial classifications have been used by courts, law enforcement, public officials, and military personnel to justify enslaving Africans and their descendants, confiscating indigenous territories, barring Chinese immigrants, interning Japanese citizens, incarcerating poor black and latinx peoples, and banning Muslims.[19] Criminal justice agencies have been key actors in many of these projects. Contradictions between liberal democratic norms and state violence are rationalized by authorities and throughout the public sphere through stereotypes about nonwhite criminality.[20] A core task of the present study is to shed light on how this indispensable part of the racial state, the criminal justice system, has adapted to the digital revolution.

The state—whether at the national, regional, or urban scale—is a site of constant conflict.[21] Political theorists have shown that the state is best described as a network of *apparatuses*—census apparatuses, city planning apparatuses, criminal justice apparatuses, homeland security apparatuses, military apparatuses, public housing apparatuses, social security apparatuses—each of which possesses capacities to "capture, orient, determine, intercept, model, control living beings."[22] To effectively institute policies, these apparatuses need knowledge—demographic knowledge, economic knowledge, spatial knowledge, and so on. While economists, criminologists, political scientists, sociologists, and technical experts have traditionally provided such knowledge, it is increasingly supplied by computer systems. Part of this book tells the story of how state officials mobilized computer science to produce tactical knowledge for crime and drug war efforts. It shows how the knowledge produced in this process is a priori political, as its purpose is to assist the implementation of specific policies.[23] It also shows how academics and technocrats who justify crime and drug war policies through computer models are the latest generation of intellectuals to sanctify exclusionary state violence in the scientific vogue of the day.

Police command a great deal of attention in this book. Most influential works on mass criminalization in the United States rightfully focus on the colossal expansion of imprisonment. But the police are a central, if not understudied, part of this story, as they are the first point of contact between criminalized subjects and the carceral state. Moreover, the police have always been ahead of courts and corrections with respect to integrating technological innovation and collaborating with technology industries. Relations between police departments and IT capitalists have deepened considerably over the past three decades, which has created lucrative opportunities for the IT sector. To be sure, the constitutive role that police play in capital accumulation is well known. Marx saw policing as one extra-economic tactic among others used by capitalists to "protect their acquisitions" and emphasized how classical economists promoted the economic benefits conferred by the modern police department. In a similar vein, Michel Foucault and Mark Neocleous drew attention to how the *Polizeistaat* and its *Polizeiwissenschaft* were central to forging the conditions necessary for a free market society. Police administered the consumption, health, festivities, funerals, public infrastructure, and weddings of the propertyless populations in efforts to maintain healthy labor pools.[24] During the rise of the market society, statistical data, which were invented by states to manage populations, became valuable resources for police.[25]

The aforementioned analyses only scratch the surface of the police function in capital accumulation. When set upon negatively racialized populations, police are not necessarily programmed to administer welfare, mold subjects into docile balls of clay, or establish productive workforces. In the United States, the police represent an alien force that helps impose alien property regimes.[26] In the United States, police are quite simply a military apparatus for whom the Posse Comitatus Act (1878) never applied.[27] In United States–Mexico border zones, policing often involves blocking the entrance of racially stigmatized labor migrants or deliberately funneling them into lethal deserts. In U.S. cities, the focus of this book, police owe more to eighteenth-century slave patrols than to the Duchy of Burgundy, because logics inherited from slave plantations resonate in contemporary approaches to managing black populations.[28] The present study chronicles how these logics are encoded in digital police mapping, crime forecasting, and surveillance.

The study also provides a history of cities' efforts to replace human decision makers in the criminal justice system with computer algorithms. Algorithms developed for criminal justice agencies are not merely sets of rules in software, nor are they simply mathematical objects. They are, in sociologist Francesca Musiani's words, artifacts of governance designed to achieve specific objectives.[29] It is thus important to avoid searching for the racist dimension of the state's algorithms inside of computing architectures. Such a formalist approach deflects attention from the concrete social relations in which those architectures were designed in the first place. It is not surprising that such formalism is common among the apologists of mass criminalization. If we only adjust the parameters, they tell us, criminal justice algorithms will be invulnerable to antiracist critiques. We are assured that race is not an important factor in newer crime prediction software because the software does not analyze demographic data, only geographic data. Predictive policing software company PredPol's cofounder emphasizes that the company's algorithms are based on statistical models designed to predict seismic activity, which means that they cannot introduce racial bias.[30] But to be clear, our thesis is not that such tech companies cause racist law enforcement but that they capitalize on its ongoing legacy.

THE PRODUCTION OF CRIMINAL JUSTICE DATA

Criminal justice data, like all data, are not merely collected; they are *produced*. They are produced to serve practical ends, such as documentation or measurement for bureaucracies, individuals, or private companies.

But if classification is the first step to structuring data, by what means are classificatory schemes determined? Who decides which categories are included—or excluded? If tabulating data and their derivatives comes second, what gets lost in the acts of filtering, reformatting, and sorting? Questions like these were at one time of interest to police reformers, race reformers, social scientists, and welfare activists. But big data hype has grown such that these questions rarely enter into contemporary academic or public discussions about crime data. Yet while city officials and IT firms promote data analytics as a means of achieving scientifically neutral crime control decision-making, the data they crunch are overdetermined by politically charged policies and practices.[31] It is consequently important to pay attention to relations between political projects and the way criminal justice data are produced, encoded, and used. It is also important to foreground the historical contexts that establish the conditions for criminal justice data production. These dynamics are increasingly important, since the future of policing, legal scholars tell us, "is data: crime data, personal data, gang data, associational data, locational data, environmental data, and a growing web of sensor and surveillance sources."[32]

The book is an attempt to clarify the historical significance behind the explosion of criminal justice data. Such an analysis departs from philosophical conceptions of data whose roots lay in electrical engineer and mathematician Claude Shannon's information theory. Working for the telecommunications industry in the middle of the last century, Shannon devised a groundbreaking theory of communication that explored the statistical structure of messages. Meaning, or any other semantic property of communication, was immaterial from this perspective. All that mattered was formal structure. Shannon's *The Mathematical Theory of Communication* established the epistemological foundations for the information revolution and a gold mine for the telecommunications industry. In addition to new information and communication industries, his theory spawned an intellectual heritage in which information, data, and knowledge were conceptualized in kind.[33] But it is necessary to look beyond the formal properties of data and information to understand their political significance. Attention must be directed toward the actual conditions in which they are produced and put into action.

A bevy of social factors prefigure the types and amounts of data that are produced.[34] Such factors are at once material and discursive. In materialist terms, the logics of capital valorization cannot help but impose themselves upon big data production in the context of a capitalist society. The devices that generate big data are commodities, which are produced in the first instance to yield profit.[35] A goal of the book is to highlight how the propulsive force of valorization influences the mass production of criminal justice data and technology. In terms of discourse, digital data are increasingly important in representing, understanding, and organizing social reality.[36] This discursive aspect comes on full display when data are organized into dataset matrices made up of rows and columns. In crime databases, the rows are populated by crime incidents reported by police. The total number of these incidents can never account for every act of lawbreaking in society. The number is constrained by who reports incidents, where patrols are located, and whom they choose to report. Moreover, the state acts as a gatekeeper over what qualifies as an incident. In point of fact, the Federal Bureau of Investigation has never developed a protocol for collecting data on incidents where police kill civilians. The columns in criminal justice databases are often populated by demographic classifications, for example, age, race, and sex. Racial attributes were first included in crime reports under the assumption that race was causally related to criminal behavior (see chapter 1). The overrepresentation of nonwhite groups in crime datasets continues to be exploited by white supremacists to indicate that nonwhites are more deviant, and hence deportable, displaceable, and disposable. But black radical theorists have shown that this overrepresentation of nonwhites actually exposes racism immanent to the criminal justice apparatus.[37] These theorists show how statistics are manipulated and how white crime is excluded and sometimes erased from official datasets. Such a viewpoint is increasingly important in an age when data analytics legitimize racial governance.

Digitize and Punish shows that criminal justice datasets are matrices not only in the sense of being rectangular arrays of rows and columns. The datasets act like what Patricia Hill Collins terms *matrices of domination,* as they assist the state in its endless efforts to hierarchize populations.[38] American studies theorist Lisa Lowe has demonstrated how state databases facilitated hierarchization in British Hong Kong.[39] Lowe points to an 1844 English ordinance that required Chinese persons to register in databases

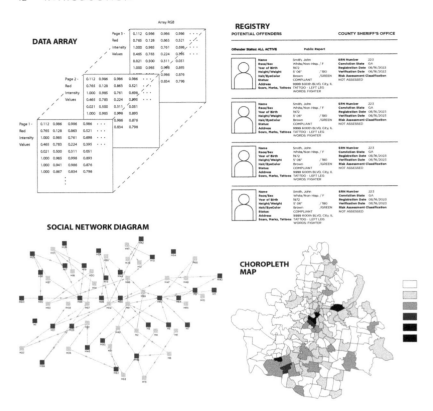

FIGURE 1. Criminal justice data visualization. Police datasets are organized, analyzed, and visualized in multiple ways. These figures depict incident report data in arrays, lists, networks, and maps. It is important to stress that the social or spatial characteristics in these data are to a large extent determined by whom police patrol and report. In this way, the datasets may be viewed as archives of police activity. Image by Keenan Dailey. Adapted from Laura Kurgan, Sarah Williams, David Reinfurt, and Eric Cadora, *The Pattern* (New York: Spatial Information Design Lab, 2008).

as part of a public safety initiative that involved curfews, checkpoints, identification cards, and constant surveillance of living quarters. The registry made the colonial subject legible through attributes including pirate, political, radical, and vagrant—each of which was outside of waged labor markets.[40]

Kim TallBear shows how private-sector companies benefit from building racialized databases. Specifically, she shows how IBM, Gateway Inc., and the National Geographic Society profited from a DNA database that stored genetic data about indigenous groups.[41] Just like these databases, those belonging to the carceral state are designed to assist capital in generating considerable gains. Such datasets are never used to rationalize improving the material conditions to which criminalized populations are subjected but rather only to justify more surveillance, more patrolling, more control. Crime databases are used to formally mark individuals for banishment from democratic institutions and housing and rationalize policies of immersing their living quarters with patrol forces and surveillance cameras. Despite this political character, or better yet, because of it, the constant churn of criminal justice data is passionately consumed, picked apart, and debated throughout academia, entertainment, everyday conversation, government affairs, and think tanks. This book aims to disrupt the all too common practice of discussing these data apart from the material conditions from which they emerge.

UPLOADING CARCERAL POWER INTO URBAN INFRASTRUCTURE

A point of emphasis in the book is that carceral power is silently spreading through infrastructures of cellular towers, datacenters, fiber-optic cables, smart sensors, and video cameras. Carceral functionality is becoming a key attribute of the smart city. This is not meant to say that the prison–industrial complex is being wholly supplanted or that it is bound to disintegrate. Even though incarceration rates have reached their lowest points in decades, the history of carceral management is not one of a linear development. Nor is it a history of a changeless institution. Carceral space has manifested in the form of extraordinary rendition sites, immigrant detention centers, and internment camps. This book traces an emergent form of carceral space that is characterized by machines that traverse human anatomy, public housing facilities, public schools, transportation systems, telecommunications systems, and street networks in U.S. cities. The book also emphasizes that the deeper telecommunications and IT firms entrench themselves in crime control policy, the more likely it is for these infrastructures to continue to expand.

The extension of carceral management through the Internet of Things

(IoT), or networks of devices that communicate with each other, is greatly influenced by the movement of capital.[42] On one hand, the carceral state's circumscription of black and latinx communities was partly catalyzed by the flight of industry from cities, which rendered entire groups deskilled and unemployable. Decades of revelatory research demonstrates how cities turned to mass criminalization to manage the enormous economic, political, social, and medical problems arising from deindustrialization.[43] On the other hand, in addition to outbound industrial capital, the carceral state's digital architecture owes its existence to inbound information capital. The infrastructure sector has emerged as one of the most important sectors in finance, knowledge, and technology industries.[44] IT companies have insinuated themselves in seemingly all facets of urban life, including government agencies, private businesses, social networks, transportation systems, workplaces, and infrastructure. These companies have also nestled their way into criminal justice administration, which is reshaping geographies of carceral governance.

A central argument in this book is that the criminal justice system's smart infrastructure is creating new geometries of carceral space. On one hand, carceral space is incredibly centralized. Extraordinary rendition sites, detention centers, jails, and prisons, which are designed to monitor, discipline, governmentalize, punish, and sometimes execute or torture those caught within their grasp, are a few examples. IT firms have penetrated these spaces. For instance, technology corporations sell geographic information systems to help custodial authorities organize cell arrangements according to demographic categories, predict inmate movements and behaviors, and identify potential escape routes (see chapter 2). Yet, on the other hand, carceral space is incredibly decentralized. Carceral geographers highlight the elaborate logistics required to shuttle humans, information, and resources across prison facilities and entire landscapes.[45] Architects have characterized rural prison facilities as urban exostructures, as they provide relief to the city's overburdened criminal justice apparatus.[46] Technology firms have also infiltrated this decentralized dimension of carceral management. Wireless networks of smart cameras, phones, sensors, and tablets extend the reach of the carceral system. At the scale of the city, smart cameras and environmental sensors send alerts to patrol vehicles dispersed throughout street networks. On regional scales, real-time crime centers receive data and transmit them throughout states and, increasingly, between them. Owing to their portability, criminal justice technologies also circulate on international scales. Today there exists a global market for public security technology that traverses capitalist, communist, and socialist nations. On yet a grander scale, electronic forms of monitoring probationers depend on Global Positioning System satellites, which extend the reach of carceral technology all the way into low Earth orbit.

Taking the carceral state apart and making it less recognizable through the lens of smart infrastructure helps short-circuit illusions that it is neatly bounded in terms of geography and functionality. While the illusion of a monolithic carceral Leviathan echoes modern theories of the state that never seem to fade away, carceral statecraft is an open, dynamic, and variegated sociotechnical process of quarantining human beings. As such, our understanding of carceral state power, Katherine Beckett and Naomi Murakawa observe, "must be as capacious, complex, and adaptive as the policies and institutions involved in it."[47] The present study insists that analysis of this power's sociotechnical substrate is also necessary to understand carceral conditions in the twenty-first century.

DESIGN OF THE BOOK

Digitize and Punish retells the history of mass criminalization by focusing on technology corporations and technology bureaus. The book's objects of analysis are not criminalized communities but rather the computer programmers, corporate-bureaucratic intellectuals, state officials, and technologists who update the tools that criminalize them. It tells untold stories of the contingencies, failed projects, unintended consequences, and technical breakthroughs involved in constructing the digitized carceral state. It illustrates how these efforts have simultaneously augmented the carceral state and created new avenues of subverting it.

This project employs an intersectional approach to understand the nexus of carceral power, racism, and IT capital.[48] The perspective was notably captured by the Combahee River Collective and Kimberlé Williams

Crenshaw, who demonstrated the inadequacies of understanding social hierarchy through one measure, or axis of division.[49] As such, structural analysis of the relations between racial difference, technological development, and political economic mutation is necessary to understand the relevant factors in racial criminalization in the digital age. The question is not if racial criminalization behaves in a structural manner but rather how it maintains, if not increases, its structural integrity from generation to generation. This book therefore seeks to explain how information capital exploited the surge of racial criminalization near the end of the last century and, at the same time, how racial criminalization was exploited by the rise of information technology.

The book provides both a broad and grounded view of the computer technology's introduction to the Wars on Crime and Drugs. It takes a multiscalar approach to understanding how events on national, urban, and local levels combined to influence the development of criminal justice technoscience. A great deal of the study is devoted to analyzing these dynamics in New York City and Chicago, as the multiscalar forces at play are especially legible in these cities. In academic circles, media, and public discourse, New York City is often portrayed as the vanguard of data-driven policing. Its data-driven administrative process, CompStat, is celebrated as having revolutionized policing around the world. Political power is uniquely concentrated in the city's Mayor's Office, which maintains a national and sometimes international profile. The city council's power is organized within a borough system, which provides a unique terrain for studying how diverse interests that drive digitized criminal justice converge. The city also offers a paradigmatic example of racialized deproletarianization and criminalization under conditions of technological change. What is more, New Yorkers have a rich history of contesting racialized police violence, including, but not limited to, the Young Lords, the Justice Committee, the Malcolm X Grassroots Movement, the October 22 Coalition, and Make the Road on the grassroots level and the Center for Constitutional Rights, the New York Civil Liberties Union, and the National Congress for Puerto Rican Rights. Chicago offers an alternative case for this study. Its political landscape is different, where power is divided between a balkanized aldermanic system, the hypermarginalized Black Belt, and strong gubernatorial authority. Chicago has also pioneered the application of science and technologies in criminal justice. The Chicago Police Department was the first to use telegraph and telephone systems that linked police call boxes to precinct houses.[50] The city also resides in Illinois, one of the first states to apply actuarial methods to parole and probation procedures, which presaged today's application of computerized risk instruments.[51]

The first chapter, "Computation and Criminalization," tracks the history of calculation and computing technology in the criminal justice system and criminological thought. Beginning during the second Industrial Revolution, it charts the contingent bloc of industrial firms, nativists, police scientists, progressives, quantitative social scientists, and social reformers who influenced how urban crime is computed. The chapter explores how digital computers quietly penetrated criminal justice administration and criminological knowledge production as the War on Crime began and how these developments codified the logics, policies, and practices central to the war in languages commensurate with digital computing. The second chapter, "Dreams of Digital Carceral Power," investigates the expansive role that computer technology played in the rise of mass incarceration. It examines how each branch of criminal justice conceptualized the benefits of computers and how this transformed understandings and operations of carceral management in turn. "A Fully Automated Police Apparatus" is chapter 3. The chapter provides a detailed account of the spread of computer technology in police departments in New York City and Chicago. It directs attention to how each process drew together a new bloc of city officials, criminal justice personnel, IT companies, and university scientists determined to create a police apparatus that could prevent crime from happening. The fourth chapter, "Punishment in the Network Form," concentrates on the intersection of punishment and wireless technology. The chapter insists that this interface exacerbates penal stigma and allows cities to enroll the public to monitor and sanction offenders and ex-offenders. The fifth chapter, "How to Program a Carceral City," examines the convergence of criminal justice and smart cities, shifting attention to the criminal justice system's steady buildup of smart cameras, environmental sensors, and alarm systems and how this gave rise to its newest branch, crime datacenters. Chapter 5 concludes by considering how the rapid-fire spread of these datacenters is transforming geographies of carceral power. The conclusion, titled "Viral Abolition," explores struggles against the digital extension of the carceral apparatus. It analyzes instances when criminal justice data infrastructures have been subverted, challenged, and turned into liabilities by oppositional forces. It highlights how these counterforces spread virally in ways that are creating conditions to halt the perpetuation of the crime and drug wars through digital networks.

1

COMPUTATION AND CRIMINALIZATION

The first encounters of criminal justice bureaucrats and computing technology occurred early in the twentieth century, a time when debates raged over what it was exactly that authorities should compute. Public officials and researchers argued about which types of crime should be counted; what attributes of offenders were worth recording; and whether criminality was a quantifiable trait of people, populations, and places. It would take decades of political and intellectual posturing before criminal justice agencies would produce uniform statistical data on a national scale. It also required technical advancements. While debates intensified over how crime and criminality should be calculated, a cutting-edge technology was gaining popularity throughout state bureaucracies. The device was the electromechanical tabulating machine, ancestor to the electronic digital computer.

From the late nineteenth century through the early twentieth century, each branch of the criminal justice apparatus lobbied to establish its data as foundational for measuring crime. For most of the 1800s, different states and municipalities compiled different types of data in their official crime indexes. In the 1830s, New York, Massachusetts, and Maine produced official data on offenders using court and county attorney records.[1] The 1850 census was the first to incorporate data on the offender population, which drew from prisoner records.[2] The first debates about standardizing criminal justice data production on a national scale occurred at a National Police Association conference two decades later. Prior to the conference, Congress stipulated that the newly formed Department of Justice supply the attorney general with statistical data on crime on an annual basis. The mandate sent law enforcement and correctional authorities into a frenzied dash to establish an official data structure to be used across the country. The 1880 census designed reports by police departments in major cities that required officers to enter information on twenty-four different offenses and a dozen inquiries about arrests and subsequent dispositions.[3] The 1880 census also included a report titled *Defective, Dependent, and Delinquent Classes,* which included data on 231 offenses classified as against the government, against society, against the person, against property, and on the high seas. After launching in 1902, the Census Office commissioned a draft of a manual for preparing crime statistical data for all three branches of the criminal justice apparatus. The commission was, according to the office, issued in "response to general demand for more complete and satisfactory statistics relation to crime and criminals."[4]

This demand for statistical data was stimulated by various historical developments. It was spurred to some extent by the professionalization and bureaucratization of the state apparatus typical to the late nineteenth century. State reformers during this period placed heavy emphasis on nonpartisan scientific methods to select and evaluate civil servants and on establishing legal science according to positivist principles.[5] But the fixation with statistical data was also spurred by technological advancements, the most influential of which was Herman Hollerith's electromechanical tabulating machine. The machine was the outgrowth of Hollerith's ambition to furnish the Census Office with a more efficient and accurate way of tabulating census data. To do so, he developed a machine that punched holes in cards, each hole representing an age group, conjugal status, English proficiency, nativity, occupation, race, or sex (Figure 2).[6] The cards were then fed into a circuit-closing device where each perforation was recorded by an electromagnetized counter. This invention gave birth to "information in combination," or the ability to ascribe multiple variables (e.g., age, race, sex, occupation) to a single "instance" at a stroke. It also made it possible to search for individuals using one or several of these traits as search terms. Hollerith conducted his first census-taking pilot with the tabulator

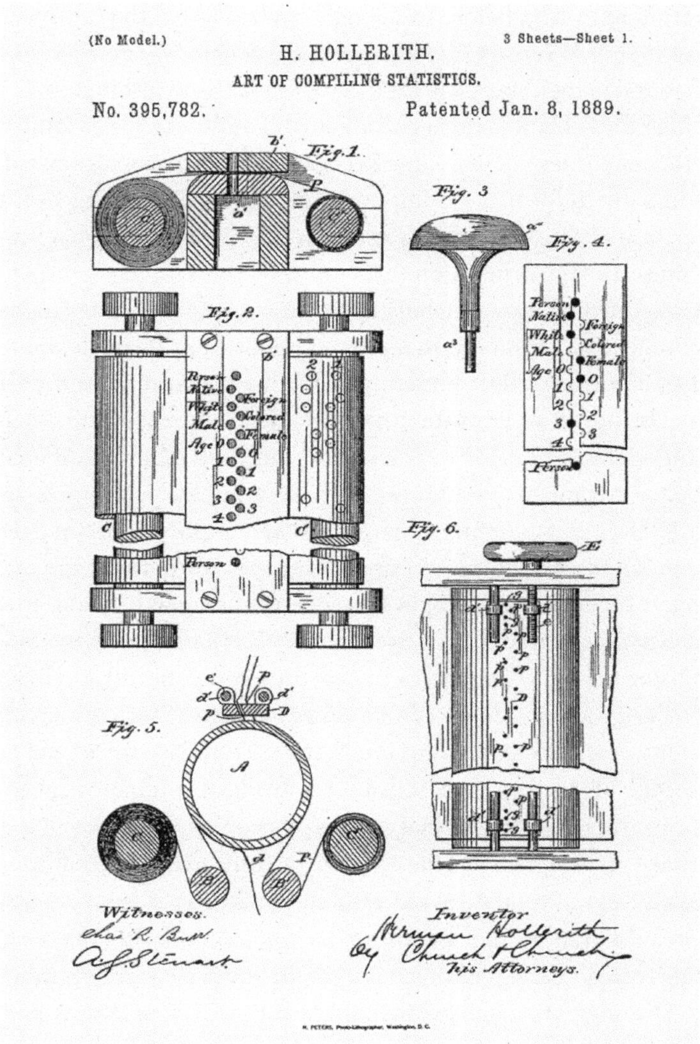

FIGURE 2. Herman Hollerith's electromechanical tabulator patent. Figures of Herman Hollerith's "Art of Compiling Statistics" in U.S. patent 395782. The patent included two classifications: one for methods or arrangements for reading patterns by mechanical means, the other for measures preceding sorting according to destination. The figures in the image demonstrate how to compile statistics about nativity (native/foreign), race (white/black), sex (male/female), and age. From "Art of Compiling Statistics," patent 395782, January 8, 1889.

in Baltimore in 1887, before receiving a contract from the Census Office for the 1890 U.S. census. Six years after the census was completed, Hollerith founded the Tabulating Machine Company in Washington, D.C. By 1911, the Bundy Manufacturing Company, Computing Scale Company of America, and International Time Recording Company amalgamated with his company to form the Computing-Tabulating-Recording Company. Fifteen years later, the company was renamed the International Business Machines (IBM) Corporation.

The electromechanical tabulator was classical epistemology made into a machine. Its function was to represent populations through *tabulation*, most of all through differentiating individuals according to predefined traits. The power of tabulation had already been put on full display in the mid-eighteenth century, when Linnaeus used tables to differentiate biological organisms and Quesnay to differentiate economics agents. With Hollerith's tabulating apparatus, state administrators nudged the differentiation of ethnoracial populations into the coming age of computing. In fact, Hollerith's application of electromagnetic theory to social differentiation proved so effective that the Nazi Party used his tabulators to register Jews and Romanies in censuses and concentration camps.[7]

The eruption of human tabulation found its way into urban administrations. Amateur statistician Frederick L. Hoffman capitalized on the new wealth of 1890 census data in a study on black criminality called *Race Traits*. Hoffman postulated that only by "thorough analysis of all the data that make up the history of the colored race" could the true nature of the so-called Negro Problem be ascertained.[8] This project was a response to the Great Migration, which witnessed 6 million blacks flee the racialized totalitarianism of the post-Reconstruction South to northern industrial cities. The migrants sought work in the factories, packinghouses, and steel mills of cities, which generated great trepidation on the part of low-waged native and nonnative European workforces. Hoffman sought to prove black inferiority using statistical methods, which could in turn justify segregating black migrants.[9] Hoffman drew heavily from the abundance of demographic data generated by the 1890 census, but he took considerable liberties with the way he tabulated and subsequently calculated the data. In one column, populations categorized as Bohemian, German,

SPECIFIED OFFENSES COMMITTED BY PRISONERS IN THE UNITED STATES IN 1890.

	MALE PRISONERS.		
Crimes Against the Person.	Total No. of Prisoners.	Colored Prisoners.	Per Cent. of Colored.
Homicide	6,958	2,512	36.10
Rape.	1,387	567	40 88
Abduction	140	32	22.86
Abortion	25	2	8.00
Assault.	8,001	3,195	39 93
Crimes Against Property.			
Arson	806	372	46.15
Burglary.	9,647	2,710	28.09
Robbery	2,350	555	23.62
Larceny	7,978	3,126	39.18
Grand larceny	6,411	1,774	27.67
Petit larceny	3,475	1,055	30 36
Percentage of colored in total population over 15 yrs. of age (males)			10.20
	FEMALE PRISONERS.		
Crimes Against the Person.			
Homicide	393	227	57 76
Assault.	346	198	57.23
Crimes Against Property.			
Arson	80	49	61.25
Larceny	425	225	52 94
Grand larceny	320	159	49.69
Petit larceny	266	99	37.22
Percentage of colored in total population over 15 yrs. of age (females)			11.09

FIGURE 3. Early racialized table of prisoner offenses, 1896. Hoffman was among a growing number of social statisticians who tabulated the U.S. population into a totalizing black–white binary. He claimed he could gain deep insights into the nature of each race by cross-tabulating types of crimes with racial identifiers. From Frederick L. Hoffman, *Race Traits and Tendencies of the American Negro* (New York: Macmillan, 1896), 220.

Irish, Italian, Norwegian, Polander, Russian, and Swedish in the census were transformed in Hoffman's tables into "Whites." In the other column, populations categorized as Black, Octoroon, Mulatto, and Quadroon in the census were transformed in his tables into "Coloreds." He used these racially binarized tables to compare and contrast data on anthropometrics, conjugal status, education, imprisonment, literacy, occupations, populations (e.g., state, city, county, ward), religiosity, and vital statistics (birthrates/death rates) between the populations (Figure 3). Although Hoffman's study omitted socioeconomic data, lacked controls, and was bereft of intragroup comparison, it nonetheless spread throughout the disciplines of anthropology, demography, sociology, and even history. It also shifted the center of scientific racism from anthropometry and biology into the domain of statistics-based social science.[10]

As the nineteenth century turned, statistical tabulation slowly made its way into the production of criminal justice data and criminological knowledge. Within a couple of decades, the FBI received annual statistical reports from almost all national and state adult reformatories, penitentiaries, and prisons. But the quality of the data was under scrutiny, particularly for lack of controls for sentencing variations across municipalities.[11] Many statisticians argued in favor of using court data from reports made by clerks and state's attorneys working in criminal courts.[12] Others lobbied to make arrests and complaints to police the bases for crime indexes. Advocates for police data argued that they provided a more direct, unadulterated view of conditions on the ground.[13] Toward the end of the 1920s, police incident report data finally emerged as new fundaments of criminal justice datasets. The ascent of these data was partly due to the influence of the police professionalization movement, which trumpeted the application of sciences and technologies to reduce police graft and break up ethnic nepotism in urban police departments.[14] Champions of police professionalization made the case that the application of technology to policing could also enhance criminal apprehension. Considerable energy was spent on standardizing criminal justice data production at the annual meeting of the International Association of Chiefs of Police (IACP) in 1927.[15] It was there, during the police professionalization movement, that the idea that "objective and scientific counting of crime" could be used to enhance police legitimacy was first articulated. Influential reformers, such as Leonhard Fuld, Raymond Fosdick, and Bruce Smith, argued that scientifically cultivated incident report data could counter sensationalized crime reportage and the iconic status of criminals that permeated popular culture at the time.[16] The fruits of the meeting bore in subsequent attempts by the Bureau of Hygiene, the FBI, the Laura Spelman Rockefeller Memorial, the Social Science Research Council, and urban police departments from across the country. The meeting was called to devise a national crime reporting system. After rigorous debate and dissension, the parties decided to base the system on offenses known to police, which were divided into crimes against persons and against property. Architects of the system's data structure, which was eventually called the Uniform Crime Reporting (UCR) system, decided against including property offenses like counterfeiting, embezzlement, fraud, and forgery.

Two years after the IACP's fated meeting, the association declared that "the need for compiling and analyzing persons charged by means of tabulating machines [was increasing] with the size of the city."[17] Electromechanical tabulation, reported the association, was the only practical solution for metropolitan police departments to record and analyze the social characteristics and dispositions of their arrestees. "If it were desired to know the sex and color of persons charged," an IACP researcher explained, "the cards [could] be sorted in numerical sequence for this field."[18] "With aid of automatic tabulating and listing devices," continued the association, "the facts punched on the cards can be tabulated in any manner desired. The machines are almost human in their accomplishments; they list grand totals, totals, and subtotals for any fact or combination of facts."

For the police apparatus, the curiosity with computing technology was to a great extent a response to the surge of Eastern and Southern European immigrants into industrial cities. These groups were blamed by city officials for the ills of industrial urbanization. The focus on European immigrants was precipitated by the fact that some 27 million immigrants, notably from Germany, Italy, Poland, and Russia, entered the United States between 1880 and 1930. The so-called Negro Problem was not once mentioned at the IACP conventions of 1919 and 1920 and scarcely touched upon by key figures of police professionalization.[19] With the Second World

War looming, the new European immigrants were construed in political rhetoric as security threats. The flames of anti-immigrant sentiment were also fanned by ethnicized labor conflicts, the Red Scare, and the surge of anarchist violence punctuated by Leon Czolgosz's assassination of President William McKinley. Police experts across the industrial North convened to devise ways to manage those "ignorant of our language, laws and customs [and possessing an] inborn suspicion of all police officers."[20] Police officials in districts where reports on crime were higher complained that they were up against immigrants for whom "liberty had no meaning other than gross license."[21] Some police officials ascribed 85 percent of all crimes to Jews.[22] Others ascribed crime to the broader population of immigrants who "can't talk the English language . . . don't know our customs . . . and are in general the scum of Europe."[23] Influential police reformer August Vollmer, himself the son of German immigrants, reported that excessive urban growth and so "many millions of immigrants, ignorant of our language, laws and customs, and necessarily adhering in their racial segregations," made criminal detection increasingly difficult for police.[24] And so police reformers envisioned the electromechanical tabulator as a means of administering these stigmatized surplus workforces. Vollmer explored different uses with Hollerith tabulators as early as 1921,[25] for he belonged to a larger movement convinced that more descriptive and reliable data were necessary to transform urban "social waste" into "desirable and useful social beings."[26] But tabulating machines were not yet widely available. Two vendors, the Computing-Tabulating-Recording Company and Powers Accounting Machine Company, controlled the market, and their main clients were limited at the time to census bureaus, businesses, and railroad companies.

SPATIALIZING CRIMINAL JUSTICE DATA

While it would take another half century for automated computing technology to be integrated into the criminal justice apparatus, the first part of the twentieth century saw significant developments in the way that urban criminality was computed and analyzed. The most influential developments in this regard arose from University of Chicago sociologists who chronicled the supposedly criminogenic characteristics of poor and stigmatized parts of the city. In retrospect, one of the more striking characteristics of criminal justice datasets during the nineteenth century was their general lack of spatial data. This seems peculiar given that the UCR system was originally designed to highlight crimes associated with urbanization.[27] What is more, several nineteenth-century theories about urban crime included observations of the social spaces in which they clustered. André-Michel Guerry's statistical maps, Henry Mayhew's rookeries, Archibald Alison's low neighborhoods, John Glyde's poor law unions, Charles Booth's poverty maps, and Breckinridge and Abbott's Hull House maps are some examples. Even criminologist Cesare Lambroso, a key architect of biological racism, considered village profiles when examining criminality in Italy. But although police scientists and state reformers began to explore the electromechanical production of crime data, they remained for the most part preoccupied with compiling data about social rather than geographic characteristics.

While police reformers and social statisticians contrived biological and cultural explanations for urban crime indexes at the turn of the nineteenth century, the University of Chicago's social ecologists offered sociospatial ones. Founded in 1892, one year before Hollerith received a runner-up prize at the Chicago World's Fair for his machine, Chicago's sociologists formed their historic school. It was during a period of urban mutation. Between 1890 and 1930, the city's population more than tripled. During this period, as much as 77 percent of the city was first- or second-generation immigrant.[28] The city itself was a factory for ethnoracialized proletarianization, which lured labor power from Czechoslovakia, Germany, Greece, Ireland, Italy, Norway, Poland, and Sweden. A hub for low-waged labor, almost one-third of the city's workforce was funneled into manufacturing and construction. Workers from Mexico also arrived in large numbers, accounting for nearly one-quarter of the railroad labor force by 1920.[29] And although the city's population was under 3 percent black, Drake and Cayton calculated that black labor power made up 60 percent of garage work, 60 percent of railroad labor, 40 percent of coal yard labor, 50 percent of packing and slaughterhouse work, and 35 percent of stockyard work.[30] The Chicago School emphasized interactions between physical environments and social values to decipher criminality in the hope of moving beyond the biological racism that dominated research on urban crime.

One-time police beat reporter and founding member of the Chicago School Robert E. Park boldly asserted that if you "reduce all social relations to relations of space [it] would be possible to apply human relations to the fundamental logic of the physical sciences."[31] Density, distance, proximity—these emerged as the central variables of a new, spatially inflected science of urban crime. To be sure, such a spatial perspective was not completely without precedent. The Chicago School's conceptual framework traces at least back to Adriano Balbi and André-Michel Guerry's 1829 tract *Statistique comparée de l'état de l'instruction et du nombre des crimes*. Published just two years after French mathematician Charles Dupin invented choropleth maps, or maps that display average values through shading, Balbi and Guerry represented crime data cartographically to provide new ways of interpreting criminality. Guerry, an amateur statistician who invented a mechanical device that generated statistical summaries and data correlations, went on to publish an internationally renowned manuscript using district-level data to study correlations between crimes, motivations, and social characteristics.[32] Several aspects of his method—its data sources, scales of analysis, variables, perceived casual connections—resonated in the Chicago School. But where space was static in Guerry's work, the Chicago School saw it as something dynamic. This was due in no small part to the fact that industrialization was warping Chicago's landscape.

In devising a data structure that could account for the highly dynamic character of industrial urbanization, Park imported concepts of invasion, dominance, and succession from ecology. Population density, diversity, and turnover, both tabulated according to ethnic/racial categories, emerged as dominant data points. Their data structure, which omitted how the behavior of the criminal justice apparatus influences crime indexes, established parameters for understanding cities, crime, and race that persist in today's crime-mapping software (see chapter 2).[33] Though ethnoracialized divisions of labor were acknowledged by the Chicago School as having influence on geographic distributions of urban crime, the ecologists lacked an adequate theory of why labor markets were partitioned as such in the first place. The sociologists thus identified self-interest and personal preferences as the causes of racially differentiated labor markets. Burgess viewed racial labor segmentation as the effect of racial temperaments. Park argued that clusters of unemployed people were naturally formed aggregates of people who specialized in begging as a vocation.[34] These heaps of "human junk" were seen as organic products of individual choices enacted within the conditions of industrial urbanization.[35] The Chicago School's focus on the neighborhood scale reinforced the tendency to blame industrialized poverty on impoverished communities. While the notion that crime was an intrinsic property of poor urban neighborhoods was expressed before by several British proto-urbanists, the Chicago School developed a standardized system for quantifying how criminogenic an area was. The system classified neighborhoods by ethnoracial composition, homeownership rate, median income, and turnover rate, among other variables. This assumption that one can understand crime solely by calculating neighborhood-level phenomena was present throughout the classic ecological works of William Thomas, Florian Znaniecki, Frederic M. Thrasher, and E. Franklin Frazier (a notable exception is Edwin Sutherland).

Social ecology achieved its most iconic expression in Burgess's concentric zone model, which taxonomized urban space according to social composition and economic functionality (Figure 4).[36] Located simultaneously in the urban core and at the periphery of the urban social order, Burgess's infamous Zone II was where the most disposable elements of the industrial workforce resided. Clifford Shaw and Henry McKay looked for correlations between juvenile delinquency and the physical, economic, and demographic characteristics of Zone II. A central goal in their landmark work was to conduct a comparative analysis at unprecedentedly small geographic scales. Building on Park's natural areas and Burgess's concentric zones, the duo drew data from fifty-six thousand court records to make multilayered cartographies of delinquency. The project was an immense undertaking for the time, involving manually plotting the home addresses of some twenty-five thousand juvenile offenders who had passed through the Cook County Juvenile Court between 1900 and 1933. The Department of Political Science was the university's only department using Hollerith tabulators to code and analyze voter surveys at the time.[37] The university did not own a tabulator at this point. Faculty had to use

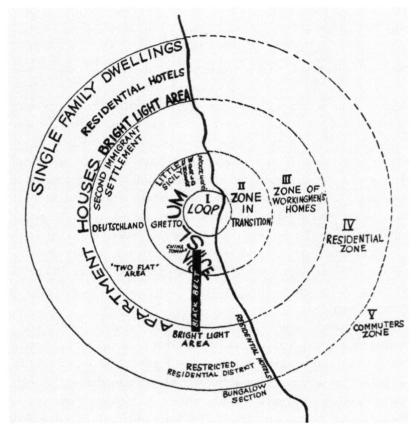

FIGURE 4. Model of concentric zone theory. Ernest Burgess's concentric zone diagram is the most iconic image in urban studies. It is invoked across disciplines in studies on urban crime, housing, labor markets, pollution, and so on. From Robert Park, Ernest Burgess, and Roderick McKenzie, *The City* (Chicago: University of Chicago Press, 1925), 55.

research grants to use a machine in the Comptroller's Office in City Hall. Chicago's sociologists did not use electromechanical tabulation until the late 1930s in studies to predict marriage success and failures. Shaw and McKay thus made spot maps of the home residences of alleged juvenile delinquents with overlays of Burgess's concentric zones, demolished buildings, vagrancy, rate maps of alleged delinquents (in square miles), and zone maps based on the concentric model (Figure 4). Delinquency was interpreted as a function of proximity to these territories, which were typified by ethnic heterogeneity, high residential turnover, and low income. Shaw and McKay argued that these traits engendered antisocial values, incentivized deviance, and ultimately normalized criminal behavior.

It is difficult to overstate the influence of social ecology on the discursive construction of negatively racialized, criminalized urban areas. From the Chicago School onward, these sectors were seen as intrinsically criminogenic, while the broader politics of crime and punishment was brushed aside. Through the ecological model, discriminatory laws, police profiling, prosecutors, judges, and sentencing biases were all barred from consideration. As if by methodological injunction, the very mechanism of criminalization, that is, the *criminal justice apparatus,* was excluded from statistical measurement. Datasets on police–juvenile contact did not include information about geographic dispersions of police patrols; the data on juvenile court referrals were not scrutinized for evidence of juror bias; and the data on youth commitments were not examined for sentencing bias. Published not even a full year after passage of the Johnson–Reed Act (1924) and its national origins quota system, in the immediate aftermath of the Red Scare, Burgess's genre-defining 1925 article had nothing to say about the systematic criminalization of immigrants and migrants. None of this context was factored into the ecological framework, yet it emerged as the dominant model for understanding social and spatial patterns in criminal justice datasets and was easily codified into geographic information systems in decades to come.

CRIMINALISTICS AND INSTRUMENTATION

Physical scientists introduced industrial technologies into the production of criminal justice data while social ecology made its ascent. Long before the computer-managed environmental sensors in contemporary cities, criminal justice institutions measured aspects of physical environments through criminalistics. The criminalistics movement of the early twentieth century opened new doors for linking criminalization with cutting-edge science and technology, and added scientific credence to law enforcement. In fact, by 1923, the U.S. Supreme Court had ruled that evidence obtained through criminalistic techniques were admissible if they were accepted in scientific communities.[38] What made criminalistics unique was its emphasis on instrumentation, which generated so much information that relations between science, technology, and criminalization began to alter. The merging of science, technology, and criminalization is attributed to the FBI's premier director, John Edgar Hoover, a technophile who staked his legacy on suppressing the Mafia and Black Power, civil rights, and various labor movements. After assuming power in 1924, Hoover promptly announced that his main objective was to inject scientific and technical analysis into the heart of criminal detection and identification. He added scholastic modules into agent training, opened a criminology library in the bureau, and took over the administration of UCR data from the IACP. Hoover also funded academic programs, such as the Scientific Crime Detection Laboratory at Northwestern University, which served as a model for the FBI's Technical Laboratory.[39] Technical evidence was the raw material of criminalistics. Fancying themselves natural scientists interested in how science could be employed in the juridical sphere, pioneers in the field embraced techniques from analytical chemistry, ceramics, geochemistry, organic chemistry, metallurgy, and thermochemistry. Blood, fingerprints, hair, paint specimens, residues in fire remains, semen, subatomic particles, and vapors were its fundamental elements. This development was an effect of applying industrial-sector technologies to criminal justice identification and apprehension. Electron microprobes, emissions spectrometers, gas chromatographs, nuclear scalar counters, ultraviolet and infrared spectrophotometers, and X-ray diffractometers emerged in forensics laboratories as choice instruments. Going a step beyond the Chicago School, which studied topological urban space, criminalists studied space in its physical dimension. Combined gas chromatographic–mass spectrographic analysis, differential thermal analysis, and neutron activation analysis provided methodological support for these new scientists of crime. Consonant with wider developments in the Second Industrial Revolution, the electromagnetic field was wielded by forensic scientists as a medium through which criminal investigation and apprehension could be extended. By the early 1930s, most major cities had some type of crime laboratory for criminalistics.

Biometric technologies were also central to criminalistics. The FBI designed polygraph machines that measured and recorded blood pulses, pulse rates, and, eventually, respiratory rates to detect criminal guilt. The bureau's core accomplishment involved establishing the first national fingerprint database, which introduced the large-scale registry into the heart of the criminalization apparatus. Many of the basic principles of modern fingerprinting were established in the late nineteenth century by English statistician Francis Galton, who also invented the mathematical correlation while working on criminal identification techniques for a eugenics project.[40] But it was French police administrator Alphonse Bertillon's fingerprint system that first arrived in the United States in 1887 in a penitentiary in Illinois. His system, *bertillonage,* marked the birth of modern criminal identification by arranging anatomical measurements and photographs of offenders in statistically organized filing systems. The Henry fingerprint identification system, which originated in Calcutta's Anthropometric Bureau for colonial administrative purposes, also became common in the United States at the close of the nineteenth century. By 1915, the International Association for Criminal Identification appeared in Oakland, California. Nearly a decade later, the FBI unveiled its Identification Division, which was made up of thirteen hundred fingerprint technicians who matched more than one thousand prints with criminal files per day.[41] The bureau's position was that identifications were necessary given the anonymity of the urban condition, and by the time President Lyndon Johnson announced the first War on Crime in 1967, the division had generated more than 15 million fingerprint cards. At the time, this made for the largest biometric database in human history.

RACIAL DEPROLETARIANIZATION AND THE WAR ON CRIME

The great surge of interest in criminal justice departments for digital computers was a result of many contingent, contradictory developments that followed World War II. On one hand, it occurred during a period of incredible technological advancement. Ambitious criminal justice technocrats and technology companies demonstrated great zeal for applying computers to crime control alongside the arrival of microprocessors, integrated circuits, high-level programming languages, and eight-inch floppy magnetic storage disks, not to mention the internet's forerunner, ARPANET. On the other hand, while computing technology was rapidly developing, black and latinx enclaves were systematically underdeveloped through policies of benign neglect and planned shrinkage. The "black ghetto" fully eclipsed Zone II in the eyes of urban criminologists, law enforcement, and urban researchers. The shift was a function of several contradictions. First, the pools of black labor power furnished by the Great Migration grew functionally obsolete as manufacturing industries relocated from major cities to suburbs and rural areas. A national Commission on Civil Rights reported that between 1940 and 1960, labor participation for black males between the ages of twenty-five and sixty-four years decreased at four times the rate their white counterparts experienced.[42] By the 1960s, the former were twice as likely to be unemployed as the latter. By the middle of the decade, according to a Labor Department study, almost 15 percent of "nonwhite separated women" were unemployed, compared to twice as many "Negro males."[43] Nearly 15 percent of children classified as Negro received American Families with Dependent Children assistance, compared to 2 percent of children classified as white. The numbers were indicative of a social crisis of such proportions that it catalyzed the technological restructuring of urban administrative power.

Various mechanisms of racialized dispossession and containment emerged amid the flight of industrial capital. Post–World War II urban renewal programs and the extension of the highway system supplemented the economic marginalization of urban blacks with physical marginalization. Redlining strategies by banking, insurance, and real estate agencies coded blackness as unfinanceable in redevlopment projects from the late 1940s to the 1960s. Moreover, racially distributed mortgages and home equity loans accelerated the depreciation of housing markets in black communities. Though billed as a low-income housing program, the Housing Act (1949) fueled the massive displacement of black and latinx populations via so-called slum clearance projects that destroyed more low-income homes than they created. These programs to revalorize urban economies of space displaced tens of thousands of families across deindustrialized cores to make room for new commercial centers, luxurious apartments, university facilities, and other risk-averse land uses. Such processes were at odds with the massive suburbanization projects that paralleled urban renewal following World War II. Through concerted efforts by the Federal Housing Administration, Veterans Affairs, and Federal Deposit Insurance Corporation, municipal governments established a distinct form of racial segregation in the industrial North via suburbanization. Between 1950 and 1970, the country's suburban population increased 30 percent, which put considerable strain on city revenue generation.[44] This was to a large extent due to the racial state accommodating the exodus of white professionals from deindustrializing cities. New suburban businesses, labor markets, and property markets gestated through this colossal welfare program, which redistributed rates of homeownership, state funding, and wealth to cultivate the white middle class that we witness disintegrating today.

But the story of urban blacks would not be one of passivity. Revolts erupted across industrial cities throughout the middle of the 1960s. Dozens of insurgents mobilized in Rochester, New York City, Philadelphia, Jersey City, Paterson, Chicago, Watts, Cleveland, San Francisco, Newark, Detroit, Houston, Milwaukee, Minneapolis, Baltimore, and many other cities. These revolts signified socially stigmatized and economically discarded populations rejecting the material conditions foisted upon on them once capital no longer needed their labor and proved unwilling to support their social reproduction. In spectacular fashion, tens of millions of dollars' worth of urban capital was destroyed. The episode signified a not-so-subtle shift from civil rights tactics exemplified by the Conference on Racial Equality, Southern Christian Leadership Conference, and Student Non-Violent Coordinating Committee to those of the Black Power movement. The upheaval involved nearly a half million people, 60,000 arrests, 10,000 serious injuries, and 250 deaths. These insurrections represented negative moments of urban accumulation in the very heart of capitalism's precious cities. This episode was so fraught with implications for the political economic system in cities that it demanded a digitially enhanced mode of urban administrative power.

Some of the most spectacular transformations in urban administration to arise in reaction to black insurgency in the 1960s occurred at the interface of social and penal policy. In the economic field, the fusion of social policy and penal policy had already been under way under John F. Kennedy's New Frontier programs. Historian Elizabeth Hinton demonstrates how the antidelinquency programs of the Juvenile Delinquency and Youth Offenses Control Act of 1961 acknowledged the role of racism in economic disparity, on one hand, and codified racialized theories of social pathology in policy, on the other.[45] Despite Progressive encouragement from the Civil Rights Act of 1964, Office of Economic Opportunity, and Voting Rights Act of 1965, Kennedy's successor, Lyndon Johnson, nevertheless framed the urban rebellions in New York during summer 1964 as a matter of law and order. He formally announced the War on Crime the following year. Though some liberals warned of choosing between a social state and police state,[46] it was the latter that arose from the turmoil, and it was on such a grand scale that it required the powers of IT to build and administer it.

Urban administrations were fortunate that a model for enrolling criminal justice apparatuses to suppress political movements already existed. Southern segregationists fashioned a suite of juridical instruments to criminalize civil rights activities a decade prior. The exportation of this "southern strategy" to northern industrial cities was inaugurated with Republican presidential candidate Barry Goldwater's 1964 pledge to save northern cities from the "bullies and marauders" of the civil rights and New Left movements. Not to be outdone, President Johnson announced the War on Crime shortly thereafter. Politicized criminalization was further advanced in the North by Richard Nixon, who, completely lacking for irony, exhorted the need to militarize law enforcement lest the country become the "most violent in the history of the free peoples."[47] Nixon announced the War on Drugs two years into his administration. In the university apparatus, "black ghettoes" emerged as analytical objects of social scientists. Lawrence Mead, Patrick Moynihan, and Charles Murray were the most visible ghettophiles. It is not enough to point out the pseudo-scientific nature of their work. What is important is the strategic function of their publications in the context of the crime and drug wars.

Much like Hoffman in the post-Reconstruction era, theorists of black social disorganization provided rationalizations for racialized forms of governance. But unlike Hoffman, the social disorganization theorists of the 1960s had the bipartisan support of the racial state.

DIGITAL COMPUTING ENTERS THE WAR ON CRIME

In 1968, a year in which assassinations, electoral realignment, imperial frictions, and social conflict sent shockwaves across the U.S. political field, computer scientist Melvin Conway published an influential article in *Datamation* magazine that laid the groundwork for what eventually became known as Conway's law.[48] The piece belonged to a wider though barely noticeable development taking shape in universities during the turbulent 1960s—the birth of computer science. Conway's law stated that the communicative structure of an organization shapes the way its members conceptualize systems. The thesis resonated deeply with state bureaucrats and provided a guiding principle for criminal justice restructuring following the violent contradictions of the decade.

The police apparatus was the first branch of the criminal justice system pegged for computerization in the 1960s. Before digital computers arrived, the communicative structure of the police was command and control, a system where designated commanders exercised unidirectional authority over adjunct agents to execute assignments. Drawing from the military, police incorporated command and control with the assistance of the Federal Communications Commission and American Telephone and Telegraph Company (AT&T), who teamed to implement a centralized service call system (911) in the late 1960s. The calls were routed to a communications center, analyzed for relevant details, and then used by commanding officers to direct patrol units. This system was envisioned as a "nerve center controlling the minute-by-minute deployment of the police force."[49] Reformers of police administration, such as O. W. Wilson, aggressively promoted the expansion of automatic dialing equipment to lessen the workloads of human switchboard operators. Telecommunications systems were also regarded by Wilson and others as mediums to bolster coordination between administrative offices and motorized patrols.[50]

Such a communicative infrastructure, law enforcement bureaucrats and technologists maintained, would blend seamlessly with command-and-control logics found in computing. With computers, command functions emanated from logic boards instead of human commanders. Technology corporations and technocrats quickly took up the stance that automated command posts would make the police apparatus unbelievably more efficient. Companies saw a new opportunity on the horizon, so they joined forces to stimulate effective demand.

Lyndon Johnson's Law Enforcement Assistance Administration (LEAA) was at the center of programs to insert digital computing technology into the police apparatus. Initiated by the Omnibus Crime Control and Safe Streets Act of 1968, the LEAA was formed in response to the rising incident crime reports associated with the civil rights movement, second wave feminism, resistance to urban renewal, and Vietnam protest. One of the conclusions drawn from Johnson's Commission on Law Enforcement and Administration of Justice was that urban police would benefit greatly from a digitized command-and-control system.[51] In such a system, the computer would maintain records of street address locations and the current whereabouts and availability of patrol units to determine which unit was best positioned to respond to the call (Figure 5). It would also automatically send a dispatching order to the selected patroller via computer-generated voice messages or teletype. If the patrol unit did not acknowledge the message within a specified period of time, the system would contact another unit.

Johnson's commission also recommended a "computerized data bank of policy information" and identification network for line officers and supervisors. At the time the commission's report was released, the Justice Department was the sole cabinet department that did not receive research and development funds. Speaking at a hearing on the Law Enforcement Assistance Act of 1965, Edward Kennedy (D-MA) bemoaned the Justice Department's technological deficiencies. Kennedy was especially critical of the fact that there had been a "revolution in technology and in the behavioral sciences over the last 30 years. [Thus] the corpus of knowledge necessary to explain and cope with antisocial behavior has grown tremendously."[52] Research communities made similar observations. For

A Possible Computer-Assisted Police Command-Control System.

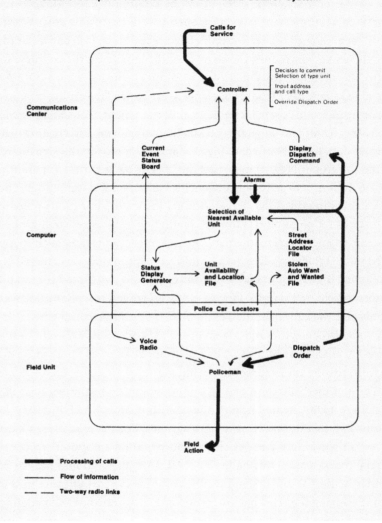

FIGURE 5. Diagram of police command, control, and communications system. Many police experts in the LEAA saw rapid and rational patrol deployment as the main benefit of computer automation. From *The Challenge of Crime in a Free Society: A Report by the President's Commission on Law Enforcement and Administration of Justice* (Washington, D.C.: U.S. Government Printing Office, 1967), 253.

instance, IIT Research Institute's Law Enforcement Science and Technology Center chronicled how the scientific community recognized that courts, corrections, and law enforcement were not using post–World War II technology,[53] nor were criminal justice technocrats in conversation with the wider community of scientists and engineers in the country. To rectify the situation, the Office of Law Enforcement Assistance (OLEA) assembled a task force whose core objectives involved reforming criminal justice agencies to foster technological development, translating crime control problems into languages of quantitative analysis, and creating new types of data to accommodate these changes. Moreover, the Organized Crime Control Bill (1970) increased the LEAA's budget from $75 million to $500 million to expand police agencies equipment and technology. The LEAA recommended that large criminal justice organizations prepare themselves for computerization by creating operations research groups made up of engineers, mathematicians, scientists, and statisticians. One of the more influential ideas the administration proposed was centered on developing digital command-and-control systems that linked command centers to field patrol units. Once a universal emergency phone line was established, the administration exclaimed, information coming from cities could also be autonomously analyzed via computers and sent to the nearest available patrol units. The police apparatus was finally privy to the third revolution in computer technology.

The commercialization of digital minicomputers beginning near the end of the 1970s created opportune conditions for the IT industry to burrow its way into the crime and drug wars. The introduction of hard drives, silicon thirty-two-bit chips, and personal computers to commercial marketplaces was hailed by the LEAA, the National Bureau of Standards, the FBI, and law enforcement officials as a cost-effective means of modernizing the criminal justice apparatus. Authorities and fledgling IT companies, such as Advanced Data Systems, Bendix Corporation, and Northern Research and Engineering Corporation International, explored ways of instituting information systems in everything from background checks to sentencing. In merging criminal justice, science, and technology, the OLEA proselytized *systems analysis,* the modeling of large complex systems to regulate relations between their constituent parts, as the new administrative matrix. Systems analysis had its roots in industrial science. It was centered in the principle "carried out in the factory system, of analyzing the process of production into its constituent phases, and of solving the problems thus proposed by the application of mechanics, of chemistry, and of the whole range of the natural sciences."[54] This principle was formalized and further developed by the Ford Motor Company and the Midvale Steel Company, the creators of Fordism and Taylorism, respectively. Following World War II, computer-operated systems analysis—pioneered largely by Jay W. Forrester, who designed computerized management systems for AT&T, Air Defense Command, Air Material Command, Air Research and Development Command, IBM, and Western Electric—was used in the Department of Defense to assess cost-effectiveness. Assistant secretary of defense, economist, and RAND Corporation researcher Charles J. Hitch also developed models for the Defense Department, which culminated in the highly influential Planning, Programming, and Budgeting System. Systems analysis was also introduced to welfare reform in the late 1960s to ensure public assistance satisfied the criterion of cost-effectiveness. The figure of the system became so central during this period that it was ascribed an almost mythical autonomy by thinkers as different as Niklas Luhmann, Talcott Parsons, and Michel Foucault.[55]

The mid-century explosions of systems theory cannot be understood apart from the emergence of the digital computer, whose strange life began to take shape during military research to calculate atomic implosions and ballistics trajectories. The framework of the system, which fused political logics of warfare with economic logics of cost-effectiveness, eventually came to define the logistical dimension of the crime and drug wars. And logistical knowledge, political geographer Deborah Cowen has shown, is characterized by harnessing the tactical logics of the military to accommodate circulations of capital. Thus, as political economic mutations and social antagonisms intensified in the 1960s, the LEAA reformers embraced computers as tools of applying systems analysis to criminal justice to make it more streamlined, and more martial. Technocrats in the administration encouraged law enforcement officials to reimagine criminal justice apparatuses as an enormous complex of operations working in harmony across space and time. Efficiency was understood in market terms. At the first National Symposium on Law Enforcement Science and Technology in 1967, sociologists asserted that the "passage of offenders from one agency to the next, from arrest to release, somewhat parallels the passage of raw materials from one firm to another as they are converted into finished products and are distributed to consumers."[56] In the final analysis, making the criminal justice system look like a digital computing system was part of broader projects to establish a logistically sound form of racial management.

The combination of computers and systems analysis left its imprint on the ways technocrats conceptualized criminal justice administration. Many insisted the War on Crime be firmly rooted in the principles of positivist science and conducted logistically with the aid of digital computers. One of the main benefits of this new approach, argued the LEAA, was that it could economize the many criminal justice activities required for Johnson's impending War on Crime. For one, computers were meant to economize the amount of brainpower that criminal justice personnel expended on making decisions. A report from the Criminal Courts Assistance Project enthusiastically explained that one of the benefits of using computers in courts was that, for court personnel, "it is not necessary to learn how a computer is engineered or constructed, nor is it advisable for court management to learn how to program or operate computer equipment."[57] Another benefit was that using computer-aided system analysis was construed as a way to help authorities appraise the cost of internal operations throughout the criminal justice apparatus. Everything from low-level employees to large-scale initiatives were valuated with an eye toward streamlining War on Crime operations. Moreover, system analysis was seen as a means of revealing the projected costs of new practices and policies. It was used to predict, for instance, how increasing clearance rates or providing treatment to convicts would affect the overall efficiency of the criminal justice system. But to achieve this thoroughly rationalized apparatus, high-level criminal justice activities first had to be translated into mathematical equations.

Applying the analytic of the system to police administration was the first order of business for the LEAA. This was because police were determined by federal officials to benefit from computerization the most.

An LEAA task force considered how methods of scientific analysis and experimentation could be used to evaluate data from case clearances, emergency calls, incident reports, and patrol field activity. It also called for the development of new mathematical models to assess individual patrol forces. The task force criticized distributing patrol forces on the basis of incident-to-officer ratios and emphasized the need to distribute them on the basis of data analysis instead. Patrol dispatch was thus one of the first areas of the police apparatus to be exposed to the ideology of systems. Up until the late 1960s, patrol dispatch was performed by human operators who manually filed, examined, prioritized, and transmitted information from emergency calls to patrol units. Computer-aided dispatch (CAD) systems changed this. CAD was first developed and most fully elaborated by the South Bay Regional Communication Center, California Crime Technology Research Foundation, and Planning Research Corporation in the late 1960s.[58] The original CAD system automatically extracted and prioritized information from emergency calls while simultaneously tracking the movement and activities of patrol units. It also recommended specific patrol units to respond to specific calls in an efficient manner.[59] CAD represented one of the earliest attempts to determine the relative policeability of urban areas through digital computing.

TECHNOLOGY FIRMS AND THE LEAA

The LEAA's commitment to computerization created new opportunities for technology firms. Giants of industrial production and emerging technology corporations eagerly offered their expertise and services.[60] California was naturally a hub for private firms working on criminal justice information technologies. For instance, the California-based System Development Corporation offered its own vision of how criminal justice agencies could capitalize on advancements in digital computing. Such a union, corporate enthusiasts maintained, was not simply a matter of automating existing criminal justice practices. It was also regarded as the birth of a new vision of criminal justice where activities, machines, personnel, and procedures were modular components in a rationally administered process. The corporation asserted that increased crime rates would lead to increased criminal justice activities, which required increased computing power. In the late 1960s, the Alameda County Data Processing Center unveiled a real-time "police information network" that involved almost seventy law enforcement agencies. Lockheed Missiles and Space Company, a former California-based branch of Lockheed Martin, inventoried data items in each state's criminal justice agencies and offered to analyze them to maximize efficiency. Hughes Aircraft Company designed an automated filing system replete with addresses, aliases, distinguishing marks, driver's licenses, fingerprints, racial descriptors, and Social Security numbers. The Department of Defense also aided these corporations and California in rolling out an information management system to respond to rapid urbanization, increased individual mobilities, and an "aggressive sensitivity for civil rights."[61]

Such developments were not confined to the West Coast. As the War on Crime kicked into gear, the New Jersey–based firm Computer Technology Incorporated developed a digitized ballistics identification system for investigative units throughout urban departments. The system combined computers, electromechanical scanning, and applications that assigned numerical values to ballistics markings. It stored the values on magnetic tape and could match new markings against previous files. In Connecticut, the Woodley Company explored equipping patrol units with car locator devices to further optimize the dispatching system. The company evaluated how efficient patrol units were—in terms of arrests, fuel, and response times—by analyzing police incident data, call box sensors, and car-borne position reporting. Some of these systems were fully automated, while others required the active participation of humans. One example of the latter type involved using geographic information systems to divide jurisdictions into quarter square mile patrol areas.[62] Each area was assigned a number, which patrol units were required to report manually as they moved about the city. IT was also used to optimize this movement. In Maryland, the IIT Research Institute was contracted by the LEAA to design a semiautomated dispatch system for the Washington, D.C., Metropolitan Police Department. The result linked nearly four hundred cranes, cruisers, harbor patrol boats, motorcycles, patrol wagons, and scout cars, each route of which was partially determined by computers in control rooms.

IBM also figured prominently in police computerization. Specifically, it demonstrated the far-reaching powers of the database to police departments gearing up for the War on Crime. Record repositories date back to Scotland Yard in 1829, the first professional police department in the Western world. For more than a century, repositories were used to store information about cases prosecuted and incarcerated persons. The New Orleans Police Department was the first to use an electronic arrest and warrant data processor in 1951, which was made from a vacuum tube–operated calculator connected to a punch card sorter and collator.[63] But following the popular insurrections of the 1960s, IBM showcased a database that could provide patrol forces access to digitized files on people (e.g., criminal records and warrants) and places (e.g., property owners and building blueprints). In prescient fashion, IBM outlined a future where digital computers analyzed geographic, temporal, and type-of-crime patterns in incident data; evaluated personnel performance; managed the allocation of manpower; and processed inquiries sent from remote data terminals. It also prototyped a system that applied military command system technologies and techniques to apprehend criminals, prevent crimes, and inhibit social unrest. The system revolved around a Communications Input-Output Center that circulated to and from geographically tracked patrol units. But the application of such systems at the time was limited as they had to be maintained manually, could only be afforded by large departments, and had to be shared with other state entities.

Biometric technologies also evolved during the 1960s, most of all through advanced criminalistics. Three decades prior, the FBI's Identification Division developed a punch card system for searching fingerprint files using the same system as British colonizers. But each print was identified by ulnar loops, a pattern found on only 60 percent of all fingerprints. As a result, the technique, dubbed the Henry system, was not adequate for the War on Crime. One of the LEAA's main tasks was to develop a new system based on ten-digit fingerprint files. Moreover, the administration sought to automate the entry and retrieval of high-resolution fingerprints given the impending expansion of offender processing. In achieving this, the FBI and the New York State Identification and Intelligence System teamed with titans of engineering, energy, and research, including General

Electric Company and IBM's Center for Exploratory Studies, to investigate digital fingerprint recognition technology. The FBI also collaborated with the Bureau of Standards, Department of Commerce, and U.S. Air Force to design a device that automatically identified the position and orientation of bifurcations and ridge endings in fingerprint cards and convert the information into digital form. Alongside these endeavors, the Bureau of Standards outlined a plan to develop a computer-aided system to automatically read, categorize, serialize, and store ink-based fingerprint cards.[64] Other biometric technologies were developed in Illinois, where the Argonne National Laboratory prototyped automated optical scanners that scanned fingerprint files, translated them into code, and then fed them into datasets. Also during the same time, a division of Litton Industries prototyped the Fingerprint Automatic Classification Technique, which linked fingerprint card scanners, criminal record databases, data terminals, mainframe computers, and printers into an integrated machine. General Electric went so far as to explore ways of using holography to enhance fingerprint recognition. In 1963, a special agent called Carl Voekler realized that the national fingerprint database was so vast that it was no longer humanly manageable. As a result, he approached the National Institute of Standards and Technology to help automate it. Cornell Aeronautical Labs Inc. and North American Aviation Inc. were awarded government contracts to develop digital processes of detecting, encoding, measuring, comparing, and matching fingerprint minutiae. Development continued until the mid-1970s, when the bureau digitized its mushrooming fingerprint database.

As arrest rates escalated toward the end of the 1960s, attention within the state–technology nexus turned to finding ways that technology could be used to expedite processing felony defendants through courts. The vanguards of digital restructuring looked into computer simulation techniques to explore how to enhance court procedures. Juridical technologists were determined to find ways that information communications systems could slash the time it took offenders to go from appearances to dispositions to receiving grand jury indictments. Professors from Harvard's medical and law schools sought ways to integrate scientifically irrefutable proof into the judicial process. The National Center for State Courts' Court

Improvement through Applied Technology initiative and the Criminal Courts Technical Assistance Project explored how to use the information about felony offenders in databases to expedite criminal processing and how the information could be analyzed to determine which counselors were best suited for trial and appellate counsel.

Applications of IT in corrections also gained headway following the rise of the LEAA. Technocrats throughout parole agencies devised disciplinary reporting systems to assess the outcomes of correctional supervision program. In 1964, the interstate Advisory Council on Parole of the National Council on Crime and Delinquency devised a standardized data collection system for correctional assessment. Some advisors suggested that dataphones be installed in each decision maker's office to provide information on whether an offender was a latent recidivist. The rising enthusiasm for categorizing offenders according to demographic and latent characteristics marked the first step toward the database becoming the central technology of the punitive state. In fact, the rise of this trend roughly paralleled the rise of Edgar F. Codd's relational database management system, whose key innovation was to organize data in compounds (Figure 6).[65] Before Codd, database systems arranged data in trees or graphs that required high levels of technical competence to maneuver. Different databases structured data in different ways, making data sharing quite a laborious task. To further complicate things, before relational databases, criminal justice agencies relied on city- or state-controlled data-processing centers.[66] These higher administrative levels were responsible for distributing processing power throughout public agencies, which generally did not privilege police departments.

Codd's invention changed this state of affairs. Much like Hollerith's machine, the relational database tabulated data such that organizing, querying, and retrieving data became unimaginably easier. Codd's relational system laid the foundation for Structured Query Language (SQL), a programming language that allows one to add, search for, combine, and manipulate different data tables within and across multiple databases. With SQL, creating new datasets and cross-tabulating old ones became effortless. In fact, the language is so proficient in organizing data that it enabled low-storage databases to store millions of rows and columns of

TRAFFIC CRIME MAP

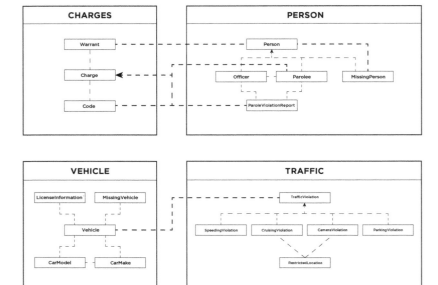

FIGURE 6. Transit authority relational database model. One of the relational database's most revolutionary features was its ability to enable users to access and reorganize data from different datasets. In the criminal justice domain, this meant that various public and private institutions would be able to share data about individuals to authorities. Image by Keenan Dailey.

data. This made the size of database files into an afterthought, which allowed for the production of structured data on unprecedented scales. Such technologies allowed agencies to interface with each other's databases and even populate each other's data fields. The technology was a revelation for the FBI's identification record system. It allowed users to search for and extract data irrespective of the location or structure of the database. This provided a technical nucleus for the National Crime Information Center (NCIC), a centralized database that absorbs data from enforcement agencies all over the country (see chapter 4). The NCIC database houses information on property (e.g., articles, guns, securities, vehicles) and persons (e.g., gang affiliates, fugitives, immigrants, missing persons, sex offenders, terrorist suspects). These files were hailed by the ascendant generation of criminal justice technologists for containing the "most valuable information currently available for the differentiation of offenders," including type of offense, age, race, and sex.[67] Urban police departments also began to implement these new systems for warrants in the 1960s, such as with the Los Angeles Police Department's Automated Wants and Warrant System and San Francisco's Police Information Network.

For correctional apparatuses, the appearance of relational databases came during a period when "theoreticians, practitioners and researchers increasingly [sought] some classification system—some meaningful grouping of offenders into categories" so as to manage them more effectively.[68] Parole administrators developed scientific methods for evaluating parole board decisions. In 1964, a consensus emerged from the National Advisory Council that parole boards needed to develop common data-reporting systems, vocabularies, and standards of evaluating programs. This took place during a time when technocrats began to conceptualize the organizational structure of the correction apparatus as an integrated, multimodal system. And while computer-aided evaluation and tabulation slowly permeated the correctional field at the dawn of the War on Crime, a series of research articles toward the decade's latter half offer a glance into the rational kernel of an increasingly digitized mode of social management. In a revelatory treatise, criminologist Harland Hill laid out a prophetic vision of digitized correctional power toward the end of the 1960s.[69] At a 1967 meeting of the Commission on Law Enforcement Science and Technology, he lamented how far corrections departments were behind the private sector with respect to IT. Hill proposed several ways of closing the gap. One of the more interesting applications of information systems he imagined involved computerizing correctional case management. He painted a picture of how digital computers could optimize receiving, diagnosing, disciplining, monitoring, and evaluating the burgeoning offender population. This included perfunctory tasks like assessing custodial, counseling, educational, and medical practices. It also included feeding correctional decision makers, diagnosticians (educators, social workers, psychiatrists, psychologists), and staff continuous updates on evaluations, recommendations, and relevant details for each individual prisoner. But the most intriguing part of Hill's document is where it outlines a digitized form of correctional control inspired by air defense systems. He imagined the day when the correctional apparatus would be made up of a "sensing system which will maintain surveillance over all offenders, whether in institution or in the community, so that . . . those who are deviating from expected behavior, either in a positive or negative sense, will be called to the attention of correctional authorities."[70]

Hill's vision represented a new way of thinking about criminal justice, whereby criminalized human was but an element of an increasingly automated logistical apparatus designed to shuttle human beings from one institutional node to another. Hill advanced the concept of the "correctional sequence" to illustrate how crime control could be understood as logistical management. In this sequence, the criminalized subject was an object to be secured, transported, processed, and distributed with maximum efficiency. Just like the economic field, surmised the new technologists of racialized punishment, crime control involved collecting, bulk processing, packaging, labeling, storing, and transferring human-made products. This convergence—or, even better, collision—of systems analysis and criminalization reflected what sociologist Alain Touraine called *social rationalization,* as it articulated criminal justice as complex machinery in which each individual component (decision maker, correctional officer, criminal suspect, police officer, prisoner) became progressively interchangeable. This established conditions for an interlocking chain of state apparatuses steered by bureaucrats and technology corporations. Such a state of affairs was touted as the beginning of an unprecedentedly efficient ability to intercept, classify, and micromanage people, populations, and places targeted in the War on Crime. One is almost tempted to think that the overproduction of racialized criminality, which crystallized in the form of the mass incarceration, was inevitable given the newfound emphasis on efficiently patrolling, intercepting, processing, and transporting human subjects.

THE EMERGENCE OF COMPUTATIONAL CRIMINOLOGY

Plans to import digital microcomputers into criminal justice did not only include representing criminal justice processes as mathematical abstractions to maximize their functionality. They also included mathematically representing criminalized territories. Thus the slow introduction of digital computing into the War on Crime went hand in hand with the quantitative modeling of the "black ghetto." Enter a new generation of architects, criminologists, sociologists, and urban planners devoted to modeling, analyzing, and representing criminalized communities to aid War on Crime initiatives.

One of the most impactful transformations during the early phases of criminal justice computerization occurred in the sphere of police knowledge production. Academic researchers across disciplines were mobilized as appendages of the police apparatus, tasked with finding elegant solutions to patrolling the criminalized territories. The living spaces of poor minorities were subsequently dissected and analyzed with unprecedented granularity by social scientists as the War on Crime kicked into gear. Streets, sidewalks, and housing units slowly but surely eclipsed the city-scale and concentric zones as the focus of criminological knowledge production.[71] It is not a coincidence that geographic information systems made a forceful entrance into the criminal justice apparatus at the onset of the War on Crime. Using grant money from the Law Enforcement Assistance Act (1967), the St. Louis Police Department's Resource Allocation Research Unit was among the first to use geographic information systems to organize beat structures according to statistical analysis of incident report data (Figure 7).[72] This involved creating new nine- to twelve-block areas to cultivate and assess emergency call and incident data. These so-called Pauly Areas, named after the unit's project implementation officer, were then correlated with street locations using a computerized street file system in which each street had a unique code number based on recorded incident activity. The unit then turned to Harvard's Laboratory for Computer Graphics and Spatial Analysis to translate the data into contour and flat-tone maps, which was made possible by its vaunted Synagraphic Computer Mapping Program.

The St. Louis Police Department eventually adopted IBM host and communication computers, IBM 1050 computers, and remote teletype terminals to enter and retrieve data on adult arrests, bench warrants, and vehicles. The department also developed a centralized mainframe computer that generated statistical reports on arrests, dispatch call frequencies, and patrol response times. Inasmuch as the system analyzed

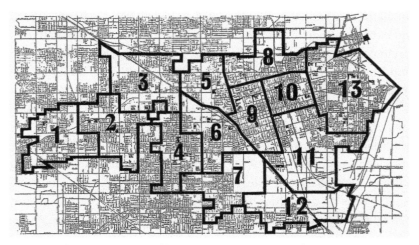

FIGURE 7. Computer-generated beat structure, 1973. Mitchell's computer-generated beat structure presages predictive policing by nearly forty years. For Mitchell, each beat was to be analyzed to determine its relative crime incident rate. This in turn was meant to help police administrators decide beat patrol officer distributions. Mitchell never analyzed correlations between number of beat patrollers in a district and the district's relative crime incident rate. From Phillip S. Mitchell, "Optimal Selection of Police Patrol Beats," *Journal of Criminal Law and Criminology* 63, no. 4 (1973): 582.

police data on scales that were smaller than the department's existing beat structure, it became possible to create a new grid for policing. Each cell in the grid was defined by its number of reported incidents, which in turn was supposed to dictate how intensely it was patrolled. The spread of digital patrol maps preceded geographer Stan Openshaw's articulation of the modifiable area unit problem, which explained how patterns in spatial data were partly determined by classification schema and geographic scale.[73] For instance, analyzing incident data at the level of precincts will yield one number of "high-incident areas," whereas analyzing them at the level of census tracts will yield another. Thus high-incident areas, their size, shape, and density, are partially determined by the idiosyncrasies of geographic information science.

The practice of reducing criminalized territories to matrices of policing and capture brought about new modes of criminological knowledge production. This conceptual shift occurred alongside the birth of *crimes of place theory* and *hot spot criminology,* both based on criminologists' discovery that incident reports are not spread evenly across urban space. Following Claude Shannon's disregard for understanding the meaning of the information at hand, these criminologists deliberately abandoned sociological understandings of crime rates.[74] Understanding why incident reports were geographically clustered was of no interest to these criminologists. From the start, the social function of computational criminology was to produce targets for patrol forces; it is one-dimensional thought operating in two-dimensional space. Thus, by way of Reagan's War on Crime, the spread of personal computers and user-friendly mapping software such as MapInfo established technology as the unmoving mover of criminological knowledge. "Quite soon," criminologists predicted, "[digital] crime mapping will become as much an essential tool of criminological research as statistical analysis is at present."[75] Banishing all context from consideration, ignoring all discoveries in human geography in the past four decades, these theories introduced their own scalar terminology suited for the geographically concentrated War on Crime. *Macro* denoted census tracts, neighborhoods, and square blocks; *meso* denoted block faces and street segments; and *micro* denoted facilities, specific addresses, and street corners. And it is the microscale that reigns supreme in computational criminology. The fetish for the micro—which rippled across biology, material science, and physics—had not only proven a lucrative source for criminologists documenting the details of criminalized microspaces. Preoccupation with the micro also formed a shield against structural analysis. No thought was given to the relations between hot spot microareas and the externally imposed social and punitive policies used to manage them. All sources of illegal activity are seen as intrinsic characteristics of microspaces. Even the physical characteristics of these communities have been construed as if they were causes of criminogenic behavior (Figure 8).[76]

Criminologists' affinity with mathematical abstraction seemed to hold a negative correlation with their interest in the social forces behind rising crime rates.[77] Their veneration for geometry provided an intellectual framework for a pseudo-physics that attributed increased levels of criminalization to attractive forces created by vectors between the

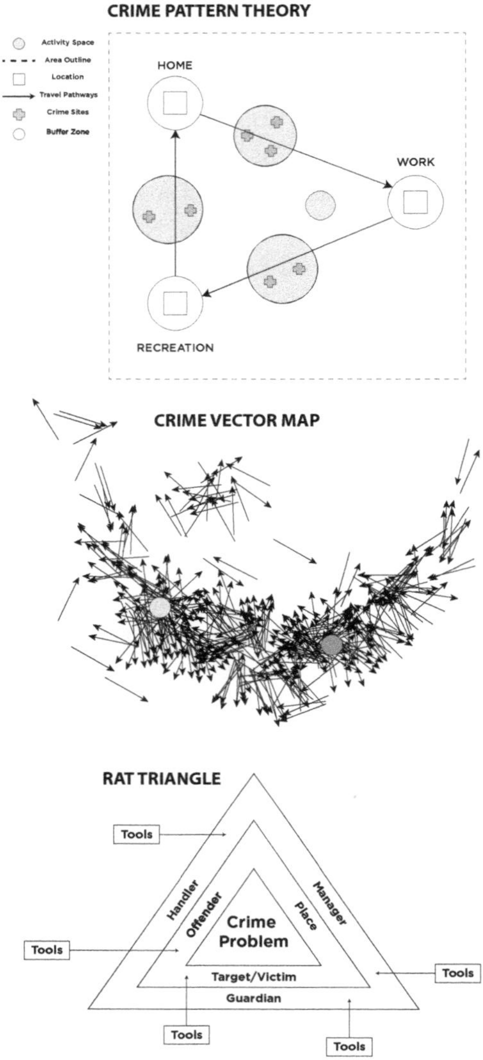

CRIME PATTERN THEORY

Activity Space
Area Outline
Location
Travel Pathways
Crime Sites
Buffer Zone

HOME

WORK

RECREATION

CRIME VECTOR MAP

RAT TRIANGLE

Tools

Handler

Manager

Offender

Place

Crime
Problem

Tools

Target/Victim

Guardian

Tools

Tools

Tools

FIGURE 8. War on Crime era representations of crime and space. Criminologists have produced an abundance of analytical, conceptual, and visualization techniques for incident report data. Such productivity has increased considerably with computerization. The representations give the uncritical eye the impression that the patterns are intrinsic characteristics of space rather than War on Crime artifacts. Courtesy of Keenan Dailey.

residences of offenders and crime locations.[78] Some social scientists invoked astrophysics to explain patterns in crime datasets.[79] Such approaches are of course absurd applications of Newtonian mechanics and explain virtually nothing about geographic patterns found in police datasets in the age of mass criminalization. By completely ignoring the influence that criminal law, crime control policies, and criminal justice data generation techniques have on incident report rates, crime science forecloses its own scientific pretense. But we would do well to avoid underestimating arbitrary uses of science to legitimize apparatuses of state violence.

The political function that underlies the steady march of digital computing into criminological knowledge is twofold. The process is conservative, as it ignores the conditions in which populations are criminalized, and liberal in that it does so in the name of scientific objectivity. What is more, the application of programming languages to criminological knowledge production also maintains a barrier against critical thought. Like any language, programming languages like SQL cannot help but warp the social phenomena they represent. The inherent differences of social phenomena get lost in databases as they are dissected and organized in classification systems, data dictionaries, data models, and the like.[80] Such systems must, as a matter of technical necessity, divide that which they catalog into predefined categories. True differences give way to false equivalences during this process of translating social reality into programming language. "Equivalence itself becomes a fetish."[81] As such, computational criminology is incapable of grasping internal differentiations within the classes of offenders it tabulates. No distinctions are made between the individual who sells narcotics to support a family and the individual who sells them for a gun cartel in computational criminology's system of reference, yet both are coded as targets for heightened police scrutiny. Nor can this criminology grasp the qualitative differences between the crime events it analyzes. No meaningful distinction is made between a chemically addicted person who commits a drug offense, the homeless person who steals food, or the youth who murders for sport. Each subject is an interchangeable target for differential patrolling and punishment. This is extreme positivism, as that which is posited, that which is given, that is, the state's datasets, establishes the limits of intelligibility. By simply sticking to the facts supplied by police departments, computerized criminology "repels recognition of the factors behind the facts, and thus repels recognition of the facts."[82] Between 1975 and 1990, the quinquennial growth index of carceral populations in county jails and in state and federal prisons tripled.[83] From 1980 to 1989, the total number of drug arrests increased by nearly 133 percent.[84] From 1980 to 2000, mandatory minimum sentences quintupled.[85] But such processes fall beyond the purview of corporatized-bureaucratized criminology, as its essential function is to assist population management. This radical erasure of the state's influence on the demographic and geographic patterns in criminal justice datasets is so conspicuous as to be informative.

The convergence of state power, information capital, and positivist social science begat a distinct form of racialized information power in which the incessant measurement, classification, and evaluation of criminalized populations and territories became central to statecraft. In the field of knowledge production, computerization facilitated the century-old practice of decontextualizing the outcomes of racialized governance, this time through digital computing architectures. Criminal justice policy, criminal law, discriminatory profiling, and a century of racist criminal justice practices had absolutely no place in computational criminology. From 1985 to 1990, state expenditures on corrections increased over 150 percent.[86] By claiming that the causes behind rising crime indexes are internal to criminalized communities and unrelated to the detonation of punitive legislation, policies, and practices, bureaucratic criminologists, themselves functionaries of the crime war, erased the criminal justice system from criminological thought. One can draw a straight line from deindustrialization-era criminology to the demonological theories of early modern Europe in terms of ignoring the social processes that determine who is labeled a criminal. But the Americans also made out criminality to be an intrinsic, measurable property of social space—in particular, the social spaces typical to superfluous and socially stigmatized labor power. This set the grounds for an entire criminological knowledge industry based on calculating the attributes of criminalized urban areas on ever smaller scales. The more data that are produced in this industry, the more reasons there are to flood such areas with patrol forces.

The use of statistical data to rationalize racist deployments of criminal justice is not new. Khalil Muhammad powerfully demonstrates how the statistical method allowed the racial state to move away from explicitly racist rationalizations of racial criminalization to covertly racist ones.[87] But in computerizing the criminal justice field, the tripartite force of bureaucrats, technology corporations, and intellectuals did more than reproduce the legacy of racialized criminal justice. Statistical data were not merely signifiers produced and circulated to legitimize anti-blackness. Upon being geocoded and time-stamped, the data were reborn as lifeblood for a digitized complex of patrolling, monitoring, cataloging, evaluating, predicting the behavior of, and intercepting unwanted elements in the most marginal sections of cities.

2

DREAMS OF DIGITAL CARCERAL POWER

The technological veil conceals the reproduction of inequality and enslavement.

—HERBERT MARCUSE, *One-Dimensional Man*

It is tempting to view the explosion of criminal justice technology in the 1990s as inevitable given the digital revolution. But the inordinate amount of resources that have gone into designing, developing, and deploying these technologies cannot be explained by the engineering laws of Gordon Moore or Mark Kryder.[1] The flight of industrial capital, racialized deproletarianization, social struggle, the crime and drug wars, and the rise of information capital each played a role in triggering the criminal justice system's multi-billion-dollar digital metamorphosis. Since the final quarter of the twentieth century, northern industrial cities have undergone a slow and uneven shift from manufacturing sites into sites of conspicuous consumption, financial exchange, real estate development, and IT industry. Some prime features of this shift included the privatization of public services, criminalization of poverty, and the ascent of information infrastructure. The digitization of the carceral state cannot be understood apart from these developments.

For city governances, large-scale projects to establish digital infrastructures for criminal justice were rooted in efforts to manage contradictions specific to postindustrialized urban space. On one hand, the forces of global economic power bunkered inside urban arcologies made up of banks, condominiums, financial firms, gentrification, high-end shopping, and tax abatements. Urban administrations, no matter their party composition, funneled development capital, tax concessions, and zoning bonuses to various industries characterizing upstart global cities. Urban decision-making was slowly but steadily handed over to business improvement districts, special purpose development corporations, and tax increment financing districts insulated from public oversight. Urban planning initiatives were quietly steered by technology corporations, such as CISCO, IBM, and Siemens, that charter IT-friendly "solutions" for architects, city planners, engineers, and public officials in charge of cities.

On the other hand, the "territories surrounding these nodes play an increasingly subordinate function."[2] Indeed, the formation of securitized centers of urban wealth went hand in hand with the formation of deindustrialized, devalued neighborhoods. Upscale lofts came to coexist with dilapidated housing projects, and the latter spread at extraordinary rates. Between the 1980s and 1990s, sociologist William Julius Wilson calculated industry jobs for workers without high school degrees decreased by 73,000 in Baltimore, 89,000 in St. Louis, 172,000 in Philadelphia, and 492,000 in New York City.[3] Public workforces were also significantly downsized. Between the 1970s and the 1980s, unemployment in some predominantly black neighborhoods increased at quadruple the rate of city averages, and in some cities, as many as 80 percent of black families lived in poverty.[4] As the outmoded labor force's economic function declined, so too did the state's inclination to support its social reproduction. Cities hemorrhaged affordable housing, as contractors prioritized high-income housing to abet gentrification over low-income housing for obsolete workers. In 1970, there was a surfeit of almost 2.5 million low-income housing units in the United States. By 1985, there was a deficit of 3.7 million. From 1978 to 1988, the Department of Housing and Urban Development's appropriations for subsidized housing were slashed by 70 percent. Homeless populations expanded, which were disproportionately made up of female victims of domestic violence, displaced elders, the mentally ill, and undocumented immigrants. Mass criminalization was one solution to managing the political radicalism and social problems that sprang from these conditions.[5]

All of these mutations took place alongside the revolution of information capital. On the technical side of things, this world-changing event was made possible by the combination of the internet, microprocessors, personal computers, relational databases, and the World Wide Web. For the business sector, the digital landscape established new horizons to conduct exchange, segment consumer markets, and optimize logistical chains. New profit margins were discovered through data mining using Gregory Piatetsky-Shapiro's knowledge discovery in databases techniques. Businesses wielded these techniques for everything from employee scheduling to micromarketing to price strategizing, among other practices. Knowledge industries that emerged from these developments were centered in cities: Cambridge, Raleigh-Durham, San Francisco, San Jose, Seattle, Washington, D.C. In fact, the steady expansion of urban tech hubs exacerbated the obsolescence of the very populations whom IT companies eventually designed technologies to digitally carceralize.

SEEDS OF POLICE COMPUTERIZATION

Geographic information systems were crucial to police initiatives to incorporate computer technology during the 1960s. The systems, which manage spatial data, were trumpeted by police officials and software companies as means of patrolling criminalized areas with greater cost-effectiveness and efficiency. Spatial data were touted as being especially valuable for police units dispatched to suppress urban uprisings. Political radicalism was on the offensive. As the 1960s raged on, civil rights and black nationalism drew closer to Third World and labor movements, spreading their influence through Chicanx, feminist, indigenous, and queer struggles. Speaking in 1964 in front of the Militant Labor Forum, Malcolm X argued that "America's strategy is the same strategy as that which was used in the past by colonial powers: divide and conquer."[6] In the political field, this strategy involved gerrymandering, sabotage, and the installment of a police state. "Algeria was a police state," X observed. "Any occupied territory is a police state; and this is what Harlem is. . . . The police in Harlem, their presence is like an occupying army. . . . They're in Harlem to protect the interests of the businessmen who don't even live there."[7] This radical interpretation of racialized governance as a mode of internal colonialism was foundational for the Black Panther Party for

Self-Defense, which was forged to establish a human infrastructure that included, among various services, the armed protection of civilians from the Oakland Police Department following a bloody rebellion in Watts, California, in 1965. One way that the state responded to the surge of black radicalism involved restructuring its enforcement apparatuses. The most totalitarian expression of these reactions was the Counterintelligence Program (COINTELPRO), infamously devised to "expose, disrupt, misdirect, discredit, or otherwise neutralize the activities of black nationalists."[8] COINTELPRO was handled by cold warriors whose conception of policing technology was mostly limited to wiretaps. But near the same time, more sophisticated technologies began to appear at the state level.

The introduction of geographic information systems into the police apparatus was to a great degree a function of happenstance. Geographic information systems first appeared in police departments in the 1970s, alongside the quantitative revolution in the discipline of geography. This significant disciplinary development catapulted spatial science to the forefront of academic spatial knowledge production. The revolution was led by a post–World War II generation of geographers seeking to establish a universal ontology of social space through descriptive statistics, inferential statistics, probability theory, and social physics. This new perspective, in which human geographies were seen as calculable, predictable, and controllable, was deeply appealing to police departments leading the crime and drug wars.[9] The first attempt to fuse quantitative geography with policing was undertaken in the early 1970s by Phillip S. Mitchell, an expert in mathematical programming and public systems working for the California Council of Criminal Justice (CCCJ).[10] An associate of the International Association of Chiefs of Police and board member of the CCCJ's Research Development Task Force, Mitchell pushed for using spatial clustering methods to decide where police should concentrate patrol forces. Mitchell's work was just a few years removed from the founding of geographic information software companies Esri and M&S Computing (now Intergraph). Mitchell was perhaps too far ahead of his time. The cost of mainframe computers and relative lack of updated geographic base files during the 1970s limited digital police mapping from spreading to most departments for a few decades.[11] Nevertheless, Mitchell's work was

```
                                                                      0.0  0.0  0.6  0.0  0.0
                                              0.1  0.4                0.0  0.1  0.2  0.1  0.0  0.1  0.0  0.1  0.0
                  0.0  0.1                     0.4  0.2  0.1  0.2  0.1  0.0  0.0  0.1  0.0  0.1  0.0  0.1  0.0  0.0  0.1
            0.1  0.4  0.5  0.6  0.9  1.0  2.0  2.0  0.4  0.3  0.3  0.2  0.0  0.1  0.0  0.0  0.2  0.1  0.1  0.1  0.1  0.0
            0.5  1.1  1.0  1.9  1.6  1.6  0.6  1.6  1.4  2.0  0.2  0.4  0.0  0.1  0.0  0.0  0.2  0.1  0.0  0.0  0.0  0.0
  0.2  0.8  0.4  1.4  0.5  0.3  0.9  0.8  1.5  0.9  1.6  3.3  0.5  0.1  0.0  0.0  0.2  0.0       0.0  0.0  0.0  0.0  0.0
0.2  2.8  0.9  1.3  1.2  0.6  1.0  0.9  0.8  1.5  1.2  3.4  1.1  0.4  0.1  0.1  0.0  0.0
0.3  0.9  0.7  0.8  0.8  0.8  1.1  0.7  1.8  1.4  1.0  1.1  1.3  0.6  0.7  0.1  0.1  0.0
0.6  0.3  0.1  0.1  0.3  1.0  0.3  0.6  0.5  1.0  0.3  0.4  1.6  1.0  0.9  0.5  0.1
            0.3  0.7  1.3  0.6  2.4  1.7  1.4  0.7  1.1  0.4  0.1
            1.0  1.0  0.7  2.2  0.6  0.4  0.4  0.5
            0.3       0.2  1.2  0.5  0.7  0.3  0.0
```

FIGURE 9. Reported incident and patrol deployment matrix. Phillip Mitchell presented a new way of looking at the urban field. Here city space is reduced to relative rates of reported incidents. Areas with higher rates would be targeted for extra patrolling. From Phillip S. Mitchell, "Optimal Selection of Police Patrol Beats," *Journal of Criminal Law and Criminology* 63, no. 4 (1973): 580.

foundational in bringing differential policing into programming language. With Mitchell, the rationalization for concentrating patrol forces in already criminalized areas was expressed as

$$L(k') = S(k') \sum_m \sum_{j \in R(k')} t(k') p(j, m),$$

where p represents the expected number of incidents of type m based on past events, $t(k')$ the average driving time required to respond to an incident for patrol unit k, and $S(k')$ the average incident load for the unit. Equations like these signified the dawn of a new conception of urban space. The city was rendered a grid of rationally distributed patrol forces (Figure 9). Of course, the idea that the police apparatus should be the choice instrument to manage social problems and struggles was itself a political invention. But where southern segregationists normalized racialized policing through biological racism, explicit laws, and overt racial demagoguery, northern powers normalized it through mathematical formulas.

The geographic information industry slowly expanded during the 1980s, which saw the establishment of companies such as Autodesk, GE Energy/Smallworld, and MapInfo. Different state apparatuses, such as the

U.S. Defense Mapping Agency, played a role in assisting these companies. Founded in 1972, the mapping agency was a Vietnam War invention for generating digital maps, charts, and positional data for military operations and weapons systems. The emphasis on spatial data production reached the domestic police apparatus in the face of mounting opposition to police violence brought about by Reagan's War on Drugs. Antagonism between police and the negatively racialized poor became increasingly volatile and reminiscent of Fanon's description of a colonial "compartmentalized world." Black separatism began to reappear through a revitalized Nation of Islam. Cedric Robinson published *Black Marxism* in 1983. Hip-hop music morphed into ethnographic analyses of racial criminalization, punctuated by Niggaz Wit Attitudes' (NWA) 1988 billboard success "Fuck the Police" and Ice T's "Cop Killer" four years later. These tensions boiled over following the acquittal of Los Angeles Police Department (LAPD) officers who brutalized Rodney King while being recorded in 1991, which detonated revolts on a massive scale. Fanon could have easily predicted what happened next: the result was not a rational confrontation of viewpoints but rather some seven thousand federal troops deployed to suppress popular insurrection, twelve hundred of whom were Marines.[12] Approximately one thousand people lost homes, twenty-four hundred were injured, twenty thousand lost jobs, ten thousand were arrested, and $1 billion worth of capital was destroyed.

As computing became cheaper and more powerful, urban police departments turned to geographic information systems in efforts to convert insurgent spaces into rationally managed microspaces. The practical effect was to mark off stigmatized territories, classify them according to varying levels of policeability, and codify uneven distributions of legalized violence with the aid of spatial statistics. Geographic information systems provided technical support for these objectives. The federal government subsequently poured funds into the Institute for Intergovernmental Research, International Association of Directors of Law Enforcement Standards and Training, and National Training and Technical Assistance Center to develop its spatial data infrastructure. Drawing inspiration from the blossoming subdiscipline of automated geography in the academy, these collaborations unleashed a series of projects to integrate geospatial visual analytics, spatial econometrics, and three-dimensional simulations of cities for police.

Programs to reorganize the police apparatus around geographic databases spread like wildfire as the millennium's end approached. In the 1990s, the National Institute of Justice (NIJ) launched its Crime Mapping Research Center (CMRC) in the behavioral sciences division. CMRC teamed with Esri to create a suite of software including a free application that enabled police to record geocoded information and display it on digital maps, crime analysis extensions for standard geographic software, and regional crime analysis application enabling information sharing across police jurisdictions. Five years following its launch, the CMRC was renamed Mapping and Analysis for Public Safety (MAPS), and it shifted its focus to developing artificial intelligences to find new types of patterns in police geographic systems. This digitized production of knowledge was not intended to deepen understandings of criminal behavior. Police mapping was rather meant to produce logistical knowledge to suppress urban radicalization and social disorders. Such knowledge arose amid city efforts to manage the racial and spatial contradictions inherent to the accumulation of capital. As Henri Lefebvre discovered, capital overcomes crises by producing new types of spaces—not only material space but also *representations of space*. In the case of policing, legions of city authorities, computer scientists, criminologists, and software firms created a boundless variety of cartographies to aid patrol units: raster maps depicted densities of reported incidents through shaded census tracts, police precincts, and zip codes; density maps subdivided urban space according to reported incident rates; kernel density maps displayed reported incident densities in a continuous fashion that superseded administrative boundaries; standard deviation ellipses differentiated hot spots according to their size; and kernel smoothing represented hot spots through a type of geocoded thermal vision. What these representations of space held in common was that they all mapped something inhibiting urban redevelopment—the growing mass of devalued populations. And whereas the maps of social ecology begat archetypal zones, those of computerized criminology begat *targets*.

Heat mapping was only one aspect of police computerization; the latter also involved populating databases with information about criminalized populations. In 1987, the Los Angeles Sheriff's Department and Law Enforcement Communications Network introduced the Gang Reporting, Evaluation, and Tracking system, a database of two hundred thousand purported gang members and affiliates. The database, later renamed CalGang, included more than two hundred data elements about suspects (addresses, acquaintances, gang monikers, names, physical descriptions, photographs, Social Security numbers) and gangs (racial makeup).[13] By the mid-1990s, 40 percent of incarcerated juveniles, 25 percent of incoming male inmates, and nearly 15 percent of nonaligned inmates were registered in gang databases.[14] At the time, somewhere around 70 percent of large police departments were using gang databases as well.[15] Though legal definitions of gang member often are not written into state legislative codes, they are nevertheless written into computer code. Individuals observed in photographs with known gang members or who have corresponded with known gang members, have gang tattoos, or write about gangs in books, in papers, or on walls are susceptible to being categorized as gang members.

Between 1995 and 1996, Congress appropriated $67.5 million of defense funding to transfer military technology to police departments.[16] The Virginia-based Rapid Prototyping Facility, managed by the FBI and Advanced Research Projects Agency, designed an automobile tracking system made up of a grid of hidden sensors strewn throughout a city that tracks vehicles in real time. The 1990s also saw the government and technology companies explore ways to cybernetically enhance patrol units. In an effort to compress urban space-time for patrollers, police turned to the fledgling field of mobile computing during the War on Drugs. Automated vehicle locators coupled with portable terminals were first used to match emergency calls with patrol units in the 1970s. But moving into the following decade, companies including Motorola and Tyler Technologies began entering into the computer-aided dispatch systems market. These firms demonstrated how patrol officers could access local and national criminal history databases and databases in other bureaucracies. By the late 1990s, the Texas Transportation Institute had prototyped the first smart patrol car, equipped with touchscreens providing access to GPS vehicle locators, radar, and video feeds.[17] This was the beginning of the transformation of the patrol unit into a miniature and mobile control room. The idea was for officers to sit behind neon screens as they navigated the criminalized territories. This meshing of officer and machine found its subjective expression in technologies devised to enhance the "situational awareness" of patrollers. Situational awareness was a martial theory about relations between human perception and environments. It is anchored in the notion that the lack of environmental knowledge is the root cause of human errors. Integrating digital computers into these activities, according to technocrats and IT companies, could simultaneously increase human environmental knowledge while decreasing mental workloads. The emergence of situational awareness in the policing domain was a boon for information capitalists. Technology companies like L-Tron Corporation designed webinars to help police departments minimize potential distractions for beat patrols; corporate–academic associations such as the International Symposium on Wearable Computing and consulting companies such as the New York State Technology Enterprise Corporation designed augmented reality training programs where officers interact with three-dimensional simulations and wearable technology. Large telecommunications companies like Verizon and small ones like WirelessUSA Inc. rebranded old information communication technology as situational awareness enhancers.[18] The Violent Crime Control and Law Enforcement Act (1994) provided broad support for cutting-edge identification systems, criminal records systems, fingerprinting systems, and mobile digital terminals to further abet digitally enhanced situational awareness (see section 210501 of the act). In 1998, the Clinton administration signed the Crime Identification and Technology Act, which authorized $1.25 billion in state grants to develop information and identification technologies so that patrol units could gain better awareness of who occupied the environments they patrolled.

The large-scale production of policing technologies brought the state, technocrats, and the IT sector closer with respect to mass criminalization. By the end of the 2000s, teams of criminologists, computer scientists, police personnel, and state officials had established journals, quarterlies, and websites to address police technology issues ranging from tutorials for software to tips for implementing systems. Crime science for the digital age was born. The decade also saw the federal government fund private policy consultants to develop crime mapping analysis software to be provided freely to police departments across the country. Police began to produce and circulate journals espousing the virtues of affordable commercial GIS packages, SQL compatible databases, and statistical software. The Police Foundation introduced a quarterly forum for crime cartographers to keep abreast with "timely topics that are well written and practical for application—perhaps even written by some of you reading this column!"[19] Magazines such as *Government Technology, Law Enforcement Technology,* and *Law Enforcement Product News* appeared to exploit the technofetishism that permeated police circles. Academic journals such the *Journal of Quantitative Criminology* and *Crime Science* emerged under the banners of "crime forecasting" or "prospective hot spotting" for the expressed purpose of assisting police in adapting computer technology. This lucrative enterprise became a central site in reproducing the symbolic violences inherent to racial capitalism as it upheld a legacy of restricting the legibility of the racially stigmatized urban poor to signifiers of deviance and punishment. Thus the computerization of the police apparatus was key in broader projects of urban administration to turn deproletarianized minority neighborhoods into administrative units characterized by, to borrow from Charles Pinderhughes, a "geographically-based pattern of subordination of a differentiated population."[20] Although the era of digitized policing was rolled out under the pretext of precision targeting, it spread alongside the increasingly differential and invasive policing of these populations in their *entirety.*

COMPUTERIZING CORRECTIONS

The introduction of digital computing to the correctional apparatus simultaneously centralized and decentralized the production of carceral space. This contradictory process was spurred by the responses of city authorities, federal technocrats, and a nascent IT sector to prison overpopulation, the prisoner's rights movement, and the Great Recession. On the quantitative side, any number of facts might be recited to cast into relief the sheer scale of the carceral project to contain these urban problems. From the 1980s to the mid-1990s, the prison population increased threefold, correctional spending increased fourfold, and drug convictions increased almost tenfold. So racialized was the carceral explosion that black males ended up 6 times more likely to be incarcerated than white males, latinx males were 2.3 times more likely to be incarcerated than white males, and indigenous youth were 3 times more likely than white youth to be held in juvenile detention. The total number of black women incarcerated eclipsed that of any male population in other Western capitalist nations.[21] And although the United States accounts for only 5 percent of the human population, it came to account for nearly a quarter of its prisoners.

On the qualitative side, old forms of stigma were reactivated and adapted to the times to normalize the rise of the carceral state. Social scientists were key in this regard. Urban black youths were cast by criminologists, political scientists, and public officials as "superpredators" belonging to an underclass that posed an existential threat to the whole of civilization.[22] Such dehumanization was perhaps necessary given the inhumanity of the carceral apparatus. The barbarity of this apparatus was made abundantly clear in a 1999 report by Amnesty International, *Not Part of My Sentence: Violations and Human Rights of Women in Prison*.[23] The report found that more than eighty thousand incarcerated women were mothers who were separated from more than two hundred thousand minors. By the late 1990s, some twenty-two hundred pregnant women were in jail, and more than thirteen hundred babies were born to incarcerated mothers. What is more, each state established laws that allowed for the termination of carceral captives' parental rights. And in many instances, this cruel machine exacerbated the everyday violences experienced by criminalized minority women. Amnesty International found that black and latinx inmates in New York—the majority of whom were incarcerated for drug-related reasons, minor property crimes, or public order offenses—had significantly higher likelihoods of experiencing domestic violence, incest, and rape than the wider population.

The introduction of computer technology into correctional facilities was jump-started by a surge of organized resistance to these conditions. The first systematic programs to computerize corrections took place during the 1970s, which witnessed the prison population increase by nearly 50 percent. The political dimensions that underwrote prison growth during this decade were captured in Black Panther Party member George Jackson's prison letters, *Soledad Brother,* which chronicled the politicization of incarceration following the urban revolts a few years prior. Jackson documented in vivid detail the crippling effect that politicized prisons had on the Black Power movement, American Indian Movement, and labor struggles made by rural white workforces. Shortly after *Soledad Brother* appeared, the Manhattan House of Detention (MHD) was jolted by resistance. Though MHD was designed to hold 925 inmates, it held more than 2,000.[24] It was so overcrowded that almost half of its one-person cells contained three inmates. Inspections found that the complex was grossly underfunded, which resulted in shortages of beds, medical accoutrements, and soap, and frequently had scourges of rats, roaches, and lice. In August 1970, inmates detained five prison guards, demanding the city respond to inedible food, brutality, overcrowding, racism, and indefinite pretrial detention periods. Several participants in the MHD revolt were transferred to Attica Prison, which erupted in 1971 into the revolt of one thousand prisoners early in September. The Attica Prison Liberation Faction emerged at the forefront of the rebellion to issue the state with a manifesto of demands that included, but were not limited to, adequate medical attention, constitutional protections, minimum wages for prison labor, democratically elected parole boards, the right to legal representation at parole hearings, more sanitary conditions, and ending punishments on the basis of political views. The manifesto captured the radical subjectivities generated by revolt in Soledad Prison, Folsom Prison, and San Quentin around the same time. Administrative brutality was the most visible aspect, though not the only aspect, of the state's response to these basic demands.[25] What also ensued was the simultaneous centralization and decentralization of carceral space courtesy of digital computing networks.

Installing Computers in Cages

One of the ways that state authorities grappled with the carceral explosion was by centralizing administrative functions through computer technologies. Database management systems were embraced by prison administrators in efforts to expedite inmate processing. Before these databases, prison intake involved entering data on each incoming inmate's aliases, birthdate, criminal record, fingerprints, medical/mental records, security threats, sex, and sexual offenses, among other factors. As the imprisoned population increased, screening each individual inmate became so burdensome that it led to overcrowded intake facilities. The state of affairs threatened to bottleneck the entire carceral machine. Inmate management databases were thus promoted by technocrats at the Justice Department, at the National Institute of Corrections, and by private firms, such as the SEARCH Group Inc., as remedies for these administrative challenges. As early as 1980, the National Consortium for Justice Information and Statistics began compiling directories for corrections management information systems.[26] One of its first moves was to inventory the types of hardware, programming languages, and staff personnel (data entry operators, operations supervisors, programmers, systems analysts, terminal operators) in use at correctional facilities throughout the country (Figure 10). The consortium's central goal was to create a knowledge community of technocrats and companies to brainstorm how technology could be put in the service of mass captivity. In 1982 in Illinois, the Criminal Justice Information Systems Division and Statistical Analysis Center initiated the Correctional Institution Management Information System Data Project to appraise the use of database management in the Cook County Department of Corrections.[27] The project focused on finding computerized solutions to cleaning and circulating inmate data. Shortly thereafter, the Association of State Correctional Administrators, Bureau of Justice Statistics, Corrections Program Office, Federal Bureau of Prisons, and NIJ joined forces to design standardized templates for digital inmate processing. They proposed automation as the cheapest, fastest, and most effective way to slash the amount of time incoming prisoners spent in intake facilities. Carceral technocrats also developed classification rubrics to analyze these data to determine an inmate's disciplinary, housing, and security requirements. Toward the end of the 1980s, the Office of Justice Programs and Bureau of Justice Statistics conducted a series of reports, such as *Strategies for Improving Data Quality*, to make data entry, data maintenance, and regulatory functions more efficient.

COMPUTER SENDS MEDICAL INFO FROM COOK CO. JAIL TO IDOC

by PAUL ZOMCHEK
Editorial Assistant

A COMPUTER system developed y the Illinois Criminal Justice Information Authority is being used to eport diverse medical information bout inmates transferred from Cook county Jail to the State prison ystem.

The Correctional Institution Management Information System CIMIS) was recently expanded to enable staff at the jail's Cermak Health enter to send more detailed medical ata to the Illinois Department of orrections (IDOC) reception center n Joliet, and to transfer the information much faster. Previously, medical nformation transmitted via CIMIS as limited to tuberculosis and xually-transmitted diseases, two ommon problems among inmate opulations. In addition, the system ent data about special diets for inmates.

Dr. John Raba's Cermak's medical irector, said his staff can now use IMIS to send data on nine separate iseases or conditions, with more ategories planned for the future. nd for the first time, CIMIS terinals have been placed in the medical center itself, allowing a faster ransfer of medical information to OC, he said.

udit Reveals Most CIMIS Data ighly Accurate," Page 11.

THE AUTHORITY first developed CIMIS in the early 1970s to omputerize a variety of correctional nformation. Two versions of the sysem were originally designed: one, installed in 1974, specifically for IDOC; he other for the Cook County Department of Corrections (CCDOC), nstalled in 1977. Four counties in ther states also use the CIMIS oftware.

The CIMIS medical information omponent was created so that medial data about inmates sentenced to tate prison from Cook County could e sent automatically, said Authority ssistant Director Edward F. Maier. le said the system allows IDOC to uickly recognize and treat pending nedical problems of convicts from ook County.

Statistics show that more than alf of all prisoners sentenced to OC adult institutions each year ome from Cook County. All risoners committed to IDOC are first rocessed at the Joliet Correctional enter before they are sent to other tate correctional facilities.

A medical assistant at Cook County Jail's Cermak Health Center enters medical data into the CIMIS computer system. Information about inmates transferred from the jail to the State prison system is then transferred electronically to the Department of Corrections reception center in Joliet. (Photo by Paul Zomchek)

TREATING INMATES' medical problems at the Joliet facility can help prevent the spread of infectious diseases at other IDOC institutions, which in turn can save tax dollars, said Marie Hall, IDOC's administrator of health services.

She said that getting proper medical data on inmates sent from CCDOC may have taken more than a week before the CIMIS medical component was implemented. Immediacy is important, she stressed, because certain diseases that a new prisoner has upon entering a prison can spread easily throughout the facility's population.

"In two instances within a three week period, we had discovered, as a result of this information, individuals who had been tested for venereal disease, but who had not yet completed treatment," she said. "This early knowledge allowed us to complete treatment on these individuals prior to their entering a general population."

Ms. Hall said she could not "put a dollar figure on the possible savings to the department and to the taxpayers of Illinois," but estimated it was significant.

ALTHOUGH CIMIS can now transfer to IDOC more information on a variety of diseases, Dr. Raba said

the system cannot be used for sending complete medical histories. "For medical-legal reasons we cannot send a complete record," he said.

"But it is absolutely vital that we send down a list of [an inmate's] current medical problems and current medications," he said. "Not to do that would be unethical, and would set the person up for so many medical problems that it would be of tremendous legal culpability."

After a CCDOC inmate is examined, a medical assistant at Cermak enters into CIMIS data about any current medical problems the person has. Next, the information is sent to one of the Authority's computers in Chicago, where it is reformatted so the codes from CCDOC can be translated for IDOC. The Authority's computer then sends the data to Springfield, where the State's central computer makes the information available to the Joliet reception center. In all, the transfer takes only a few seconds for each inmate's record.

"I think it's terrific," said Dr. Raba. "Without computers, in the long run we would have to tie up so many people. A computer can do the work efficiently, quickly and neatly. It frees up staff to do more hands-on work as opposed to paper work."

FIGURE 10. Correctional Institution Management Information System. The introduction of computer processing to prisoner management brought new secretarial practices to the carceral state, with all their gendered implications. In the Kafkaesque machine that is the computerized prison, administrators generate an exhaustive record trail in the process. From Paul Zomchek, "Computer Sends Medical Info from Cook Co. Jail to IDOC," *Compiler*, 1984, 3.

The slow creep of IT extended to one of the most totalitarian expressions of mass criminalization—the supermax prison. These hypersecuritized "prisons inside of prisons" were reserved for political dissidents and violent inmates. While the notion of indefinite administrative lockdown dates back to Alcatraz circa the Great Depression, it achieved broad normalization in the 1990s. Carceral power achieved its densest state in supermax facilities, thanks in part to tech firms. These facilities were designed with control rooms as nerve centers, where correctional officers could check each individual cell using radio frequency monitoring. Internal detection technologies including electrical circuit systems, light beam intrusion systems, motion sensors, and sound detection systems were installed to securitize ceiling crawl spaces, mechanical rooms, and ventilation openings.[28] Computer-operated lock operating systems were put into cell doors so that they could be opened remotely. Telephones and intercom systems were fit with automated recording systems to listen in on conversations. Remote-controlled surveillance cameras were stationed to overlook elevators, living unit access, living unit day halls, pedestrian circulation corridors, and sally ports. These hyperregulated compounds were further fortified by automated perimeter security systems composed of electric field sensors, infrared sensors, seismic sensors, and video motion detectors. Wardens across the country championed computer-managed lighting and sensors as cost-effective substitutes for expensive watchtowers.[29] Lethal fences capable of conducting up to ten thousand volts of electricity also emerged as common perimeter defense technologies at the edges of supermax apparatuses.

Prison administration could not escape some measure of technological displacement under these conditions. The RAND Corporation proclaimed that the mergence of computer technology and correctional management "changed the nature of prison functioning and of prison construction and design. The transition moved many prison functions from being personnel-intensive to technology-enabled."[30] In point of fact, as early as the mid-1980s, Denning Mobile Robotics Inc. began development of robotic prison guards. Standing three and a half feet tall and weighing two hundred pounds, the Denning Sentry was designed to detect intruders and smoke using Motorola 68000 microprocessors. The dream of digitally administered inmates was further pursued the following decade. One example involved using radio frequency identification tracking devices to conduct roll calls, notify staff when inmates were approaching restricted areas, and alert correctional officers when rival gang members closed in on one another. The NIJ and Space and Naval Warfare Systems Center sought ways to combine location-aware prisoner tracking, biometric devices, and CCTV surveillance to keep constant watch over inmate consumption and movement.[31]

As the 1990s progressed, the IT sector was offering products and services for a myriad of prison processes, from access control to prisoner monitoring. For instance, the company GTL, which markets itself as the "corrections industry's trusted, one-stop source for integrated technology solutions," unveiled a database to provide "end-to-end prison management" throughout the cycle of sentencing, intake, cell assignment, meal planning, and release. New markets also emerged for a myriad of technologies to monitor staff and visitors. Backscatter imaging, electric field tomography, low-dose radiation body scanning, and orifice-scanning machines are some examples. By the mid-1990s, as the carceral population surpassed 2 million people, prison technologists, bureaucratic social scientists, and IT companies scrambled to understand how digital technology might best help manage the unwieldy scale of mass incarceration. Much of the development in this sphere was assisted by the National Law Enforcement and Corrections Technology Center (NLECTC), which grew out of the NIJ's Office of Science and Technology in 1994. NLECTC's main objectives included establishing equipment performance and technical standards, providing research and development support to the NIJ, and overseeing the transfer of information communication technology from the prototyping stage out into the correctional and law enforcement fields. A new market was born. Companies as big as Motorola and as small as Syscon took to designing software for corrections management, offender management, and jail management.

During NLECTC's early days, federal and state-level prison administrators organized a country-wide report on correctional databases (Figure 11). The report gave birth to a standardized rubric of more than two hundred data elements, including information on inmate behavior, convictions, fees and fines, risk assessments, sentences, and socioeconomic profiles.[32]

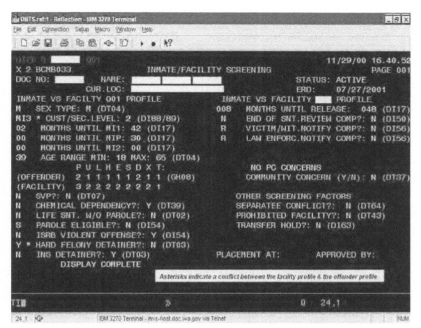

FIGURE 11. Automated Prison Classification System. Inmate Facility Screen
Prisoner classification systems were co-constituted alongside an entire carceral
logistics. Database management systems allowed for granular classification schema
to help administrators determine the most cost-effective means of managing
inmates. From Tim Brennan, David Wells, and Jack Alexander, *Enhancing Prison
Classification Systems: The Emerging Role of Management Information Systems*,
ed. National Institute of Corrections (Washington, D.C.: U.S. Department of
Justice, 2004), 171.

Taking advantage of the growing carceral data environment, Federal
Prison Industries, which oversees manufacturing in federal penitentiaries, developed a database that used Microsoft's SQL Server 7 for data
warehousing, electronic commerce, and enterprise resource planning
to identify emergent security risks, prison transfers, and punishments.
Correctional institutions in Colorado, Illinois, North Carolina, Pennsylvania, and Washington developed risk-assessment algorithms to predict
inmates' risk of recidivism, violations, and violence. These were intended
to aid administrators in deciding cell assignments, security precautions,
and disciplinary programs for inmates.[33]

Carceral algorithms calculated inmates' risk of violence and recidivism based on factors such as educational attainment, gang affiliations, language proficiency, mental health evaluations, socioeconomic background, and work history. They also calculated the relative significance of each factor for a number of possible scenarios (e.g., collusion or escape). Additional algorithms, such as the psychological assessment technology firm PAR Inc.'s Inmate Personality Assessment Inventory and the PAI Interpretive Report for Correctional Settings, were also developed during this period to assess the emotional and psychological states of inmates.

In addition to managing individual inmates, carceral technologists looked to digital computing to manage the arrangement of space. As the millennium neared its end, the American Probation and Parole Association convened in New York to explore how geographic information software could be implemented to organize carceral space, time, and subjects.[34] The summit laid the groundwork for a geographic information database system called Correctional Mapping (CORMAP), which classified inmates by risk factor to assist prison administrators in determining cell and housing arrangements. CORMAP tracked the age, ethnoracial category, religion, and gang affiliation composition of each cell and housing unit. Some later versions of the software generated predictions of potential escape routes based on the architectural layout of the facility, group affiliation data, inmate locational data, and inmate interaction records.[35] CORMAP also generated visualizations of the locations of gang members and sites of repeated disciplinary incidents. When linked to surveillance equipment (e.g., ankle bracelets, CCTV cameras), it could receive and map the locational data of an inmate's every movement. NLECTC toyed with versions of CORMAP that kept logs of every person with whom an inmate has been in contact during incarceration.[36] As the twenty-first century advanced, the carceral state's technologists began to explore how prison space-time could be represented in three-dimensional models. During the same period, the California Department of Corrections and Rehabilitation (CDCR) joined forces with the LAPD to integrate geographic information databases into prisons. Police saw a great deal of potential for integrating digital mapping into prisons, as they were the "functional equivalent of precincts."[37]

The efforts on behalf of administrative technocrats and eager IT companies amounted to the dream of a truly totalitarian apparatus. Their imaginations ran wild with ideas to add biometric, disciplinary, family, financial, legal, locational, medical, and physiological information about inmates to the carceral state's database infrastructure. They eventually summoned the image of a computerized cage in which all behaviors, movements, and risks were quantified and analyzed in real time. Early into the new millennium, the NIJ and Space and Naval Warfare System Center began to investigate how biometric technologies could be implemented in correctional facilities to manage access to different areas. Fingerprint and iris scan technology would regulate the movements of inmates, prison officers, and visitors. Florida State University's Center for Criminology and Public Policy collaborated with the state's Department of Corrections to optimize its Correctional Operations Trend Analysis System (COTAS), which analyzed both historical and real-time data concerning individual inmates, institutional performativity, and prison incidents. The system, whose origins lie in the state's Bureau of Research and Data Analysis in the late 1990s, made a series of predictions by probing a multiplicity of databases, including the Fast Access Secure Tracking system (for inmate visits and volunteer activity), the Human Resources Database, the Management Information Notes System, the Offender Based Information System, the Inmate Gang Database, and the Use of Force Database. One of the most celebrated features of COTAS was its purported ability to determine an inmate's threat level based on age, bed category, drug tests, gender, involvement in violent events, number of violent events, time served, and racial identity (which only included "white" and "nonwhite").[38] NLECTC and the U.S. Energy Department's Savannah River Technology Center prototyped more advanced versions of similar software that provided real-time, multilevel, three-dimensional simulations of prison facilities and the people inside, replete with data on parolees, prison facilities, prison officers, probationers, and inmates.[39] Similar systems were installed throughout prison facilities for information on booking, cell checks, inmate movement, medical records, and visitations. Some companies, such as Kiosk Information Systems, Keefe Group, SeePoint, SmartJailMail, and TurnKeyCorrections, dove into the automated kiosk industry to grant inmates access to email, conduct commissary transactions, participate in video visitations, and schedule appointments, sometimes for a fee.

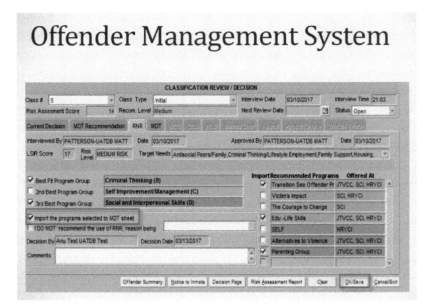

FIGURE 12. Offender Management System: Risk/Need/Responsivity Module. This screen grab of an offender risk management system shows how it generates a score for each inmate and recommends treatment programs to stabilize or lower the score. The score incorporates medical, physiological, and psychological values. From Joanna Champney and Samantha Zulkowski, *Implementing a Risk/ Need/Responsivity Framework into an Offender Management System* (Dover, Del.: Department of Correction, 2017).

Marx's analysis of large-scale industry helps us to understand this other Satanic Mill, the computerized prison. Indeed, the promise of digital technology companies was a prison managed like an orderly factory. The continuous automation of mechanisms that captured the criminalized subject, drove it from point to point through the criminal justice system, and regulated its movements and distributions through space was supposed to give way to a "vast automaton" of great efficiency and scale. On the micro level, computerization was intended to help optimize the prison's architectural, functional, and hierarchical political anatomy. Information systems were intended to assist carceral administrators in distributing devalued humans through cells and corridors; organizing carceral enclosures according to sociological and penological categories;

enhancing abilities to supervise, immobilize, and capture inmates; and ranking inmates and prison personnel according to normative baselines pertaining to race, educational background, employment history, and numerous other attributes (Figure 12). What is more, the technologies were said to enact a type of time discipline similar to the factory through automated lighting, roll calls, and daily regimens determined by risk-assessment tools. But the metaphor stops here, and racial difference is the reason. The computerization of the carceral apparatus was not driven by extracting surplus from production processes or manufacturing docile consumer-workers; rather, it was driven by cities determined to quarantine economically devalued populations and by information capital seeking new profit frontiers.

Digitized Detention

In addition to provoking new ideas about establishing total control inside correctional facilities, digital technology has facilitated the diffusion of carceral power over public space. Prison development siting has become increasingly influenced by computer software over the past two decades. Near the turn of the century, planning agencies such as California's Office of Planning and Research started to design location-siting algorithms to help determine where to construct new halfway houses, jails, and prisons.[40] The algorithms identified construction sites based on a series of factors, including land uses, infrastructures, and transport connections. For existing prisons, municipal planning agencies also used management applications to monitor the conditions of correctional land holdings, buffer zones, and wastewater fields.

Digital computing has also come to play a role in determining where inmates are released once their sentences terminate. As the Great Recession placed increased strain on public expenditures, some state officials turned to risk algorithms to defray the mammoth costs of mass incarceration. Algorithms designed to assess inmates' likelihood of recidivism were embraced by courts, prisons, and juvenile detention centers to help determine which inmates ought to be eligible for early release or work programs. To be certain, risk assessments have been applied in social service apparatuses since the 1920s.[41] In the 1970s, risk scores were used to predict future behaviors of juvenile offenders. Two decades later, the Office of Juvenile Justice and Delinquency Prevention released its Comprehensive Strategy for Serious, Violent, and Chronic Juvenile Offenders, which expanded the practice to identify low-risk inmates and relocate them into parole or probation programs. But the epic scale of the carceral crisis saw to it that these algorithms were computerized. University programs like the Center for Evidence-Based Corrections and public agencies like the New York City Criminal Justice Agency worked diligently to codify risk instruments. These were designed to help administrators determine release eligibility based on "static values," such as gender, mental/health problems, and prior record, and "dynamic values," such as age, education level, employment, and marital status, in languages amenable to computer programming.[42] Developed in conjunction with criminologists, these algorithms typically coded eight variables as the most powerful predictors of criminal tendencies: antisocial associates (association with offenders), antisocial personality pattern (adventurous, impulsive, pleasure-seeking behaviors), antisocial cognition (negative attitudes toward legal authority, rationalization of criminal activity), family/marital status (estrangement from parents or spouse), history of antisocial behavior (arrested at young age, large number of prior offenses), leisure/recreation (low participatory levels in recreational activities), substance abuse (alcohol or drug abuse, save tobacco), and school/work (low participation and/or achievement in educational institutions or labor markets). Companies such as the Northpointe Institute Orbis Partners and Multi-Health Systems turned these instruments into software packages that quickly spread across the country.[43]

The Herculean efforts to make the carceral state digital went hand in hand with the extension and thickening of the parole and probation apparatus. This was due in no small part to the fact that between 1980 and 2015, the probationer and parolee populations increased fourfold and fivefold, respectively. As a consequence, a variety of geographic information-based systems crafted to manage parolees and probationers throughout public space began to appear on the market. In 2001, the New York City Department of Probation (NYCDOP) unveiled the Statistical Tracking and Reporting System (STARS), which employed geospatial software to help probation offices manage information on sixty thousand adult probationers and twenty-five thousand juveniles. City officials boasted that STARS generated forty thousand pre-sentence investigations for the U.S. Supreme Court and criminal courts and seven thousand investigations and recommendations for family courts.[44] By 2008, NYCDOP had adopted geographic information systems to produce digital maps of recent arrests, gun stores, drug trafficking areas, liquor stores, and other probationers to assist parole/probation boards in determining where probationers should be released and were authorized to travel. To coordinate the geographies of correctional supervision, software company MapInfo created an application to optimize the distribution of parole and probation officers throughout city space.[45] The company adapted an older application to generate districts based on caseload distributions of parolees and probationers. The districts were meant to help administrators select caseloads for probation/parole officers (PPOs) and determine home visitation assignments. In a similar vein, Esri repackaged older software packages to determine route sequences for PPOs during home visits. Software applications like these were designed to minimize the amount of time it took for PPOs to establish contact with parolees and probationers. The overriding objective was to establish a logistical correctional apparatus whose capillaries spread across urban space.

Technological displacement came to loom over PPOs under such conditions. Companies like DynaTouch, Napo, and Northwest Ohio Regional Information System have taken to producing automated kiosk terminals exclusively for probationers to report themselves. Usually located in courthouses, police precincts, and probation offices, the terminals allow parolees and probationers to check in via biometric identification and then answer questions pertaining to drug tests, employment, and housing. Technology firms, including AnyTrax and Fieldware LLC, offer automated telephone- and internet-based reporting for low-risk subjects living in remote areas. Some of these remote reporting terminals come equipped with a breathalyzer, polygraph, voice stress analyzer, and voice recognition technology.[46]

The most significant development in the digital extension of correctional supervision has been the use of the Global Positioning System in parole and probation management. This location-aware form of correctional supervision has quietly advanced the correctional management of everyday life. Early forms of electronic correctional supervision using radio frequency technology first appeared in the 1960s in Cambridge and Boston, Massachusetts. Dubbed "electronic parole," the program involved parolees wearing portable transceivers. A researcher from Harvard's Science Committee on Psychological Experimentation who assisted with the technical side of the procedure saw the radical implications of this new dimension of supervision. "When specific offending behaviors," he asserted, "can be accurately predicted and/or controlled within the offender's own environment, incarceration will no longer be necessary as a means of controlling behavior and protecting society."[47] It would be some time before electronic monitoring was truly unleashed. In 1983, a district state court in New Mexico ordered multiple parole violators to be supervised through GPS tracking. This revival of electronic supervision was also stimulated by Reagan's Military Cooperation with Civilian Law Enforcement Act (1981), which allowed military technology, such as GPS devices, to be transferred to municipal law enforcement. Not only did the act contribute to the militarization of racial criminalization but it also extended its field through electronic correctional supervision.

Three catalysts would expand electronic supervision even further, moving further into the present century. The first was organized resistance against mass imprisonment. Public awareness for prison reduction gained national traction through the formation of the Sentencing Project in 1986 by Malcolm C. Young and of Critical Resistance by Angela Y. Davis, Ruth Wilson Gilmore, and Rose Braz in 1997. Over the next decades, momentum from these struggles carried over into mainstream political discourse. This was due in no small part to the appearance of Michelle Alexander's influential book *The New Jim Crow* and the *Brown v. Plata* (2011) U.S. Supreme Court ruling mandating the observance of population limits in prisons the following year. Moreover, a 2015 federal report exposing the excessive force, rape, and solitary confinement at Riker's Island prison contributed additional fuel to resistances against the carceral state. To pacify mounting social forces, federal, state, and municipal authorities across the country slowly began to recommend electronic supervision as a humane alternative to imprisonment. The second catalyst in the spread of electronic supervision was the Great Recession and the inertial force of austerity politics that followed. As state budgets across the country dried up, line items were scrutinized with extraordinary care. In 2010, the average annual cost of imprisonment was revealed to be more than $31,000, a figure that exceeded the labor market value of inmates. The Vera Institute reported that states spent more than $43 billion on prison expenditures in 2015 alone.[48] Electronic supervision was touted as one means of cutting these expenses, as the total number of probationers rose to quadruple of it what it was when the Reagan administration commenced. The third catalyst was information capitalists, who, with the cleverness of a parasite, seized the opportunity to profit from decarceration. For instance, the Center for Media Justice discovered that ankle bracelet suppliers Attenti, BI Incorporated, Satellite Track of People, and Sentinel Offender Services alone generated more than a billion dollars of revenue on an annual basis.[49]

Electronic supervision inscribes the correctional apparatus deeper into urban space and interiorizes it in the lifeworlds of criminalized populations. Upon enrollment in the electronic monitoring apparatus, one is given a digital shackle to wear that radiates locational data to PPOs, nearby police patrols, and, in some instances, real-time crime datacenters (see Figure 13). The device is meant to ensure that one is at an authorized location, which Africana studies scholar James Kilgore has shown usually involves house arrest.[50] Should the monitored subject enter unauthorized space or tamper with the device, an automated alarm is sent to the parole/ probation office, nearby police patrols, and victims in cases involving domestic and sexual violence. Digital supervision programs like these were pioneered in California. Early in the 2000s, the CDCR used risk-assessment tools to identify the most violent people registered in its gang database.[51] The individuals were then tagged with GPS shackles and told where in the city they were (dis)allowed to go. The shackles were also used to generate data to help authorities map gang turf more accurately. For instance, the GeoShadow initiative of the Oklahoma Department of Corrections, NLECTC, Office of Science and Technology, and University of Oklahoma's Center for Spatial Analysis used similar methods to track high-risk subjects. With location-aware supervision, mobility, not visibility, is the trap. In some instances, people enrolled in these pro-grams are permitted travel to specified locations for specified amounts of time.[52] In some cases, monitored subjects must attend rehabilitation centers, school, psychological evaluations, or workplaces. In many cases involving juveniles, data produced from the monitored subject's drug tests, home visits, school/work reports, and psychiatric session are also fed into software programs that scan for fluctuations in risk ratings. In these instances, the technology helps the correctional apparatus modulate rehabilitation centers, schools, and workplaces into disciplinary satel-lites. Electronic supervision cases involving domestic, gang, and sexual violence often involve establishing *exclusion zones,* or electronic barriers that trigger alarms when breached. Exclusion zones bisect urban space into areas in which parolees or probationers may and may not travel and thus form an electronic grid for carceral urbanization. Disciplinary society and control society collapse in such a scenario. The digitized expression of carceral space does not replace discipline with control; it cross-fertilizes the two.

It would not be unreasonable to see electronic supervision as a new horizon of carceral statecraft. This apparatus that combines uninterrupted monitoring and evaluation invokes images of the Public Safety Bureau in Gen Urobuchi's manga *Psycho-Pass.* In it, the bureau uses proprietary technology to monitor the physiological states of citizens for deviant vectors. Urobuchi's dystopian vision was partially realized in juvenile electronic supervision programs in New York's Division of Probation and Correctional Alternatives. Some of these programs required juveniles to regularly submit "status of life" evaluations that provided information about drug tests; living situations; time spent in job training, school, or work; and psychiatric diagnoses.[53] The information was entered into digital profiles that were analyzed for emerging risk. Here we see a glimpse of a type of carceral power whose audacity is only matched in Urobuchi's fictional account. One mistake, and you are forced into a cage. In fact, in 2014, more than one-quarter of all prison admissions were for technical violations of parole or probation, such as associating with known offenders, failing a drug or alcohol test, failing to report to a parole/probation officer, missing appointments with social service agencies, or violating geographic

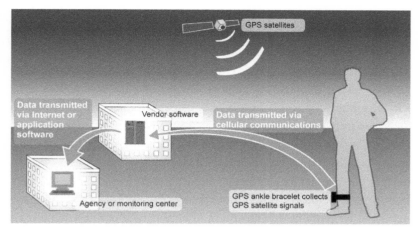

FIGURE 13. Early Global Positioning System–based offender tracking system. Mostly used for house arrest, electronic ankle monitors endowed the carceral state with location awareness. Originally, parole and probation officers were alerted when a monitored subject left her premises. Subsequent versions alert patrol units according to various factors, including proximity to the monitored subject and present activity. From *Electronic Monitoring: Draft National Standard for Offender Tracking Systems Addresses Common Stakeholder Needs,* ed. Committee on Science Subcommittee on Oversight, Space, and Technology (Washington, D.C.: U.S. Government Accountability Office, 2015).

restrictions. Unlike Urobuchi's account, however, electronic supervision is not applied universally throughout the body politic. It is instead reserved for tracking the economically devalued and racially stigmatized populations who dwell in the cracks of urban centers of global capital.

By the mid-2000s, an estimated one hundred thousand parolees, probationers, registered gang members, sex offenders, and work release program participants were under GPS-based supervision.[54] This represented a ninefold increase in the number of electronically supervised subjects in just over a decade. Cases involving domestic violence, drunk driving, undocumented immigration, sex offenses, truancy, and a range of minor offenses including ordinances violations and trespassing are now punishable by digital detention.[55] Increasingly, the electronic bracelets are equipped with blood alcohol detectors and breathalyzers. Academics eager to get a piece of the industry have already explored ways of equipping the bracelets with conducted energy devices capable of electrocuting monitored individuals who violate parole/probation conditions.[56] In 2006, California Proposition 83, also known as Jessica's Law, mandated that sex offenders be placed under GPS supervision for life. Four years later, thirty-three states had begun to employ electronic supervision for sex of-fender tracking. Electronic monitoring has also been adopted by New York City's Immigration and Customs Enforcement branch for its alternative detention initiative. Used primarily on undocumented immigrants from Central America, the initiative is part of a nationwide program used on more than forty thousand criminalized immigrants.[57] In addition to GPS devices, the program uses voice recognition software so that employers may verify a monitored immigrant's presence at workplaces. Here digital networks are mobilized as a conduit of border relations and something resembling privatized prisoner labor.

PROGRAMMABLE PUNISHMENT

The inefficiency of the court system during the apex of the War on Drugs was prodigious. But this state of affairs was propitious for software com-panies. The utopian vision of a court apparatus that operated with clock-like precision peddled by these companies was captured by the Illinois Criminal Justice Information Authority in 1993:

> A criminal-court judge sitting in her chambers mulls over a difficult fraud case. She picks up a pen-like device attached to a computer to select a case from an on-screen list. The computer displays videotaped trial testimony with captioned text. Using the computer pen, the judge writes a key phrase onto the screen and the computer fast-forwards to that portion of the testimony. After reviewing the video passage, the judge switches to a criminal records database before calling up an artificial-intelligence-based software program to determine the appropriate punishment.[58]

Or perhaps

> artificial intelligence, in which a computer replicates the knowledge and reasoning of a skilled professional, may someday assist judges in sentencing or attorneys in selecting jurors. While development of those applications is just beginning, a number of courts are already using a

sophisticated computer program to evaluate the likelihood of substance abuser rehabilitation.[59]

Though digital technology has not penetrated courts to the same extent as the other branches of the criminal justice apparatus, it is still important, because courts play a vital part in determining the size, profile, and, in some instances, geography of criminalized populations. The rapidity with which the carceral state expanded during Reagan's War on Drugs in the 1980s placed heavy strain on criminal processing procedures. Human Rights Watch reported that the decade saw drug arrests increase from 376,155 to 981,381, about 160 percent.[60] And as the War on Drugs raged, it became all the more important for courts to pronounce judgments and punishments swiftly and to distribute those whom it convicted between community supervision, house arrest, and jail in an efficient manner. If the court was not up to this task, many bureaucrats worried, the carceral colossus would buckle under the pressure of its own weight.

Originally, the computerization of judicial power revolved around digitizing documents to reduce trial time and provide judges access to the internet to cross-verify references and participate in remote deliberations.[61] It was, however, the application of database management systems to criminal proceedings that judicial technocrats raved about the most. Prosecutors in Los Angeles, New York City, and St. Louis were using computer-aided transcript systems already in the 1970s and 1980s. These systems, originally developed through Law Enforcement Assistance Administration (LEAA) funding, were designed to manage the deluge of cases following the launch of the War on Crime. The uptick of political prisoners during this period was making it all but impossible for attorneys to process paperwork in an accurate and timely fashion. This resulted in backlogs of pretrial defendants, which threatened to overload pretrial detention facilities. Database management systems were posed by IT companies and technocrats as remedies. Justice management databases were rolled out with the promise of ushering in the age of the paperless courtroom. By digitizing records, companies such as ICON Software Corporation and Tyler Technologies marveled, courts would also be able to convert storage room and cut back on human clerks. Several technologies were also developed to hasten procedures. Early in the

1970s, the LEAA teamed with Inslaw Inc., a technology corporation that specialized in administrative database management systems, to develop prosecutorial software. The collaboration gave birth to the Prosecutor Management Information System (PROMIS), which offered dozens of functions for legal proceedings. PROMIS was designed to administer data about court costs, court orders, courtroom scheduling, decisions, defendants, evidence, fines, jurors, offenses, plaintiffs, and restitutions.[62] It also allowed police to transmit information about arrestees, victims, and witnesses to prosecutors and administrative agencies. Furthermore, PROMIS automated the assignment of cases to attorneys based on experience and workload. In New York, the Information Systems Department of Criminal Justice Agency Inc.—a legal service consultant founded by a New York industrialist—introduced a database that stored case-processing data from courts, demographic data about communities, and incident data from the police.

The drug war pushed forward judicial computerization. By the 1990s, the U.S. Attorney's Office had unveiled its own customized database, which organized data on cases, defendants, investigations, gang warrants, general crimes units, narcotics, and wiretaps.[63] It also had geographic information functionality so that attorneys could conduct queries by location and view spatial distributions of their dockets. These specs were meant to bolster information sharing throughout the administrative state apparatus. Videoconferencing also emerged in courtrooms to accelerate offender processing. Video technology first emerged in an Illinois court in 1972 for a bail hearing and came to be used in the majority of courts for various ends.[64] Use of the technology expanded significantly during the 1990s to alleviate pretrial overcrowding, schedule arraignments for people arrested during courts' nonoperating hours, and reduce costs of moving inmates from jails to courts. Inside courtrooms, video technology was instituted so that alleged victims could offer real-time testimonies from remote locations. Touchscreen technology was also introduced to witness boxes for witnesses to look at images and hear audio of defendants and suspects. Document scanners, email, real-time court transcripts displayed on courtroom monitors, two-way video, and wide area networks have also reshaped the materiality of the judicial apparatus. By the early 2000s, over

95 percent of federal district courts used audio conferencing equipment, evidence cameras, and internet connections.[65] More than 80 percent used bench monitors, witness stand monitors, and video conferencing equipment. In some cities, judges digitally sign orders, and trial lawyers use trial presentation applications on laptops and tablets to organize designation reports, deposition videos, exhibits, deposition transcripts, and witness/trial notebooks.

What began to emerge from the application of digital computing to the judicial apparatus was the dream of a logistical complex that processed convicted populations without interruption. This was bolstered by endeavors to digitize the transmission of evidential data to judges, jurors, and legal teams. In the late 1990s, the National Task Force on Court Automation and Integration conjured the specter of a frictionless criminal processing environment where an arraignment judge sitting behind a computer could pronounce judgment within minutes of a suspect's arrest.[66] The task force imagined a day when alimony orders, criminal history records, drug test results, fingerprints, gun purchase applications, protective orders, sexual offense registration status, and warrants would be instantly retrievable by judges. During booking, automated databases would assemble data on defendants, case characteristics, charges, sentencing, witnesses, and victims for attorneys, judges, juries, and prosecutors. These databases would be equipped with algorithms to determine a defendant's harm to society, risk of flight, and risk of future crime to help judges and prosecutors make pretrial preparations.[67] Risk-assessment tools were also proposed by judges for various decision-making tasks concerning bail, bond amounts, diversion programs, guilt/innocence, rehabilitation requirements, the mental health of accused offenders, releases on recognizance, and sentencing.[68] The Conference of Chief Justices, Conference of State Court Administrators, and National Center for State Courts all lobbied for making risk-assessment tools part of standard procedure. Their ultimate stated goal was to speed up court appearances to the point that they could take place within twenty-four hours of booking.[69]

Dozens upon dozens of corporations, including eFORCE, Exhibit-View, Moonlighting Software, Synergy International Systems, and Tyler

Technologies, have rushed to corner market shares in judicial database systems. Near the end of the 1990s, the Center for Applied Studies of the Environment, the Southern District of New York, and the U.S. Attorney's Office teamed up to create a case-tracking and mapping database system explicitly for the narcotics trade. Similar database technology is now marketed as a way to manage arrest reporting, court docketing, jail booking, mobile dispatching, and offender registries.[70] At the municipal level, which deals primarily with minor adjudications, court management systems are used for perfunctory tasks of collections, docketing, and scheduling. Appellate and juvenile courts use specialized software that has bank account applications for collecting and distributing childcare, fees, fines, garnishments, restitutions, and credits for offender work programs.

It is perhaps impossible to measure the effect that these technologies have had in adjudication. In many cases, access to the algorithms is blocked from the general public. Public safety is invoked when the software is developed by public–private partnerships; intellectual property is invoked when it is developed privately.[71] What remains clear, though, are the social categories that these algorithms are programmed to criminalize. Most propriety software generates risk scores according to the "central eight" commonly cited factors in criminal psychology.[72] These search inmate data for high levels of antisocial associates, antisocial cognition (attitudes, values), antisocial personality (stimulation, low self-control), criminal history, family problems, employment instability, low participation in social leisure activities, and substance abuse.[73] Others process data from prisoner surveys and personal records, including data on depression, educational achievement, length of unemployment, powerlessness, psychological handicaps, reliance on welfare, resentment, and minority status. These predictive tools do not explain criminality; rather, they describe those whom the carceral apparatus is literally programmed to micromanage. They describe the age, race, gender, psychological profile, and socioeconomic status of people targeted for more than a half century by the apparatus of mass criminalization. Perhaps the most insidious thing about the scientific veil is that it conceals the barbarism of the criminal justice system that it services. These digital maps, machine learning algorithms, and statistical curves are developed in service of state apparatuses that round up millions of people at gunpoint and lock them in cages; that encage young people for years at a time for selling marijuana; that are characterized by routine sexual assault; that execute people using experimental concoctions of lethal drugs; and that murder twelve-year-olds in plain sight and on camera with impunity.

3

A FULLY AUTOMATED
POLICE APPARATUS

Two years before Rudolph Giuliani was sworn in as mayor of New York City, the Committee on Information Technology of the New York Police Department (NYPD) outlined a vision for a "fully automated police department."[1] While hagiographic accounts single out Giuliani, police commissioner William J. Bratton, and deputy commissioner Jack Maple as the catalysts behind the digital restructuring of the NYPD, a much wider constellation of forces set the process into motion.[2] To be certain, what the NYPD and other police departments have realized is nowhere near being fully automated. The problems with data entry, inefficiencies, and malfunctions associated with police technology are well documented.[3] But the eruption of information technology in urban policing is an event that demands attention, for it signified a new way of normalizing racialized policing that was driven in part by a new partner—the IT sector.

Irrespective of public officials, technocrats, and technology corporations who claim that computer software results in more precise policing tactics, it has been used by cities to justify policies of establishing *blanket control* over entire populations and places. For instance, geographic information systems are used to justify the differential patrol of block corners, deployment areas, drug consumers, homeless encampments, "impact zones," night clubs, "notorious adult use locations," panhandlers, public housing units, public schools, open-air markets, sex workers, street intersections, subway stops, "squeegee men," the visibly indigent, and the visibly mentally ill. The technology has thus become a force in the production of what geographer Rashad Shabazz calls prisonized landscapes, which are managed in the first instance by the police apparatus.[4] Such was certainly the case in Chicago and New York City.

CATALYSTS OF POLICE AUTOMATION IN NEW YORK AND CHICAGO

Information capital began to rise near the same time northern cities were upended by deindustrialization. Where industrial capital ceased to find low-income minorities exploitable, information capital found a lucrative opportunity. Marx's analysis of value in motion spent a great deal of time on relations between the movement of capital and *differentiation*. He illustrated how the continuous valorization of capital requires the differentiation of circulation periods and of forms (money, constant, fixed, fluid, variable, etc.) invested in industries that constantly change over time. It is no wonder that Marx developed a preoccupation with differential calculus toward his latter years. But he critically overlooked how the movement and valorization of capital also relies on differentiating populations. Capital does so, we now know, primarily along axes of gendered, racialized, regionalized, nationalized, and physical difference. Different groups are ascribed different levels of value, be it positive or negative, with respect to rates of profit and, ultimately, the right to live. But what happens when entire communities become bearers of antivalue, that is, hindrances to the movement and valorization of capital? What modes of sociospatial differentiation rectify the situation?

Restructuring Global North urban economies toward the end of the twentieth century required transforming the police apparatus to manage devalued populations. The most problematic of the lot had to be identified, quarantined, even relocated, to make way for postindustrial forms of accumulation. Not only did this project call into being new political discourses, ordinances, and policies but it also gave rise to digital infrastructures of policing and punishment. Under such conditions, a digitally enhanced police apparatus programmed to securitize nodes of global capital from the growing mass of surplus populations began to take shape.

New York City

In New York City, police computerization emerged alongside city projects to rebuild its political economic system. Until then, police were primarily deployed to monitor and suppress drug violence and the organization of radical groups, including the Nation of Islam, the Young Lords, and the Youth International Movement. But more than a decade of social dislocations wrought by deindustrialization, multiple recessions, and stock market crashes catapulted the NYPD to the front lines of an indefinite War on Crime. From the early 1990s onward, the department would be characterized by biopolitical "quality-of-life" measures for the privileged and necropolitical "zero-tolerance" measures for the stigmatized others.

The magnitude to which the NYPD was transformed in the 1990s reflected the magnitude to which industrial and public workforces lost their economic utility. The resolution of this crisis was to a great extent dictated by the financial sector.[5] The firms that bailed out the city did so while imposing stringent conditions that reshaped its economy of space. The financial sectors obtained first claim over tax revenues, which they used to pay bondholders; implemented wage freezes; rolled back public employment and services (education, housing, transportation); and required municipal unions to invest pension funds in city bonds. This also led to an ever-increasing reliance on credit-rating agencies, municipal bond markets, and their concomitant "debt machine" governances to feed the finance sector.[6] But this rising tide of financialization proceeded in lockstep with the backwash of deproletarianization. More industrial jobs were lost in New York during the early 1990s than in any other major U.S. city, save Philadelphia.[7] Middle-wage jobs began a decade-long decline, while low-wage jobs began a decade-long increase. Between 1990 and 1991, losses in state revenue prompted a twenty-one thousand person-cut in the public workforce. Despite improvements in the national economy, the census tallied the city's unemployment rate at 12 percent, its highest since the 1975 financial crisis.[8] By the mid-1990s, one-quarter of New Yorkers received incomes below the federal poverty line, and almost 45 percent of children lived at or below the poverty line. Of the almost 2 million New Yorkers living beneath the poverty line, 33 percent were classified as Hispanic, 25 percent as black, and 10 percent as white.[9] Estimates suggest that up to fifty thousand people were homeless at one point in the early 1990s—who were 62 percent black, 25 percent Hispanic, and 8 percent white—an almost fivefold increase from the mid-1980s.[10]

Despite the sudden amplification of economic inequality, the city's private sector experienced its largest economic boom in a half-century as it approached the new millennium. New York City's IT industry grew considerably during this period. By the mid-1980s, the city had the third highest information-intensive employment location quotient, measured by the absolute size of the IT sector and its relative share of IT industries in the region.[11] As a central node of global financial power, the city required a vast information communications infrastructure. Such infrastructure was supplied by AT&T, Motorola, Teleport Communications Inc., and other technology corporations. Internet-ready real estate like the Rudin Management Company's New York Information Technology Center proliferated in the mid-1990s, which provided interactive media enclaves for the CD-ROM developers, web designers, and virtual reality artists that would come to populate emerging labor markets.[12] From 1996 to 2000, the city's private-sector employment and wage and salary earnings rose at a faster pace than the national average.[13] Service-sector employment expanded considerably moving into century's end, adding 160,000 and 110,000 new jobs in the business and consumer sectors and health and social service sectors, respectively.[14] Wages and salaries in the securities industry increased at more than double the rate of the rest of labor markets during this time.

But things looked different for the negatively racialized poor during this time, as they'd come to exercise a negative economic function in the emergent economy. By the turn of the century, the unemployment rate of New Yorkers classified as black was more than double that of those classified as white, and it was only slightly less than double for those classified as Hispanic.[15] Poverty rates among black and Hispanic subjects were approximately double and triple that of whites, respectively.[16] In the Bronx, Hispanic poverty was nearly five times greater than white poverty, whereas black poverty was about four times greater. And with the rise of Clintonian workfare programs in New York City, well over a half million New Yorkers were cut off of public assistance.[17] Removing these remnants of a bygone era from the urban core became a prime objective of the city's power structure. Crime commissions founded by the business community began to monitor the effects of crime on economic growth. Commercial and real estate capitalists were among the first advocates of hyperaggressive policing tactics to eliminate social disorder inhibiting commerce. Sociologist Alex S. Vitale illustrates how Bid Improvement Districts (BIDs) concerned with the effects of visible homelessness on commerce and rent values hired private police forces.[18] The Grand Central Partnership, an influential BID comprising property owners, tenants, and public officials, was especially determined to remove the disorder pervading Midtown Manhattan. Private patrols coordinated by the NYPD appeared in Rockefeller Center, South Street Seaport, and Roosevelt Island. In 1991, the legal bureau launched its Civil Enforcement Unit program called the Civil Enforcement Initiative, which engaged merchants and attorneys to eradicate business-threatening, low-level offenses, including visible signs of sex work, drug sales, public consumption, intemperance, and loud music, through nuisance abatement, forfeiture, and loitering laws. Such were the material conditions in which the digitized NYPD was born.

Chicago

The catalysts of police computerization were somewhat different in Chicago. Responding to the hyperviolent narcotics trade, Mayor Richard M. Daley's administration (1989–2011) proposed a flurry of ultrapunitive anticrime policies that targeted gang members. Moving into the 1990s, Daley, like his mayoral counterpart in New York City, cast anticrime initiatives in the mold of the Clinton administration's Violent Crime Control and Law Enforcement Act, which eventually passed in 1994. The administration tied Chicago's fate to the omnibus bill, as it provided Chicago almost a half billion dollars to upgrade criminal justice institutions. Daley's bill introduced a variety of provisions, including wiretaps of gang leaders, harsher sanctions for gang-related crime, and loitering ordinances that authorized police to disperse gang suspects from street corners. The mayor also proposed to implement the three-strikes rule and capital punishment for subjects convicted for federal crimes. As in New York, these laws, and the objectives they were designed to achieve, were mediated by the interests of commercial, information, financial, and real estate capital. Once a central hub for industrial labor power, Chicago was soon trying to restructure its economy around condominium construction, finance, gentrification, start-ups, and tourism.

But as the 1980s unfolded, Chicago and its core counties also established the fourth highest concentration of employment in information-intensive industries in the metropolitan United States. The dot-com boom gave rise to numerous, albeit ephemeral, consumer-facing firms. The early 1990s saw cloud services, cybersecurity, online insurance services, software consulting firms, trading technologies, and web design firms crop up throughout the city. Chicago also was home to various professional service industries for management consultation, IT/business process outsourcing, and technology consultancies that helped major corporations around the country build digital infrastructures. The slow and steady growth in new sectors stood in direct opposition to the decline of the old sectors. Once an exemplar of Fordist accumulation, Chicago's slow industrial decline spanned the 1960s to the 1980s. From the late 1960s to 1990, Chicago hemorrhaged 60 percent of its manufacturing jobs. Philadelphia was the only city to lose more. Between 1970 and 1990, the poverty rate increased nearly 20 percent, and the population declined by the same percentage. Saskia Sassen notes that during this time, the city lost over 25 percent of its factories and 45 percent of its manufacturing jobs.[19] Unlike New York, Chicago saw rapid declines in service industries, losing more than thirty thousand between 1991 and 1992. Its financial sector also contracted, evidenced by a 20 percent office vacancy rate during the period.

These contradictions gave rise to heterogeneous social responses. In the register of formal politics, in 1984, Jesse Jackson's National Rainbow Coalition made him the first black presidential candidate to make the national party's election. Black nationalism also found rejuvenation in a resurgent Chicago-based Nation of Islam, which sponsored the Million Man March in 1995. Narcocapitalism and self-medication also emerged to mitigate the material and psychological effects of deindustrialization in Chicago's Black Belt during this period (much like in the case of post–Great Recession rural opioid markets). Throughout the 1980s, the total number of recorded offenses increased by nearly 65 percent. In the next decade, the total number of recorded murders rose by nearly 40 percent.[20] The police superintendent argued that the department should adopt Chinese policing strategies and curtail constitutional rights where they encumber law enforcers.[21] Ironically, what the Chicago Police Department (CPD)—and the NYPD—helped create was a digitized mode of policing that was eventually replicated by China's Nationalist Party.[22]

DATA PROCESSING IN THE NYPD

A historically detailed account of digital computing in the police apparatus might begin in New York. The NYPD's history with computers commences in the 1960s and 1970s, which were characterized mostly by applying emerging computer technologies to internal administration. The NYPD's data processing starts in 1963, when its Electronic Data Processing Division first used an IBM 1401 mainframe computer for fingerprint files, personnel records, and Uniform Crime Report (UCR) data.[23] The division, which was renamed the Management Information Systems Division (MISD), underwent modest expansions during the following decade through portable data terminals for the patrol fleet, an online booking system, and an online personnel system. MISD, which oversaw research on emerging trends in the IT industry, eventually came to manage nine mainframe databases and more than two dozen applications for administering personnel. The databases included an automated property management system to log and track property vouchered as evidence, a fleet management system to help administer the department's automobiles, an automated alert system that notified the District Attorney's Office when former misdemeanants were arrested, and a narcotics recidivist database that connected narcotics databases throughout the five boroughs. Through MISD, police personnel, recidivists, and suspects were incrementally drawn into the NYPD's slowly evolving data ecology. The department's Special Police Radio Inquiry Network (SPRINT), which automatically assigned patrol units to incident areas, prioritized emergency calls, and kept track of available patrol forces, also underwent modest expansion during the decade. In 1975, mobile terminals were installed in a small number of the Radio Motor Patrol fleet for officers to perform license plate and name inquiries from state and federal file systems. Teletype terminals in precincts were replaced by the Field Administrative Terminal Network, a closed system that allowed NYPD personnel to send messages between commands to the New York State Information Network and National Crime Information Center. However, the city's descent into bankruptcy during this decade prevented the widespread adoption of new technology by bureaucratic agencies.

The arrival of commercial microcomputers in the 1980s established conditions more conducive to NYPD computerization. But in New York City, fiscal conservatism posed a formidable obstacle to upgrading the NYPD's digital repertoire. In fact, the decade commenced at the end of a six-year period in which the police department shed nearly 30 percent of its personnel. In terms of technology, NYPD technological advancements in 1980s were defined mostly by a new telecommunications network, FIN-EST, which connected data terminals across borough command centers, patrol precincts, and specialized units. In the middle of the decade, the department was using 50 personal computers and 204 mobile data terminals in radio motor patrols.[24] Near the end of the decade, the department began prototyping an online complaint system that captured data from incident report forms and missing persons reports. Coincidentally, one of the computers being used during prototyping had geographic mapping software. The Committee on Information Technology casually suggested that the software could be used to replace pin maps. So influential was the committee's report that the mayor conducted a private-sector survey to find out what other technologies on the market could be used for policing.

The forces of globalization encircled the NYPD and metamorphosed it in the early 1990s. This had several repercussions in terms of police technology. The early part of the decade saw the NYPD deployed to surgically remove criminalized populations from Manhattan's core. Homeless sweeps were conducted in Central Park, FDR Drive, Madison Square Garden, Penn Station, and the Manhattan sides of the Brooklyn and Williamsburg Bridges. Mayor David Dinkins (1990–93) passed his omnibus anticrime bill, Safe Streets, Safe Cities, which was cast in the mold of Clinton's Violent Crime Control and Law Enforcement Act (1994). The act was the largest crime bill in U.S. history and allocated nearly

$11 billion federal matching funds to police departments.[25] Tapping into this ultrapunitive zeitgeist, Dinkins's Safe Streets was designed to enlarge and energize each component of the criminal justice apparatus, speed up arraignment processes, and make sentencing protocols harsher. The crux of the bill involved assembling the largest patrol force in U.S. history. It made provisions for hiring three and a half thousand officers in addition to the three thousand already slated for the next fiscal year. Moreover, patrol car deployment was to increase by 80 percent, and transit and public housing police were to increase substantially as well. Some 80 percent of these new forces were to be concentrated in about a dozen precincts with the highest crime rates. This strategy was to involve the block-by-block patrolling of these precincts so as to produce twenty-five hundred extra arrests in its first six months and nearly fifty thousand in its first four years.[26]

But while the administration rattled its saber by quoting arrest statistics in public discourse, it sought other, subtle ways of reconfiguring the police apparatus. It began to expand its technical repertoire and adopt computerized modes of human and resource management. However, the NYPD's data infrastructure was far from optimal. Institutionally, police data were generated at this time to satisfy FBI reporting requirements rather than to make the department run more efficiently.[27] At this point, NYPD headquarters received compilations of precinct data in the form of quarterly Management Information History reports. All NYPD data were between three to six months old at the time of collation and analysis. To complicate matters, data visualization techniques were limited at the time to hand-made pin maps of drug and serious crimes, including grand larceny, murder, robbery, and shootings. Different precincts mapped different crimes at different time scales. Such a lack of shared standards was unsuited for a massive project the likes of urban restructuring. Despite the fact that Rudolph Giuliani and William J. Bratton feuded over credit for the NYPD's technological transformation, the Committee on Information Technology explained two years prior to their arrival that the NYPD's "vision for information technology consists of a fully automated police department."[28] The committee insisted that MISD could significantly enhance community patrol forces through new relational database architectures that allowed patrol officers to access and analyze complaint, arrest, warrant, and previous incident data. Digital computers were also regarded as mediums to enhance police administration by providing access to crime analysis, resource planning, beat redesign, and rapid response planning applications through handheld computers, mobile digital terminals in vehicles, and local area networks.

By the mid-1990s, the NYPD had launched several projects to develop database management systems for accounting, complaints, firearm ownership, fleet administration, fuel monitoring, and property tracking. It assembled a Committee on Information and Technology, which was tasked with comprehensively upgrading the department's digital infrastructure. Its recommendations were manifold. The committee suggested that the NYPD obtain an integrated relational database for all incident reports; a mainframe central processing unit to support all databases; an online complaint system to support crime analysis, criminal investigations, crime reporting, and resource planning; a precinct-to-precinct microcomputer network linked into the central mainframe; and a local area network for NYPD headquarters. The committee also recommended that the department establish automated and online warrant systems, automated communications systems, digitized beat books, and digitized court orders of protection, among other technologies. It also requested funding from the state for dozens of additional projects, including, but not limited to, bioelectrical impedance analyzers, digitized department forms, driving simulators, cellular phones, statewide automated fingerprint systems, vehicle tracking devices, and videoconferencing equipment.

In rationalizing using tax dollars for this ambitious plan, police technology was presented to the public as a means of improving NYPD–civilian communication. IT was said to be necessary to support the analysis of local problems and the subsequent development of appropriate solutions. The technological core of the project was a "computerized database of community-related information . . . made available through designated precinct terminals. Data would include local crime statistics, [and] procedures on how to report crime incidents."[29] MISD also sought to equip patrol officers and detectives with access to state liquor authority databases, cellular phones, microwave video transmission devices, pagers, and photo imaging systems, among numerous other devices. Most of the recommendations during this period revolved around the internal operations of the police. But the technocratic spirit of the Committee on Information and Technology eventually came to define the NYPD's relation to urban space.

AUTOMATING GANG WAR IN CHICAGO

While the application of IT to police patrols is widely viewed as an invention of the NYPD, the CPD was ahead of the curve in several ways. In contrast to the NYPD, computing technology was conceived by CPD personnel from the outset as a tool to establish a logistical police apparatus for the city's war against gangs. As early as the mid-1980s, the Illinois Criminal Justice Information Authority was funded by the Bureau of Justice Statistics to develop Spatial and Temporal Analysis of Crime (STAC) software. STAC laid overlapping circles on city maps and then counted the number of reported incidents in each circle (see Figure 14).[30] Police targets emerged at the center of circles with the highest rates of reported incidents. The program also used probability theory and geometric techniques to predict future high-incident areas. This was a predictive policing prototype during the era of Reagan's War on Drugs, and it was first tested in the poorest sectors of Chicago's Black Belt.

The CPD's implementation of geographic information systems was far from a seamless affair. It was retrofitted into the department in fits and starts. This lack of smoothness was due to happenstance and institutional rigidity. In the late 1980s, the CPD collaborated with the National Institute of Justice (NIJ), Chicago Alliance for Neighborhood Safety, and Chicagoland university professors to pilot the Microcomputer-Assisted Police Analysis and Deployment System (MAPADS) in the West Side community of Austin. At the time of its inception, the city classified Austin's residents as 85 percent black, 30 percent of whom were living in poverty. The MAPADS pilot was an unintended consequence of patrol officers in the CPD's Twenty-Fifth District tinkering with STAC and coming across correlations between hate crimes and stolen vehicles.[31] The officers ended up exposing an entire auto theft ring, and the district commander

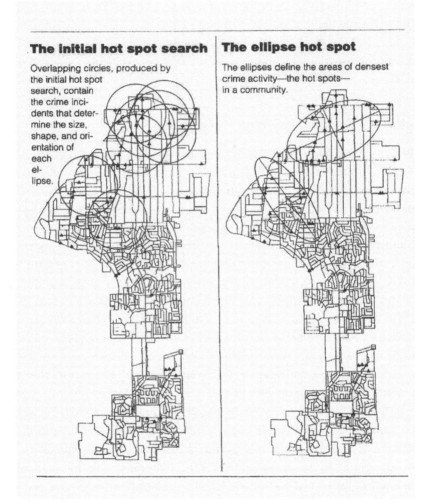

The initial hot spot search

Overlapping circles, produced by the initial hot spot search, contain the crime incidents that determine the size, shape, and orientation of each ellipse.

The ellipse hot spot

The ellipses define the areas of densest crime activity—the hot spots— in a community.

FIGURE 14. Computerized hot spot targeting. Consistent with the martial rhetoric of Daley's Gang War, CPD officials used spatial statistical analysis to produce targets for patrol squadrons. The technique, often called *heat mapping*, remains fundamental in police departments. From Margaret Poethig, "Hot Spots and Isocrimes," *Compiler*, Fall 1988, 12.

Choosing a police computer system

The number and variety of computer systems for police agencies is increasing by leaps and bounds. Here are some pointers on identifying needs and then finding the right solution.

By Maureen Hickey

How does a law enforcement agency decide that it needs a computerized information system? How does it choose the best system to fit its needs?

According to interviews with people involved in developing and using criminal justice information systems, including several police officials in agencies that are considering automation or have recently installed systems, there are three important steps: a realistic assessment of the department's information needs, a detailed understanding of how information currently moves through the department and how it should move, and a careful look at the options offered by particular information systems.

Assess your needs

"The first and most important step is to assess your needs realistically," said Edward Maier, the Illinois Criminal Justice Information Authority's deputy director for information management and research. "It is especially important in medium-sized and smaller departments to look closely at what functions must be computerized and what you may just as well leave manual."

Mr. Maier urges departments to look at

how long it takes personnel to do tasks that could be automated—such as responding to an inquiry or doing UCR reporting—to see if computerizing would materially affect the amount of time those tasks take. In addition, he said, the department should decide what investigative and management functions it would like that could be performed efficiently only by a computer, such as producing incident reports by time of day and by beat or searching a file of suspects.

What functions to automate and what not to may be difficult to determine, however.

"In law enforcement circles, you can never say that you have more than you need," according to Lawrence Burnson, deputy chief of the Matteson Police Department, which is currently enmeshed in the process of purchasing a computer system. "The more information that you can provide not only for the administrators, but for the officers on the street, the more effectively they can do their jobs. Anything we do to enhance data processing capabilities is going to enhance the officers' abilities to work more effectively on the street, and in turn that provides better service to the public."

Deputy Chief Burnson is also facing the fact that advances in computer technology have made many things possible that were unimaginable or unaffordable a few years ago. For example, databases that file a computerized picture along with text information are becoming available, allowing departments to keep "mug shots" in their computerized criminal history record.

Deputy Chief Burnson has been planning the automation of the Matteson department since 1982, but other projects, such as the building of a new police station, have

FIGURE 15. Vision of future police, 1988. Chicago's Gang War prompted CPD officials to incorporate computer technology in the late 1980s. Officials were particularly interested in using geographic information systems to create profiles for each patrol beat in high-crime areas located exclusively in the Black Belt. From Maureen Hickey, "Choosing a Police Computer System," *Compiler,* Fall 1988, 7.

was instantly convinced of the revelatory power of geographic informa-tion systems. Not before long, the police cum technocrats boasted that geographic information systems could be used to generate "institutional memories," or criminogenic rankings for each police beat in the district. "The maps," a task forcer later declared, "are the only place where one can see everything that is going on in an area. . . . Only on a map can the entire beat experience be put together and the pattern discerned from the individual incidents."[32] This epiphany was the spark that eventually lit digital transformations throughout the entire department.

Projects such as MAPADS accelerated as Mayor Richard M. Daley (1989–2011) ratcheted up Chicago's Gang War. Daley stressed that Chicago's fight against gang violence required technological upgrades to cut off in-ternational flows of drugs and firearms. Lobbying for military technology, he likened the most violent parts of Chicago to the Colombian drug war. Aldermen promising constituents high-tech policing compared violent parts of the city to Vietnam. Citizens were encouraged to organize Block Clubs to assist CPD in the street war against gangs and ultraviolent drug markets. But tooling up for the Gang War first required harnessing the power of computer technology. "For all the advances in criminal science and technology," Daley bemoaned, "ours is still a police department that is mired in the past."[33]

Soon after taking power, Daley's administration began acquiring land to construct a 61 million dollar high-tech police headquarters with the Illinois Institute of Technology. The request was made on the heels of the department revamping its incident database for beat officers. City officials spun the move as a community policing initiative, meant to assist a "wholesale transformation of the department, from a largely central-ized, incident-driven, crime suppression agency to a more decentralized, customer-driven organization."[34] "Computer-aided dispatch systems, onboard computers, in-car video systems, personal computers for report writing and other computer technologies," the state's Information Author-ity exclaimed, "are becoming part of the mainstream in law enforcement. The cyberworld of the information highway also has become part of the law enforcement technological age."[35] Using a grant from a private insur-ance company, the CPD began assembly of its Information Collection for Automated Mapping (ICAM) system. It was completed in 1995 (see chapter 4). The first public mapping interface to use Esri's digital mapping software, ICAM did not only cartographically represent CPD incident data but also overlaid buildings, citizen complaints, churches, liquor stores, schools, taverns, and other facilities. Soon after launch, ICAM emerged as a central part of CPD strategy.[36] It was quickly expanded so that detectives, narcotics officers, and the general public could access and map data. Subsequent versions were installed on laptops in each patrol vehicle, which allowed patrol officers to conduct temporal analysis and map hot spots, incidents according to different categories, and incidents according to distance to specified locations. The CPD also used ICAM to help School Patrol Units determine where to deploy security dogs, metal detectors, and school patrol cars.[37]

As the new millennium drew closer, the CPD sought consultation from Oracle Corporation to upgrade its central database, the Criminal History Records Information System (CHRIS). Oracle was founded in 1977 in California by an entrepreneur who was perusing the *IBM Journal of Research and Development* only to come across an article on relational databases. But the corporation that emerged was less an oracle than a priest, as it both pronounced the cause of evil (hot spots) and proposed a way of exorcising it (hot spot policing). At the time the CPD approached the corporation, Oracle commanded roughly three-fourths of the federal database market and was the CPD's lone consultant for computer-related matters. It also built CHRIS, with which the CPD encountered several problems because of its lack of user-friendliness and hefty training requirements.[38] Moreover, rank-and-file officers had no input in the development of its interface, and the templates on data entry screens differed greatly from incident case report sheets. After determining the potential market value of an updated database system, the CPD and Oracle set out to modernize CHRIS.[39] The corporation was given full access to CPD operations, the CPD was given ownership of the software's proprietary version, and Oracle retained ownership of the generic version. Oracle contributed $35 million to bringing the system up to date. It also committed ninety thousand consulting hours and five hundred hours of basic training to CPD staff at Oracle University. The CPD, for its part, reallocated 9 million dollars worth of funds from its Community Oriented Policing Services to the project. Over the course of research and development, the CPD stressed that the new database needed to be more user friendly, online compatible, and equipped with geographic information functionality. The result was the Citizen and Law Enforcement Analysis and Reporting (CLEAR) system, whose crown jewel was its mapping application, CLEARmap. For CLEARmap's architects, the main benefit of the program was its ability to produce targets for patrol units at unprecedentedly small geographic scales. It could also generate new categories of hot spots by correlating CPD data with data taken from other bureaucratic datasets. CLEARmap was even linked up with surveillance cameras so that maps could be supplemented with video feeds in schools, hospitals, street intersections, transportation hubs, and vanity buildings, such as the Daley Center, Sears Tower, and Shedd Aquarium, at a resolution of five hundred square feet.[40]

Digital mapping was not CLEAR's only function. Its Gang Book application provided a registry of known gang members' activity spaces, alliances, and symbols. CLEAR also sported a web-based arrest management system, the Automated Incidence Reporting Application (AIRA), which was originally used by custodial personnel to enter information about prisoners during intake.[41] Before CLEAR, CPD bureaucrats were tasked with recording arrest information. But AIRA offered patrols the ability to use wireless data portals to enter information about arrests, digital mugshots, and follow-up reports directly into the department's case reporting database. CLEAR included an arrestee-detainee tracking function, which gave officers instant access to biometric data (fingerprints, hair color, height, weight), central booking numbers, criminal history reports, demographic information, and mugshots.[42] One of CLEAR's server subsystems allowed rank-and-file officers to view and edit data in real-time. The technology effectively made patrol squads into mobile criminal processing units, which laid the groundwork for new ways of administering criminalized populations and places.

The arrival of upgraded database technologies coincided with a blitz-krieg of police sweeps, or dragnet operations carried out by patrols on street segments, at street intersections, and in housing complexes targeted by CLEAR. One such tactic, called hot spot saturation, involved infusing upward of 250 tactical officers in hot spot blocks targeted by STAC software. In 2002, the department introduced an initiative in which hot spot saturation teams were deployed for the express purpose of conducting mass arrests on a monthly basis.[43] The CPD also began to deploy personnel to talk to residents in every house or building located on hot spot blocks. Initiatives like these were used eight times within the first four months in MAPADS's home neighborhood of Austin.[44]

The CPD's computer-aided sweeps occurred around the same time that it first implemented a mapping application on its closed intranet, which was managed by the Deployment Operations Center (DOC). The DOC introduced a logistical mode of racialized policing that formed around a software application that generated a ceaseless stream of targets for patrol units.[45] The targets emerged from mining data on arrests, convictions, gang affiliations, incident reports, juvenile records, warrants, and vehicle registration and biometric data on more than 17 million entries.[46] DOC predicted future violence by analyzing data on parolees, probationers, youth offenders, and sex offenders. DOC targets appeared in the form of Level II Deployment Areas, areas where violence was deemed probable. Every week, DOC analysts identified these areas by scouring data on gang activity, local stakeholders' concerns, and the whereabouts of persons of interest, such as ex-convicts, high-level gang members, relatives of gang members, and relatives of victims of violence. The center produced hundreds of deployment areas ranging in area from 0.06 to 4.08 square miles—about 60 percent larger than police beats—on an annual basis.[47] After identifying deployment areas, the DOC also made recommendations on patrol tactics. These included aggressive enforcement of low-level disorders, the permanent patrolling of suspected drug sites, and the issuance of loitering dispersals to people in targeted spaces. Another tactic was strategic traffic enforcement, which involved stopping vehicles for traffic law violations and establishing checkpoints in deployment areas to conduct car searches. In 2003, the DOC unleashed a fifty-person Targeted Response Unit (TRU) to saturate deployment areas and exhibit zero tolerance on drug, gang, and gun suspects.[48] In 2005, the number of TRU personnel was increased by 50 percent, and the TRU conducted 4,774 missions that generated a total of 7,402 arrests. While the unit was originally assembled to focus on violence, guns, and car theft, nearly one-third of all arrests in 2005 fell into the "other" crime category.[49] Three years later, the department launched its Mobile Strike Force, a citywide unit tasked with supplementing ordinary patrol forces according to spatial analyses. In a little over a year, the Mobile Strike Force had conducted 1,190 missions, made 4,271 arrests, and impounded 934 vehicles.[50]

The DOC was used to rationalize not only uneven distributions of patrol units but also uneven distributions of police–civilian interaction. Some deployment areas were marked specifically by DOC bureaucrats for increased "contacts." In such areas, specialized units were encouraged to proactively engage civilians on the street. In these instances, patrol units were required to document interactions that did not lead to arrest on field contact cards that included the subject's name, nickname(s), vehicle information, and gang affiliation. Once digitized, the field contact cards were supplemented with fingerprints and mug shots and given a serial number. Between 2003 and 2014, the production of nongang contact cards increased by 80 percent and gang contact cards by 260 percent.[51] These increases resonated with other instances of the CPD using geospatial technology to normalize its warlike approach to suppressing narcotic activity. The department's 2003 Operation Just Cause, named after the 1989 U.S. invasion of Panama, targeted latinx gang members for minor infractions. "If they are caught drinking, urinating, or throwing a candy wrapper out the window, they are subject to arrest," a CPD spokesperson explained.[52] Computer targeting assisted similar sweeps in the Near South Side's Harold Ickes public housing, Bronzeville's Dearborn Homes, Little Village, and the Far South Side. Many of these surges took place during the Safe Summer initiative, which involved the police establishing ninety roadside safety checkpoints on Friday nights. The police attributed the initiative to a 17 percent increase in gang dispersals, a 30 percent increase in curfew arrests, and a 47 percent increase in graffiti arrests.[53] An invention of the Gang War in the 1980s, the DOC's geographic database technology was central to rationalizing a new cartography of racialized administrative power.

CREATING COMPSTAT

Much ink has been spilled on the NYPD's data-driven administrative system, CompStat. It has been praised in police circles as the "single most important organizational innovation in policing during the latter half of the 20th Century" and a "revolutionary paradigm shift" in U.S. policing.[54] Nearly every major city in the United States now uses some form of Comp-Stat, and it is spreading to urban administrations across the planet. But to be certain, CompStat was only part and parcel of a much larger project to manage the sociospatial contradictions of urban restructuring. In New York City, its ascendance signified a drive to establish a degree of territorial order against the deterritorializing effects of capital circulation. As with the urban renewal programs and organized revolt three decades prior, the city found itself confronted with the problem of populations whose hindrance on profit rates was increasing. City officials responded in part by eviscerating public aid while revolutionizing the instruments of policing.

The computerization of the NYPD gained momentum during a period when tough-on-crime hyperbole was in full effect.[55] At the time, mayoral hopeful Rudolph Giuliani, a former U.S. attorney, propelled himself into office by promising to establish social order through a militarized police apparatus. In his 1994 inauguration speech, Giuliani conveyed the image of a revitalized city "built around stricter enforcement of the law to reverse the growing trend of ever-increasing tolerance for lawless behavior."[56] Quality-of-life enforcement, zero tolerance, and broken windows theory were the policies introduced to achieve this. From the onset, one of quality-of-life policing's most vocal proponents was a business association masquerading under the name of the Citizens Crime Commission. Since 1990, the commission had implored the city to place greater emphasis on regulating low-level incivilities and victimless infractions. Its main concern was how visible drug addiction, homelessness, indigence, and sex workers hurt businesses. With support from Business Improvement Districts and residential associations, the commission recommended that municipal assistance corporations or special levy taxes fund NYPD reforms, the lion's share being allocated toward expanding the department by five thousand patrol officers who would be "permanently assigned to the same small pieces of the city, day after day, making themselves, knowing and being known by the residents, upholding the standards of civilization."[57]

Zero-tolerance policing was predicated on subjecting criminalized people and places to extraordinary levels of patrol forces. Its essence was distilled in the NYPD's Police Strategy 5 to "reclaim public spaces," which targeted lower-grade offenses across core areas in Manhattan.[58] Police Strategy 5 was directed at "symbols of disorder," such as beggars, loiterers, visibly mentally ill persons, truants, subway fare cheaters, and disruptive motorists. Upon taking office, Giuliani announced that the NYPD would begin to observe the disorderly conduct statute with renewed vigor, which, pursuant to §240.20 of New York State's penal law, stated that a person is in violation of public order for a variety of vague behaviors, including failure to disperse while in a group, unreasonable noise, or obscene language or gestures. Urban geographer Neil Smith famously called the program behind these changes *revanchism,* named after a French group organized against the liberalism of the Second Empire and the Paris Commune in the late 1800s. Giuliani recited all the platitudes of French revanchists—respect for traditional authority, fear of progressivism, resentment for disadvantaged classes. The mayor attributed the city's seven-year economic decline to gender nonconformists, homeless people, immigrants, racial minorities, pornographers, and putative "welfare queens." Giuliani claimed that these groups, along with Mayor Dinkins, the city's first black mayor, were taking the city from the white middle class. Revanchist policies, with the NYPD at the tip of the spear, were means of reversing the trend. And like twenty-first-century surges of U.S. white nationalism, the 1990s revanchist movement spread virally through heartless shaming, scapegoating, and extraordinary cruelty. The city swiftly arranged itself to cut public school funding, dismantle rent control, eliminate homeless shelters, and shutter mental clinics, on one hand, and conduct militarized homeless sweeps, squatter evictions, and subway sweeps, on the other.

Broken windows theory, which posits that criminality is a function of urban blight, was the third core logic of Giuliani-era NYPD reform.[59] First articulated in criminologist George L. Kelling and political scientist James Q. Wilson's 1982 article in the *Atlantic,* the theory explains crime as an effect of exclusively neighborhood-level phenomena, including social disorder (public intoxication, profanity), physical disorder (untended property, graffiti, litter), and anomie.[60] The theory was based on a New Jersey police department's Safe and Clean Neighborhoods initiative in the mid-1970s that found that foot patrols, in contrast to motorized patrols, increased citizens' perceptions of safety and willingness to assist police. Kelling and Wilson also drew on psychologist Philip Zimbardo's experiments in the late 1960s, which hypothesized that untended property in public spaces attracts vandalism and more serious criminal behaviors. The monumental errors characterizing broken windows methodology are well documented.[61] But what often escapes scrutiny is the racial project for which the theory was wrought. Broken windows theory was another example of corporate-bureaucratic intellectuals explaining criminal justice datasets by completely sidestepping analysis of the criminal justice apparatus—the very same apparatus that renders subpopulations unemployable, rips family units apart, and cultivates true hatred for juridical authority. Such a radical reified frame of thought translated seamlessly into computer code.

To make quality-of-life, zero-tolerance, and broken windows principles amenable to programming languages, the department had first to mathematicize the theories.[62] This occurred in the mid-1990s through spatial statistical science. In most accounts, the NYPD's embrace of computer-aided spatial analysis is attributed to a deputy commissioner, Jack Maple, who ordered precincts to make pin maps of burglaries, car thefts, gun-related crimes, murders, narcotics activity, robberies, and shootings in 1993.[63] At this point, the NYPD used acetate overlay maps of different crimes at the crime meetings. Budget cuts, however, made this approach too costly and time consuming. To defray costs, the deputy commissioner purchased a Hewlett-Packard 360 with funds from the Police Foundation, an organization founded by the Ford Foundation to research law enforcement innovation and science. At first, the NYPD's patrol borough staff used the computer to log hand counts of UCR crimes and civilian complaints. The staff compiled data for the first six weeks of 1993 and 1994 in a computer file called both "compare statistics" and "computer statistics" by department staff. Soon after its inception, the small file was renamed "CompStat Book" and integrated with the Online Booking System, a centralized repository of data coming from precincts across the department. The file was also merged with a geographic information application that extrapolated spatial patterns from precinct datasets that were not coterminous with existing administrative boundaries. These labors resulted in the translation of quality-of-life, zero-tolerance, and broken windows theory into digital dialects, which ensured that War on Crime logics persisted even if policing policy and rhetoric changed.

Soon after the birth of CompStat, the NYPD's Office of Management Analysis and Planning enrolled the expertise of the Center of Urban Research and Center for Applied Studies of the Environment at the City University of New York.[64] The team's objective was to build a new geographic information system that was capable of organizing, analyzing, and visualizing a greater variety of NYPD data. The Crime Mapping and Analysis Application was the fruit of these labors, which integrated software applications from MapBasic, MapInfo Professional, Microsoft Excel, and Vertical Mapper SDK.[65] In designing the software, the group started by vectorizing NYPD datasets to code longitudinal/latitudinal coordinates of reported incidents, which it then superimposed onto police beats, precincts, census block groups, and street grids. The group visualized police data through maps that depicted aggregations of incidents by precinct and sector; geographic distributions of incidents overlain on maps of the city; and clusters, distributions, and pathways of reported incidents. The spatial statistical analysis centralized NYPD internal operations. "Very few operations outside the Soviet Union," marveled a policy expert working with the NYPD, "were so centralized. [It was] like something dropped from outer space in terms of what it could do."[66]

For NYPD administrators, computer analysis also provided an instrument for human resource procedures that revolved around processing all types of data to evaluate commanding officers. Commanding officers were made to defend their precincts' performance in front of the top NYPD officials and under a neon canopy of charts, graphs, and tables on a biweekly basis.[67] During the notoriously grueling meetings, commanders' profiles showing their dates of appointment, educational levels, specialized training, and years in rank were displayed for all to see. They also displayed statistics on the commander's precinct, including available resources, average response time, community demographics, crime statistics, domestic violence incidents, integrity monitors, officer absences, and unfounded radio runs. NYPD headquarters began to keep digital score cards on commanders, which cultivated a new age of predatory policing. Commanders (and officers) were now tasked with producing numbers. In 2013, it was revealed that rank-and-file officers had stop-and-frisk quotas that were verified through case management data.[68] The ordeal revealed that the practical function of NYPD data was not to document crime but to provide proof of police aggression to department brass under pain of demotion or job termination. "The CompStat system," Bratton later explained, "was police Darwinism; the fittest survived and thrived."[69] Put simply, CompStat was developed in part to governmentalize police behavior.

In addition to its uses in centralization, CompStat was embraced by NYPD technocrats to decentralize decision-making. It was a key piece of the commissioner's "reengineering" initiatives, which were characterized by applying post–World War II management theories to NYPD administration. Just as police reformers of the Progressive Era adopted Taylorist principles of management, Commissioner Bratton adopted the gospel of horizontal decision-making that gained traction during the 1970s in Silicon Valley companies such as Apple, Atari, and Oracle.[70] The NYPD thus "decentralized its operations, not to the police officer on the beat . . . but rather to the precinct commander," who, because of CompStat's ability to track and analyze precinct performance, was afforded greater discretion in planning, staffing, and implementing initiatives. In a 1996 speech titled "Decentralizing and Establishing Accountability," the commissioner explained that a decentralized NYPD meant precinct commanders "were empowered to assign officers as they saw fit, to focus on the priorities of the neighborhood. Whatever was generating the fear in their precinct, [commanders] were empowered to address it by prioritizing their response."[71] Decentralized decision-making shifted the way that the NYPD allocated resources from a logic of functional specialization (detectives, forensics, youth officers) to one of territorial specialization (census blocks, hot spots, street segments).[72] Beginning with CompStat, the department began to conceptualize the NYPD as part of a larger social management infrastructure overseen by digital machines.

As management science tells us, an organization's turn to data analytics increases its demand for additional data. As a consequence, CompStat was eventually used to manage a vast and diverse ecosystem of data. In 1995, the department created the Pattern Identification Module (PIM), a team made up of the detective, housing, organized crime, patrol, and transit bureaus that scoured data in search of geographic trends. PIM used CompStat's mapping function to carve up the city into two dozen precincts with the highest quality-of-life offenses, 29 precincts with the highest sex work offenses, and more than 250 hot spot areas with "metastasized disorder."[73] Data on active bench warrants, civilian complaints, daily summonses, parole residences, parole warrants, and desk appearance tickets for minor violations and misdemeanors were mapped and scrutinized.[74] Data on drug sales, homelessness, littering, unlicensed vending, panhandling, and public consumption came next. The city also used a geographic information system in efforts to establish a "rational distribution" of unlicensed street vendors across the city.[75] Furthermore, it built geographic databases to track the movements of registered chronic misdemeanants, disorderly youth, disruptive students, drug offenders, sex workers, shoplifters, truants, and violent offenders across the city. In sum, the computerization of NYPD administration was deeply wound up in dividing urban space according to varying levels of policeability. Moreover, it allowed the city to rationalize differential law enforcement through the newspeak of spatial analysis and postindustrial management theory.

CALCULATING PROBLEM POPULATIONS AND PLACES IN NEW YORK CITY

As the millennium dawned, New York City's Mayor Michael Bloomberg (2002–13) announced that the city would take full advantage of digital technologies to expand the frontiers of the Giuliani-era NYPD apparatus. Of course, the biopolitical policy of improving life was shadowed by its necropolitical counterpart, zero tolerance. Bloomberg announced that managing "problem people and problem places" was the new centerpiece of his administration's crime control policy. One is tempted to think that the policy was the product of some mischievous reading of Foucault, who identified the problem of populations, administered through statistics, as the definitive feature of modern governance. For the NYPD, the problem people–problem places strategy was designed to exploit the "ability to mine, refine, and use data, from CompStat and other sources, about problem people and problem places."[76] The police were to do so by identifying disorderly areas, increasing tactical forces in these areas by the thousands, and tracking disorderly persons as they maneuvered about the city.

Part of the problem people–problem places initiative revolved around continuously tracking targeted individuals. In early 2002, city officials announced an initiative to intensify the surveillance of repeat quality-of-life offenders convicted of drug possession, property crime, prostitution, sex offenses, subway fare evasion, or trespassing. The NYPD also began making digital identification cards of persons of interest that, although the cards were not authorized by courts, were at times used like arrest and bench warrants. But it was the NYPD's digitally generated impact zones, or areas identified as criminogenic through spatial statistical analysis, that positioned police as permanent administrators of impoverished areas. In 2002, impact zoning was made operational through deployment of fifteen hundred patrollers in two dozen areas across the city. Through the program, police were tasked with probing areas for minor offenses, including disorderly conduct, loitering, and a range of imprecisely defined behaviors. The prime objectives of the operation included increasing summonses for homeless encamping, defecation, marijuana consumption, panhandling, public alcohol consumption, public urination, and unlicensed window washing. Between 2003 and 2006, thirty zones were marked for this type of enforcement. Two years after its launch, the initiative was proudly credited by the mayor for generating more than a half million summonses and fifty thousand arrests.[77]

Impact zones provided not only a scientific pretext for inundating negatively racialized communities in patrol units but also a rationale for micromanaging them through hyperactive tactics. In point of fact, geographic information systems supplied the police with spatial coordinates to deploy the stop-and-frisk technique, the erstwhile centerpiece of the digital age NYPD apparatus. The number of times that minorities were halted, queried, and frisked by patrol officers leaped orders of magnitude following the advent of impact zoning. From 2005 to 2006, there were nearly 510,000 stops in impact zones, a 500 percent increase from the prior year.[78] A network of checkpoints and chokepoints also crystallized in CompStat's computers. In 2010, the ten precincts with the most stops totaled almost the entire number of stops in the other sixty-six precincts.[79] In the Brownsville section of Brooklyn, an area with the densest concentrations of public housing in the city, upward of fifty-two thousand stops were executed. Males between the ages of fifteen and thirty-four in this area were stopped on average five times a year. Between 2006 and 2010, the NYPD conducted 329,446 stops on suspicion of trespassing, only 7.5 percent of which resulted in an arrest, and 5 percent in summons. Over 80 percent of people stopped were classified as black or Hispanic, though they made up a combined 53 percent of the population.[80] Only 10 percent of those stopped were issued summonses or arrested. Between 2002 and 2012, more than 85 percent of all stops were performed on black and Hispanic subjects. Patrol units in impact zones were tasked with doling out punishments for graffiti writing, littering, loud music, marijuana smoking, panhandling, and unlicensed vending. Of the twenty precincts with the largest number of frisks, eleven were majority black, six were majority Hispanic, and three were majority white. The NYPD also analyzed emergency calls to identify "high noise zones" because "noise nuisances [were] increasingly an indicator of a lack of civility and urban disorder."[81] Patrol forces were systematically deployed to eliminate noise pollution from bars, boom boxes, car alarms, clubs, disorderly persons, incomplete construction sites, and vehicle engines and horns. Moreover, the police used several technologies to enforce noise nuisance ordinances. The city proudly announced that the noise elimination program yielded eighteen thousand arrests in its first thirty months.[82]

This seemingly self-expanding apparatus of racialized policing penetrated public housing, which secreted a quasi-correctional architecture around the living spaces of the city's castaways.[83] Housing complexes located in impact zones were subjected to "vertical patrols." Drawing from the 1991 Operation Clean Halls, these patrols comprised police deployed in at least 3,895 low-rent private housing complexes and generated more than 20,000 arrests and 209,000 summonses in its inaugural year. The city justified the patrols by invoking the New York City Housing Authority's do-not-enter bylaws, which prohibited nonresidents from entering public housing uninvited. Vertical patrols stopped trespassing suspects and asked if they lived in the building or were visiting a resident, and requested identification. NYPD analysts also identified impact schools, which further carceralized marginalized communities. Impact schools were patrolled by the School Safety Division (SSD), a unit led by Patrol Borough Commands that enforced school disciplinary codes and securitized school grounds.[84] At the height of impact zoning, the SSD had increased school safety agents by over 60 percent, making the total head count of safety agents and police in New York public schools one of the largest enforcement entities in the country. Agents and police were deployed to perform a series of patrol maneuvers inside schools, such as regulating flows of students through entrances and exits, clearing school perimeters of unauthorized individuals, creating checkpoints for ID cards, conducting searches and seizures for contraband, maintaining safe and orderly cafeterias, and reporting suspicious persons and activities. Agents also performed building sweeps in bathrooms, classrooms, exits, offices, and stairwells for suspicious activity, unauthorized persons, and disorderly behavior. With the exception of two, impact schools were located in zip codes that were on average 13 percent or more black, 4 percent or more Hispanic, and 8 percent or less white than city averages.[85] Students classified as black and Hispanic made up 94 percent of all school-related arrests and were fourteen and five times more likely to be arrested than white students, respectively.[86] After seven years of impact enforcement, suspensions increased by 130 percent, which paralleled an overall decline in the black student population.[87] More than half of black students arrested were documented as having a disability.

At roughly the same time that impact schools appeared, the NYPD began developing body-scanning technology that utilized terahertz waves to detect metal objects. "If something is obstructing the flow of radiation, for example a weapon," the police commissioner explained, "the device will highlight that object."[88] Upon detecting an anomaly, algorithms determined its risk level, and levels that exceeded predefined thresholds alerted patrol units closest to the point of detection. This "sentient" dimension established conditions where machines began to play a part, however nominal, in organizing distributions of racialized police encounters by themselves. This is because the machines autonomously transmitted information that, in some instances, influenced patrol behavior. This diffusion of surveillance through automated alert systems invoked Deleuze's control society, as it very much resembled a sieve whose mesh spread throughout physical space-time. It is not only figuratively gaseous but also literally electromagnetic. But the NYPD's body and environment scanning did not replace the fact that the negatively racialized poor are prodded into *internment*. When it comes to the racial administrative state, computerization hardly equated to the disappearance of enclosures or violence.

THE NATIONAL EMERGENCE OF PREDICTIVE POLICING

If impact zoning was publicized by city officials as a way of locking down on problematic geographies, predictive policing was publicized as a way of regulating their temporality. Though there is no consensus definition of predictive policing, it obtained a semblance of coherence after a 2009 NIJ symposium spearheaded by former NYPD chief William Bratton and broken windows theorist George L. Kelling.[89] One of the symposium's core goals was to forge a "connection [between] corporate ideas and methods to policing."[90] A reccurring theme at the symposium was that criminal justice trailed far behind the business sector in the application of data analytics. And trailed it did. Infancies of data analytics first formed in the 1956 Dartmouth Summer Research Project on Artificial Intelligence, attended by W. Ross Ashby, John Nash, and Claude Shannon, among numerous other luminaries in the budding computer sciences. The workshop revolved around the idea that "every aspect of learning or any other feature of intelligence can in principle be so precisely described that a machine can be made to simulate it."[91] It took a revolution in technology and decades of information capitalists exerting influence on the administrative state for the fruits of this workshop to reach the police.

Infusing market logics into police departments was an explicit objective in many early predictive policing initiatives. In fact, the first projects used software that adapted customer-targeting and supply chain management logics to crime prediction.[92] One such example was developed by Los Angeles police and psychologists from the business technology corporation MC2 Solutions. MC2 pointed to the success e-commerce and marketing firms had with predictive analytics as a testament to its crime-fighting potential. It also proposed the application of business analytics as a technical means of shrinking police budgets while enlarging their public presence and versatility. Similar initiatives quickly replicated across the country— East Orange, New Jersey; Memphis, Tennessee; Chicago, Illinois; Dallas, Texas; Palm Beach, Florida; Santa Cruz, California; Glendale, Arizona; New Orleans, Louisiana; Baltimore, Maryland; Charlotte–Mecklenburg, North Carolina; Nashville, Tennessee; Philadelphia, Pennsylvania; New Castle, Delaware; Miami, Florida; Lincoln, Nebraska; New York City, New York; and Minneapolis, Minnesota.

From the viewpoint of the police apparatus, early predictive policing projects centered on attempts to "design a computer model that could replicate an officer's intuition."[93] The idea was that transferring high-, middle-, and low-level decision-making functions to machines, the entire department would operate more fluidly. To achieve this, a mishmash of anthropologists, biomedical engineers, business solution firms, machine-learning experts, police personnel, psychologists, and technology corporations combined forces following the NIJ's 2009 symposium. One product to emerge from these efforts was offender-based predictive software, which isolated social networks in criminalized areas and ranked the criminal inclination of each individual member. The algorithms probed criminal justice datasets for connections between victims of violence, people with violent records, and people who have been arrested at the same time as former violent offenders. Individuals with close connections to violent offenders, who have been arrested around the same time as violent offenders, or who have been victims of violence were assigned higher risk ratings.[94] Persons with high ratings populated "heat lists," which designated them for heightened police surveillance.

A mass of civil rights litigators mobilized against the compiling of heat lists. In reaction, many cities, criminologists, and software corporations invested in predictive policing spurned offender-based predictive analytics for geographic-based ones. The latter excluded individual data from analysis and relied instead on spatial analysis of police datasets. This approach also included a temporal dimension, as it analyzed time coordinates of past reported incidents (e.g., time of day, day of week, month). This type of geographic profiling had existed since the 1990s. It was then that crime geographic-targeting software was first designed to predict the probable spatial behavior of violent serial offenders by mapping their "hunting areas."[95] The software was employed by the Royal Canadian Mounted Police; the National Crime and Operations Faculty in the United Kingdom; and the Bureau of Alcohol, Tobacco, Firearms, and Explosives in the United States. Similar geography-based predictive algorithms have been devised by university professors to determine the probability of arrests for specific categories of crime in specific time frames, identify irregular concentrations of arrests, and correlate crime reports with physical characteristics of the streets on which they occur. PredPol, a California-based software company spearheaded by anthropologists, mathematicians, and the Los Angeles Police Department, was founded upon the premise that seismology could be wielded to predict spatial and temporal distributions of crime. Azavea, a Philadelphia-based firm, produced software that performs risk terrain modeling by analyzing environmental data, land uses, moon phases, school schedules, and weather patterns. There is also predictive policing software that looks for correlations between criminality with abandoned buildings, broken streetlights, liquor stores, and civilian complaints about garbage disposal and road conditions.[96] And even when criminalized areas do not have high arrest rates, there is "cold spotting" prediction software that produces z-scores to show police that they are criminogenic nonetheless.

Predictive policing software is knowledge power written in code, as it ordains differential identification, monitoring, and intervention on human subjects. Precrime maps also belong in the company of Borges's Cartographers Guild, as they precede territorial practices. Whether offender or geographic based, the proliferation of these maps goes hand in hand with normalizing policies of encircling, evaluating, and intervening in the everyday lives of populations and places bearing certain coefficients. The coefficients are the same ones found in Frederick L. Hoffman's work well over a century ago. This is why today's digital maps contribute nothing to understanding urban criminality. Against mounting suspicions that the software has no tangible effect on crime rates, clearance rates, or productivity, technology corporations have contrived selling points of all sorts.[97] IBM promotes its crime-forecasting software on the grounds that crime is becoming more sophisticated; Motorola on the grounds that the criminal world is becoming increasingly complex; and PredPol on the grounds that it saves departments money.

No harbinger of Leviathan, Urstaat, or even instrumental rationality anticipated the creation of artificial intelligence for the purpose of calculating appropriate distributions of state violence. Dead labor animates necropolitics with predictive policing, one of the IT sector's contributions to racial governance. Predictive policing's algorithms are products of the radically empiricist ideologies of corporate-bureaucratic intellectuals and computer scientists content to describe facts (e.g., arrest rates) without understanding their conditions of possibility (e.g., the War on Crime). From this perspective, social relations do not exist, only mathematical relations. No thought is given to how different crime-reduction policies, crime legislation, profiling tendencies, or sentencing biases influence the patterns found by algorithms in the data. Only negatively racialized and poor human targets exist in the functionalist logics of predictive policing software, which lays bare the scopic viewpoint of police officers.

Discursively, geographic-based crime prediction furnished police with an ostensibly evidence-based justification to immerse devalued areas with patrol units. But their replacement of individual-based software is of no practical significance. Analyzing spatial data is practically no different than analyzing individual data because urban zip codes, not to mention home addresses, are overwhelmingly correlated with racial classification.[98] And inasmuch as geographic-based crime-prediction models look for correlations in official police datasets, they are bound to yield the same practical results as offender-based models. Moreover, geographic prediction is rooted in the tautologies of criminology's near-repeat theory, which posits that areas are criminogenic because crimes occurred in those areas.[99] Such tautological reasoning, which expresses in the predicate that which was already stated in the subject, is foundational to crime science dogma. However, the real-world function of predictive policing is not to see crime before it happens but to graft scientific authority onto entrenched forms of racialized policing. But it is pointless to belabor all of this owing to the fact that predictive policing was not developed to solve first-order problems. Crime diffusion risk, hot spot matrices, nearest neighborhood hierarchical clusters, near-repeat patterns—"whatever the name used, whatever the latest expression," the point is to assist the state in managing stigmatized populations.

CHICAGO'S PATH TO PREDICTIVE POLICING

The City of Chicago's foray into predictive policing came during a moment of socioeconomic crisis. The Great Recession (2007–9) increased the monthly average unemployment rate in the Chicago metropolitan region by a staggering three percentage points.[100] The rate for black and latinx labor fractions was 7 and 3 percent higher than the city average (whites were 3 percent *lower*), respectively, both almost 1 percent higher than national averages.[101] From 2007 to 2010, the Institute for Housing Studies reported, the percentage of people out of work for twenty-seven weeks or more rose from 23 to about 50 percent in Illinois.[102] The census calculated that almost 33 percent of residents registered as black lived below the poverty line, compared to 24 percent for those registered Hispanics and 15 percent for whites.[103] Illinois teen employment dropped to about 25 percent, the lowest in the state's recorded history, 92 percent of which were classified as black males and 80 percent of which were classified as Hispanic.[104]

As part of wider initiatives to turn Chicago into the Silicon Valley of the Midwest, or the Silicon Prairie, Mayor Rahm Emanuel (2011–19) proposed big data analytics as a remedy to the social wreckage of the recession. Digitally enhanced law enforcement, he proclaimed, could stop the most destitute of neighborhoods from turning into a "lost generation that slides into crime and poverty."[105] By 2010, Chicago's chief information officer, chief technology officer, and chief data officer became the public face of the city's computer-enhanced fight against crime. The trio announced that it could reduce crime rates by applying simple spatial and temporal principles, empiricism, and statistical models to law enforcement. The chief data officer advanced predictive policing as the leading edge of this initiative.[106] To be sure, Chicago had been at the forefront of crime prediction for nearly a century and of GIS crime mapping for twenty-five years. In 1927, the Illinois parole board appointed Ernest W. Burgess and other University of Chicago sociology and law professors to apply actuarial statistics to criminal law.[107] The initiative was part of an attempt to rectify problems arising from the state's indeterminate sentences for juvenile offenders. Such sentences gave rise to overcrowding, which prompted the Department of Public Welfare to form a parole board to find ways of decreasing the number of juvenile detainees. To do this, the board needed standardized criteria to decide who was eligible for release. Enter the Burgess method, which, by 1935, was the sole parole-prediction method used in the United States. At the heart of the method were twenty-one variables related to the potential parolee's "social type" and "psychiatric personality." Social types included drunkard, drug addict, farm boy, hobo, mean citizen, and recent immigrant, while psychiatric type included egocentric, emotionally unstable, and socially inadequate. Once it was determined which variables held the strongest associations with successful parole, Burgess et al. devised a scorecard system for the parole boards.

In 2011, the CPD introduced its Predictive Analytics Group, which brought an actuarial system to the police. The group started to coalesce two years prior, during a NIJ-funded collaboration with machine-learning experts from Carnegie Mellon's Event and Pattern Detection Laboratory and the Illinois Institute of Technology. The main objectives of the collaborators included designing algorithms capable of predicting crime events a week in advance, establishing spatiotemporal resolution at the scales of blocks and days, and developing the ability to predict at scales much smaller than neighborhoods.[108] In its early phase, the group focused on identifying statistical relationships within CPD data on 911 calls and shooting statistics. The team maintained that it could extrapolate where and when future shootings would occur based on the assumption that time series in past data could be used to infer shootings in the immediate days afterward. But algorithms have a tendency to go rogue. They find new datasets to comb for correlations, new methodologies to assimilate, new hardware inside of which to embed themselves. Thus the Predictive Analytics Group's software, dubbed CrimeScan, was expanded to include curfew offenses, disorderly conduct, driving under the influence, drug offenses, liquor offenses, loitering, prostitution, public drunkenness, runaways, simple assault, vandalism, and vagrancy, among others. It identified twelve indicators of future shootings, including assaults, minor crimes, gang-related emergency calls, and gun-related emergency calls. Beyond CPD datasets, the Predictive Analytics Group also probed for spatial correlations between reported incidents and data on liquor stores, physical disrepair, and untended garbage. The group also began to use CrimeScan to test for indicators of future crime using the city's Data Portal, one of the largest public databanks in the country. The data portal consisted of more than nine hundred datasets on municipal departments, facilities, and services. The predictive analytics group adopted an open source database to incorporate unstructured data such as the area's number of abandoned buildings, or complaints about garbage disposal and road conditions, or liquor licenses. But using the data only reproduced rationalizations for flooding the Black Belt with patrol forces, as geographies of dilapidation and disrepair are unmistakably racialized.[109]

Owing to the racialized character of Chicago's War on Drugs, the expansion of CrimeScan amounted to the expansion of calculating racial proxies as indicators of future criminality. In point of fact, the CPD's own datasets for victimless crimes (vandalism, gambling, drunkenness, and disorderly conduct) between 1991 and 2009 showed remarkably consistent disparities between subjects cataloged as blacks and whites. From 1991 to 1999, 70 percent of arrestees for these categories were black, compared to 29 percent whites.[110] According to the CPD's own data, Chicagoans categorized as black and Hispanic accounted for 83 percent of all vandalism arrestees, 93 percent of narcotics arrestees, and 99 percent of all gambling arrestees.[111] In 2009, 99 percent of gambling violations recorded by the CPD involved individuals classified as black, 93 percent of recorded narcotics violations involved individuals classified as black and Hispanic, 85 percent of instances of vandalism involved individuals classified as black and Hispanic, and 67 percent of simple assaults involved individuals classified as black.

In addition to geographic profiling, the CPD went on a brief jaunt in offender-based predictions. The individual-based approach emerged through the CPD's strategic subjects list (SSL), which was generated by analyzing the social characteristics of narcotic arrestees and registered gang members. The SSL also used social network analysis to estimate a subject's relative risk of engaging in future violent crime. This technique determined one's likelihood of committing future crime according to one's links to homicide victims. The SSL was inaugurated by conducting network analyses on sixty gangs and six hundred factions to predict potential acts of retaliatory violence in the aftermath of homicides.[112] In 2013, the DOC began producing trimonthly lists of the five hundred highest-risk individuals in the city, that is, each police district's twenty riskiest subjects. Toward the end of 2013, the department created an additional list of the city's 426 riskiest subjects to circulate to district commanders.[113] By the end of the program's first two years, the total number of subjects identified as at risk had increased by more than 200 percent, including more than fourteen hundred names.[114] Some heatlisted subjects were enrolled in call-in sessions, which were originally designed by police, federal and county authorities, and the Illinois Department of Corrections. The sessions involved rounding up putative gangs members to warn them that they would be targeted in the event of a spike in violent crime. In 2015, the department began calling in groups of high-risk subjects identified on the SSL who lived in close proximity to one another. Call-ins functioned as unequivocal admissions on behalf of the police that certain individuals, geographically concentrated in certain places, were permanently subjected to differential police supervision. Predictive policing therefore not only lent the credence of data science shamans to the age-old practice of discriminatory profiling but also lent itself to new rationalizations for *extending* such profiling.

In 2014, the tech magazine *Verge* released a widely read article on the CPD's predictive policing program that compared it to a film based on Philip K. Dick's short story "The Minority Report."[115] The story revolved around a federal agency that predicted future crimes by analyzing prophetic utterances of three "mutants,"[116] which were speckled with hints of future crimes up to two weeks in advance. "Every incoherent utterance, every random syllable, was analyzed, compared, reassembled in the form of visual symbols, transcribed on conventional punchcards, and ejected into various coded slots. All day long the [mutants] babbled, imprisoned in their special high-backed chairs, held in one rigid position by metal bands, and bundles of wiring, clamps."[117] Fragments of the enslaved workers were examined and assembled in a coherent manner by data receptors and computers in the agency's analytical wing. Once clues to future crimes were distilled from the trio's ramblings, computers generated cards with the names of precriminals, previctims, and the dates and times of future offenses. The Precrime Agency worked in tandem with police units to capture precriminals before they committed crimes and send them to detention camps. The system was extolled for establishing a prophylactic precrime structure that cut down on felonies by over 99 percent, prevented murders for five years, and abolished the "postcrime punitive system of jails and fines." In Dick's story, the Precrime Agency was captured by political interests through an extraordinary turn of events. Dick's main criticism of precrime methodology revolved around the potential incongruities between precrime methodology and individual liberties.[118] However, the Precrime Agency's real-world counterpart in Chicago tells a different story. Instead of an extraordinary event, Chicago's Predictive Analytics Group was born of the normalized policies of the crime and drug wars. Moreover, real-world predictive policing does not work through preemptively criminalized individuals. Whether using offender- or geographic-based algorithms, predictive policing identifies entire demographics and neighborhoods as criminally predisposed.

4

PUNISHMENT IN THE NETWORK FORM

The network logic epitomized by the Internet became applicable to every domain of activity, to every context, and to every location that could be electronically connected.

—MANUEL CASTELLS, *The Rise of the Network Society*

The protocols of the punitive state pulsate through communications cables and across wireless networks—sometimes at the behest of an algorithm. This is because state-authorized punishment can now be administered through the internet and web applications. On one hand, the internet serves as a medium for criminal justice agencies to agglomerate information about the public through an immense number of sources. The ability to bring diverse datastreams into central databases has given rise to a massive registry of "aliens," felons, misdemeanants, political radicals, potential offenders, sex offenders, and (potential) terrorists. In some cities, the public can submit information about suspected offenders to enforcement agencies via the web, making punitive governance an increasingly crowdsourced affair.

On the other hand, criminal justice information constantly flows from state agencies into mobile devices throughout the public sphere. Before the internet, one would have had to travel to repositories in government buildings, then comb through vast paper archives to confirm that a person held a criminal record. Now, the police and corrections apparatuses publish records on arrestees, early release offenders, inmates, low-level offenders, parolee sex registrants, sex offenders, and wanted fugitives on the web. Sometimes these profiles are supplemented with photographs and personal information. Private traders of the records employ bots to farm new ones from criminal justice websites. These traders eventually formed the background-checking industry, which has grown such that it established a trade association, the National Association of Professional Background Screeners, in 2003.[1] The association consists of just under one thousand firms that sell information about convicted persons to banks, employers, insurance companies, landlords, and state agencies. Some background-checking websites charge people to remove their information from the sites. Nonprofit organizations also publish specialized registries that focus on different types of offenders. Many newspaper websites have taken to publishing photo galleries of mug shots on the web as well. Liberal websites publish galleries of people who have been accused, though not convicted, of sexual misconduct as clickbait. Never before has it been so difficult to keep a criminal record from becoming public knowledge. As a result, more institutions can work in concert with penal authorities, including educational institutions, employers, public housing administrators, and social welfare agencies.

The newfound ability to instantly identify former offenders reflects the extent to which the penal state has adapted to the information superhighway's organizational template, the *network*. In its essential form, a network is a centerless system of cells whose core command functions are distributed across various nodes.[2] Networks multiply their power by increasing the number of these nodes. "When they diffuse," notes Castells, "their growth becomes exponential, as the benefits from being in the network grow exponentially."[3] To be sure, networks of racialized surveillance have existed in the United States since at least the Fugitive Slave Act of 1850, which spawned a network of specially appointed magistrates, civilians, and newspapers to differentially monitor blacks (this in turn catalyzed an oppositional network in the Underground Railroad). Another example was the system of networks established between indigenous scouts and the U.S. Army during the Indian Wars. But none of these could match the ubiquity and inexorability of today's internet-based criminal identification networks. Today, millions of interconnected databases, cameras, human users, and smart devices stream information about criminalized populations to the entire public body in real time. Processing and sanctioning offenders is no longer confined to state facilities. In fact, now the penal state can theoretically authorize punishment anyplace there is a wireless connection.

The penal state's quiet mutation through wireless networks is creating conditions hospitable to new topologies of state-authorized punishment. For patrol forces, these networks allow officers to register sanctions into databases while they are still in the streets, thus extending criminal processing to public space. Networked criminal justice databases also have deep implications for criminal identification. By 2007, the NCIC confirmed that it processed a wanted person hit every ninety seconds.[4] What is more, web technology allows the police to mobilize the public as sentinels for surveillance and the courts to highlight those whom they convict to employers, landlords, schools, and the public at large. The mergence of the web and mass criminalization has invoked the unsettling image of a wireless apparatus that can monitor and sanction former offenders as they move from point to point across various institutional landscapes. The image, to be sure, emerged well before the internet explosion in the 1990s.

BUILDING A NATIONAL CRIMINAL IDENTIFICATION NETWORK

Throughout the turbulent 1960s, the Federal Bureau of Investigation (FBI) sought congressional approval to build a nationwide criminal identification network. It got its chance toward the middle of the decade, when the Identification Division proposed leasing data processing hardware to aggregate criminal history records, incident reports, and wanted notices from law enforcement agencies in the Washington, D.C., metropolitan region.[5] The proposal emboldened the FBI to build a computer network that connected information systems from law enforcement agencies in the country. The result was the National Crime Information Center (NCIC), a hub that brought together criminal justice databases on a national scale. The network, which comprised fifteen city- and state-level computer systems and processed fifty-five hundred transactions daily, was activated in 1967.

FIGURE 16. National Crime Information Center, 1967. Workers in the National Crime Information Center maintain a countrywide clearinghouse of crime records, mug shots, and other criminal justice information. The center, which drew in information from a variety agencies, created new opportunities for coordinated activity on unprecedented scales. From "History and Milestones," Federal Bureau of Investigation, https://www.fbi.gov/services/cjis/ncic.

A key moment in NCIC history occurred when a New York Police Department (NYPD) officer radioed the center to look up a license plate.[6] Within a minute and a half, the story goes, the officer was given the plate number and notified that the car was stolen. The incident was taken by many in the bureau as an example of the power of networks. It found that telecommunications networks established a medium through which patrol units, dispatchers, and centralized databanks could collectively form a dynamic chain of surveillance, identification, and interception. The revelation was characteristic of the zeitgeist. During the NCIC's early phases, the Information Processing Techniques Office's Advanced Research Projects Agency (ARPA) mulled over designs for interactive computing networks. The result was ARPANET, a computer network designed by the engineering firm Bolt, Beranek, and Newman courtesy of a $1 million contract with the Defense Department. ARPANET employed a revolutionary telecommunications technology developed at RAND Corporation and the British National Physical Laboratory, packet switching, which defined rules for data transmission over the internet. ARPANET made its first successful data transmission at the inaugural International Conference on Computer Communication in 1972. This established the foundation for the internet.

While computer science and technology were flourishing at West Coast universities, the national War on Drugs was beginning to take form. Political scientist Marie Gottschalk chronicled how the politics of punishment had grown to such an extent in the United States during the 1970s that it commanded bipartisan support. In addition to familiar conservative factions, activists from the American Civil Liberties Union, National Organization of Victims Assistance, and Mothers against Drunk Driving drove the expansion of penal populism in the 1970s.[7] As the penal state began to crystallize around this especially toxic populism, the NCIC embarked on a national project to link all criminal justice information systems in the country. The center marshaled LEAA funds for the System for Electronic Analysis and Retrieval of Criminal Histories (SEARCH) project to "demonstrate that a computerized criminal offender file, containing data from all segments of criminal justice, can be standardized and exchanged between States on a timely basis."[8] The project was spearheaded by the SEARCH team, a multimember firm that acted as a liaison between criminal justice information scientists and the IT sector. The group oversaw construction of the Computerized Criminal History database, which stored the aliases, arrest dates, charges, dispositions, fingerprints, names, and physical descriptions of serious offenders. In little over a year, the SEARCH project unveiled an incident report database using an IBM 360/65 central processor in the Michigan State Police headquarters. It was linked into police databases in five other states. Members of the SEARCH team downplayed the praise its database received for drastically reducing the amount of time it took to retrieve criminal records. Instead, the group, which went on to found the National Consortium for Justice Information and Statistics and SEARCH Group Inc., emphasized that it would revolutionize the state's ability to coordinate action across departments.

Constructing a database network on a national scale required standardizing criminal justice datasets. Luckily for the technocrats, the 1970s was a watershed moment for communication protocol standardization. In 1973, designs for Transmission Control Protocol (TCP) were established at Stanford University, which laid the groundwork for Transmission Control Protocol/Internet Protocol (TCP/IP). The protocols were, in essence, rules for digitally breaking down messages from one computer, transmitting the pieces, and reassembling them on another computer in another location. While these rules were being formalized, the NCIC was initiating the Comprehensive Data System program to standardize the development of criminal justice information systems on state and municipal levels. The initiative required that new software for criminal justice agencies be designed according to federal standards in order to receive financial support. In addition to technical standards, the NCIC format categorized all data into two sets: one consisted of seven property offenses, the other of twelve offenses against persons. The LEAA dispensed $207 million in categorical grants and upward of $40 million in block grants to states to build comprehensive data systems and statistical programs compatible with the SEARCH prototype.[9] Moreover, national regulations on crime data management were established in 1976. By 1980, SEARCH's database model had spread to every state, and all state governments had access to the NCIC's centralized system.

The telecommunications industry's services were summoned to transmit the coming data torrent. At the time, the largest criminal justice communication network was the Law Enforcement Teletype System. Founded in the previous decade, the network was hampered by terminal information overload, extraordinarily slow message delivery, and an inability to automatically retrieve remote data. The LEAA thus awarded $4 million to the National Law Enforcement Teletype System Inc. to "provide the technology to carry the present and predicted [data] traffic load and to make possible computer-to-computer exchanges of communication."[10] This marked the birth of NLETS Inc., which manages a network of terminals and systems for municipal, regional, state, and national criminal justice agencies to this day.

The massive project undertaken by the NCIC eventually involved upgrading the Uniform Crime Reporting system (UCR) through the National Incident-Based Reporting System (NIBRS). The new system was built using funds from the Bureau of Justice Statistics and FBI that were authorized through the Crime Identification Technology Act (1998), a bill aimed to establish an information network between eighteen thousand law enforcement agencies. SEARCH Group Inc. functioned as a go-between for the $100 million of federal funding and the IT vendors that eventually built the database network. Firms such as Crimestar Corporation, Constellation Software Inc., and Omnigo Software quickly turned to developing NIBRS-compatible software. In contrast to the UCR, which updated monthly, NIBRS took data from law enforcement the instant they were entered into databases.

NIBRS was a beneficiary to the dramatic expansion of the web. Web browsers first appeared in 1990, courtesy of programmers and engineers at the European Organization for Nuclear Research who developed hypertext languages and transfer protocols to facilitate interactions between web browsers and database servers. The FBI used Hypertext Markup Language (HTML) to link up criminal justice databases and to create unique tags for criminal justice data. So long as agencies were using the same tags, they could freely share information with one another.

Similar developments took place in the police apparatus. Midway through the decade, the *FBI Law Enforcement Bulletin* began collecting information on how municipal agencies were using the internet. The project revealed that dispatchers, patrol officers, police chiefs, students, and professors used it for researching databases and discussing current trends in law enforcement with practitioners and researchers around the world.[11] By 1992, the IACP had established a network between databases from 425 law enforcement agencies. A few years after, Chicago, Phoenix, and Sacramento had web pages to broadcast alerts, organize community policing groups, report crimes for cash, and review rewards for wanted suspects. At the same time, the FBI launched its Criminal Justice Information Services (CJIS) Division to act as a hub for the intelligence community, law enforcement, and national security. Software companies like LEA Data Technologies and Target Solutions and Power DMS were obliged. One of the CJIS's early projects was an electronic gateway for enforcement agencies called Law Enforcement Online, which facilitated online education modules on subjects ranging from forensic anthropology to antiterrorism tactics. The gateway provided multimedia libraries of documents, publications, research, and technical bulletins and a Virtual Command Center where users could submit and retrieve maps, messages, photo images, and suspect files. It also had a virtual community-building application, which included more than one thousand specialized groups. The CJIS also oversaw the implementation of the National Data Exchange (N-DEx), a repository for data on arrests, booking, computer-aided dispatch calls, incident reports, calls for service, field contacts, identification records, parolees/probationers, pretrial investigations, supervised released reports, traffic citations, and more. Corrections personnel, detectives, patrol officers, parole and probation officers, and regional dispatchers all contributed to and took information from N-DEx for everything from routine investigations to SWAT raids.

This networking of enforcement agencies slowly built up a massive database network of criminalized and precriminalized subjects. Police across states started to share access to massive gang data clearinghouses through a closed network called GangNet, a commercial, proprietary system purchased by the Bureau of Alcohol, Tobacco, Firearms, and Explosives' Information Services Division. The system, developed by Orion Scientific Systems Inc., was designed so that patrol units could supply and retrieve data about individuals in, or suspected of being in, gangs, as well as data about gang hangouts, the residences of gang members, and their vehicles. GangNet was also linked into the erstwhile Immigration and Naturalization Service, which increased the exposability of criminalized noncitizens. At this point, however, smaller jurisdictions were not linked into the national database network. To address this, in 1995, the Bureau of Justice Statistics, state-level criminal justice agencies, and the FBI launched the National Criminal History Improvement Program (NCHIP). Over the next decade, NCHIP directed hundreds of millions of dollars into establishing a national criminal justice reporting network with an unprecedented number of agencies. In its first year, it gave more than $112 million in direct awards to states and eligible territories to develop law enforcement databases compatible with NCIC's system.[12] The Crime Identification Technology Act (1998) expanded the program by transferring funds to software companies in the SEARCH Group's exclusive market niche. NCHIP helped states automate case and record databases, convert juvenile records to adult case management systems, and establish sex offender databases. It also aided states in making automated databases for fingerprint and other biometric data. Between 1995 and 1999, the number of crime history records increased nearly 30 percent nationwide, and the number of automated records accessible to the NCIC's users increased 35 percent.[13] Part of this was due to the addition of criminal immigration violations to the NCIC's central database in 1996. NCHIP also transferred millions of dollars to the National Instant Criminal Background Check System, which established instant interstate identifications to users in the system. From 1999 to 2003, the number of state records in the NCIC database went from 3,222 to 88,696.[14]

As more and more data flowed through the rapidly proliferating network, the NCIC required considerable technical upgrades. This positive feedback loop constituted a boon for information capital. Indeed, the NCIC eventually came to provide a telecommunication network to the CJIS Systems Agency in each state.[15] Smaller companies, such as Applied Technologies Inc. and Diversified Computer Systems, stepped in to fill this state-induced demand. As the new millennium drew closer, the bureau introduced NCIC 2000, which managed more than twenty-one databases and could search through others using various communications protocols and could be used on portable smart devices. This dramatically increased the data that flowed into the national center. For instance, NCIC 2000's databases stored biometric and genetic data, including DNA, facial patterns, fingerprints, irises, palm prints, and voice patterns. These data are transferred into a closed network of databases, including the Criminal History Record Information system, the Combined DNA Index System, and the Repository for Individuals of Special Concern. Patrol units in the field can search for matches through the millions of entries and submit digital photographs and fingerprints.

To manage this galactic explosion of data, technocrats went so far as to develop a new transmission and communications protocol exclusively for criminal justice agencies. In 2002, the Bureau of Justice Assistance launched the Law Enforcement Information Technology Standards Council, which—along with the Integrated Justice Information Systems Institute and a "functional standards" committee of law enforcement personnel and technology corporations—established national protocol standards for record management systems and computer-aided dispatch systems. The scope of the project was so grand that it called forth the development of a new universal markup language for all criminal justice agencies.[16] These labors materialized in the Global Justice XML Data Model (GJXDM), which established a foundation for data sharing across municipal, state, national, and international enforcement agencies. The centerpiece of the model is the Global Justice XML Data Dictionary, which is made up of two thousand unique data elements.

The War on Terror dramatically expanded the role of the federal government in the bourgeoning network of law enforcement databases (see chapter 5). In 2005, the Departments of Justice and Homeland Security mandated that tech companies that supplied law enforcement information systems had to use GJXDM to receive federal funding for research and development. This requirement gave birth to yet another data exchange model, the National Information Exchange Model, which established a standard lexicon for criminal justice agencies, homeland security apparatuses, and private corporations. (Homeland security's heightened role in the development of law enforcement databases also prompted the IACP to organize a Criminal Intelligence Sharing Summit, which eventually gave rise to an information-sharing network of police and government agencies across the Global North.[17]) The influence of network logics also penetrated the nation's largest law enforcement agency, Immigration and Customs Enforcement. In 2006, the George W. Bush administration revealed designs to augment border policing with the Secure Border Initiative's "virtual fence," dubbed SBInet.[18] Its ultimate goal was to endow border personnel with the ability to identify, track, digitally represent, and capture unauthorized subjects with unprecedented swiftness. SBInet was intended to unify and animate networks of unmanned aerial surveillance, control rooms, data terminals, ground sensors, radar and camera towers, and vehicular patrols using artificial intelligence (AI). Specifically, the AI was supposed to be designed to ascertain all security breaches into national territory, determine who or what is crossing, and notify the Border Patrol unit best positioned for interception. Boeing Corporation prototyped the ill-fated SBInet with $3.7 billion worth of federal funding.

THE NYPD'S MOBILE NETWORKS

If we zoom down to the urban scale, we see a variegated ensemble of actors and processes behind the spread of penal networks. In fact, the combination of the network form, digital technology, and differential policing and punishment predates the internet at this level. Midway through the nineteenth century, police in Boston, New York, and Philadelphia used the telegraph to coordinate quick responses to urban uprisings fueled by everything from anti-abolitionism to government graft, nativism, and rising food prices. The core function of police telegraphs was to facilitate communication between central headquarters and precincts. Near the end of the 1860s, the Gamewell Fire Alarm Company extended telegraph networks through electrical signal boxes situated throughout beat patrol routes.[19] As the century turned, police telegraph systems were integrated with telephony to multiply the number of signal booths throughout cities. These hybrid networks were used to dispatch patrol wagons to aid in the suppression of organized crime and popular uprisings. But with the unrivaled power of web technology that arrived toward the end of the century, the police apparatus could exploit the network form not only for emergencies but also for everyday patrolling and punishment.

In New York City, early attempts to implement the NYPD's web technologies were mostly for internal bureaucratic purposes. During the 1980s, the NYPD made several strides in providing personnel with remote access to its central database. Administrative staff retrieved information from mobile digital terminals that ran online booking and warrant applications. These provided personnel throughout the department summaries on cases that included arrestee names, charges, fingerprints, officer ID numbers, photographs, and information on the race, sex, and date of birth of offenders. Similar sets of interlinked databases appeared in district attorneys' offices and throughout the court system. But at the time, these systems, like those used by NYPD bureaucrats, were used for internal administrative functions.

The city's network of criminal justice databases experienced a qualitative leap in the 1990s, when technocrats started to see the greater potential of digital networks. Indeed, the mid-1990s saw the Public Access to Court Electronic Records (PACER) go online, which was intended to allow the public to obtain information on cases and involved parties. Such technology was made possible by the declining costs and increasing processing power of commercial computing. These factors placed mobile database terminals at the center of the NYPD's Community Patrol Officer Program initiative, a project to enroll the public to put their "eyes and ears on the street" to combat criminals.[20] By 1990, the NYPD estimated that it actively mobilized 65,000 civilians into 150 community patrols: 15,000 civilians into the city-sponsored block watch program, 8,864 into tenant–building civilian patrollers, 7,000 into civilian motorized patrollers, and 1,216 into on-foot civilian patrollers.[21] The department proposed publicly accessible databases as one way of organizing and harnessing the collective power of civilians. In addition to being efficient repositories, the police commissioner argued in the beginning of the 1990s, public databases could be used to augment the NYPD's ability to monitor, detect, and intercept problematic people. Just a few years before IBM released the first smartphone, the police commissioner described a world in which access to constantly updated police data was a prerequisite for being an informed citizen. Each precinct in the city was thus outfitted with a database terminal for civilians to view crime statistics, information on rules and regulations, and official procedures for crime reporting. Such was the beginning of modulating part of the public into a living and breathing appendage of the police apparatus.

The community policing initiative also involved equipping patrol officers with handheld computers to provide them with access to the police database network. Mobile terminals were installed in squad vehicles during the Dinkins administration (1990–93) so that patrol officers could tap into the NCIC and the New York State Police Information Network's databases. The city's technocrats boasted that the terminals would revolutionize patrol units, as they offered instant access to arrest records, beat books, complaint reports, court orders, information on driver's licenses, location histories, registrations, and wanted persons. By jacking into the network of databases, insisted NYPD technocrats, the department's investigations, situational awareness, and warrant enforcement would be enhanced dramatically. Accessible databases were also seen as a means by which patrol officers could capture additional data about the public during each and every police–civilian interaction. The mid-1990s thus witnessed the city transfer criminal booking procedures onto the street through digital networks. This phenomenon was made possible by wirelessly connected databases that allowed patrol units to register quality-of-life offenders almost anywhere in the city. For instance, the Transit Bureau introduced a Mobile Arrest Processing Center—the "bust bus"—a van outfitted with computers, cellular phones, and fax machines to file paperwork and execute search warrants.[22] The mobile center was meant to slash the amount of time required to process people apprehended for low-level citations during subway sweeps from twenty-four hours to a matter of hours. It was also supposed to reduce the amount of time that low-level violators spent in custody and eliminated the need to transport subjects to district commands for background and warrant checks.

Just as with the NCIC, the increased dispersion of users in the NYPD's database network mandated increasingly centralized controls. As the century closed, the city also began to centralize its IT research and development. Until then, city agencies had incorporated technology at their own discretion, leading to inefficient data-sharing practices. These factors left the city's bureaucracies far behind the private sector in terms of technical cohesion and thus advancement. In 1998, the Giuliani administration (1994–2001) issued Executive Order 43, which established the Technology Steering Committee and Office of Technology in the Department of Information Technology and Telecommunications. The committee was tasked with optimizing communications between government agencies. In the area of criminal justice, these initiatives led the city to find that the more interlinked its databases were, the more effective it was in identifying, monitoring, and capturing targeted persons. The Department of Information Technology and Telecommunications thus played a part in the rise in initiatives to use database networks to register and track graffiti artists, gun violence, narcotics offenders, peddlers, juvenile offenders, and sex workers. For instance, in 1995, the Criminal Justice Coordinator, Department of Juvenile Justice, and Law Department assembled a joint juvenile justice database, the Comprehensive Justice Information System. The Gambling Control Commission teamed with the Trade Waste Commission to assemble a database for organized crime. As the century turned, the Human Resources Administration's welfare-to-work programs for drug use offenders began using the web to facilitate information exchanges with substance abuse treatment centers.

Integrating the vast ecology of administrative databases remained a chief concern under Michael Bloomberg's administration (2002–2013), which, in 2002, appointed the first deputy commissioner of the Office of Information Technology (OIT) (now the Information Technology Bureau). As a former chief information officer from the IT sector, the OIT deputy commissioner's first major project involved the wholesale upgrade of NYPD databases and communication systems. The OIT constructed a versatile suite of analysis and investigative support applications made up of the Crime Data Warehouse, the Enterprise Case Management System, a license plate database, and the Real-Time Crime Center (see chapter 5).[23] It also established an online database that stores all data related to arrests, complaints, and summonses.

The steady proliferation of the city's database network extended to the parole/probation apparatus. The Systems Department of the Criminal Justice Agency (CJA) was a central agency in this regard, as it was made up of programmers tasked with maintaining an automated database to manage data on all arrests, court appearances, and case dispositions in the city. The Systems Department was also summoned to manage the CJA's local area network of personal computers and its wide area network of borough offices. Furthermore, the department managed the CJA's Ethernet, fiber-optic cabling, firewalls, and servers. By 2003, the CJA unveiled its own database, which contained information on almost every adult arrested and issued a summons in New York City.[24] It automatically aggregated data from the Department of Corrections, NYPD, and Office of Court Administration, in addition to community-based, criminal history, and demographic information collected by CJA researchers during prearraignment processing.

New York City officials' newfound ability to instantaneously collect, calculate, and circulate enormous data quantities through networks has quietly modified the patrol function. In fact, the database network allows the carceral state to displace many of its administrative functions into urban space through police patrols. Within an instant, patrol officers

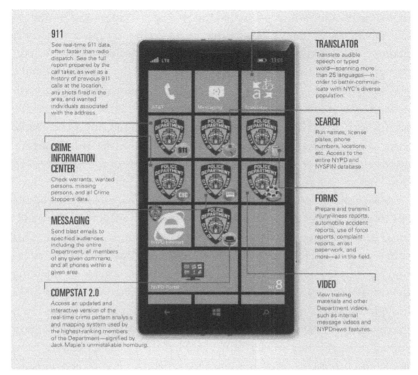

911
See real-time 911 data,
often faster than radio
dispatch. See the full
report prepared by the
call taker, as well as a
history of previous 911
calls at the location,
any shots fired in the
area, and wanted
individuals associated
with the address.

TRANSLATOR
Translate audible
speech or typed
word—spanning more
than 25 languages—in
order to better commun-
icate with NYC's diverse
population.

CRIME
INFORMATION
CENTER
Check warrants, wanted
persons, missing
persons, and all Crime
Stoppers data.

SEARCH
Run names, license
plates, phone
numbers, locations,
etc. Access to the
entire NYPD and
NYSPIN database.

MESSAGING
Send blast emails to
specified audiences,
including the entire
Department, all members
of any given command,
and all phones within a
given area.

FORMS
Prepare and transmit
injury/illness reports,
automobile accident
reports, use of force
reports, complaint
reports, arrest
paperwork, and
more—all in the field.

COMPSTAT 2.0
Access an updated and
interactive version of the
real-time crime pattern analysis
and mapping system used by
the highest-ranking members
of the Department—signified by
Jack Maple's unmistakable homburg.

VIDEO
View training
materials and other
Department videos,
such as internal
message videos and
NYPDnews features.

FIGURE 17. NYPD patrol mobile application. The NYPD's mobility initiative not only put more information at the fingertips of patrol officers; it also exported criminal processing to the street, as patrol units quietly morphed into a network of weaponized data producers. From *The Five Ts: Taking Effect* (New York: New York Police Department, n.d.).

dispersed throughout the public sphere can access federal databases, license plate reader databases, New York State's Office of Court Administration databases, and state databases. Moreover, the ability to remotely enter information into databases increased the record-keeping tasks of police patrolling, which is increasingly defined by "producing numbers." For instance, in 2014, the Information Technology Bureau equipped thirty-five thousand officers with smartphones and two thousand patrol vehicles with tablets in a $140 million mobility initiative. In the mobility initiative's initial rollout, officers were given Nokia mobile phones. But Microsoft discontinued support for the operating systems used in the models soon after, which prompted the Strategic Technology Division to take advantage of the NYPD's contract with AT&T to replace the Nokia phones with iPhones under the pretext of a hardware upgrade. Wasteful though the ordeal was, city officials confidently told the public that mobile platforms were the "single largest driver of information technology growth in the Department."[25] One goal of the mobility initiative was to provide patrols with access to the NYPD's Crime Information Center and enable them to perform fingerprint scans; check information on Crime Stoppers, missing/wanted persons, and warrants; and translate non-English speech into English (see Figure 17).[26]

The mobility initiative represented how network power allowed the city to relocate offender processing procedures from administrative buildings, jails, precinct station houses, and prisons onto the streets. This shift was evidenced by eruptions of recorded disorderly conduct violations, quality-of-life offenses, and victimless misdemeanors. By enabling the transference of offender processing to the police, wireless networks brought the bureaucratic side of the punitive state into city space. From the time that NYPD patrol units had mobile database terminals until 2003, annual misdemeanor arrests for drugs other than marijuana went from 19,082 to 37,460; arrests for marijuana went from 5,221 to 60,190; person-related charges went from 18,186 to 33,600; and vehicle-related driving violations went from 6,783 to 24,000.[27] In the process, the police built up a massive database of low-level offenders. Moreover, from 2000 to 2010, the city made an average of 136,954 major felony and 68,620 non–seven major felony convictions per year.

The city's capacity to register offenders and violators on such massive scales enabled it to exclude large segments of the population from the formal channels of social reproduction. In New York, felonies can lead to a termination of parental rights; in employment, felonies can restrict one from federal office and employment by the U.S. government; in federal aid, they can restrict one from federal assistance if one was receiving aid during the conviction; in housing, they can lead to evictions; in terms of marriage, life sentences render one ineligible to marry; in public benefits, they can disqualify one from receiving cash assistance, contracts, commercial licenses, grants, loans, and professional licenses funded by the

United States. Some felonies also exclude some subjects from the public sphere: in jury service, they can restrict one from federal grand, state, and petit jury. In short, the punitive state's network is a necropolitical network, as it is designed to maintain barriers between criminalized populations, formal avenues of social reproduction, and political rights.

CRIMINAL JUSTICE DATABASE NETWORKS IN ILLINOIS

In contrast to New York, Chicago's database network was assembled for the most part at the level of the state. Since the Criminal Identification and Investigation Act (1931), the Illinois State Police (ISP) has managed the central repository for all criminal justice data in Illinois. Four decades after the act appeared, the ISP took part in NCIC's Comprehensive Data System program to develop a crime database network that traversed all criminal justice agencies in Illinois. Called the Computerized Criminal History (CCH) system, the ISP's model was originally built for internal purposes. The overarching goal was to establish a repository for corrections personnel, law enforcement, judges, and state attorneys to retrieve criminal records. Attorneys used the database for recommending bail; correctional officers used it for determining security levels; law enforcement used it for investigations; probation officers used it for determining supervision techniques and treatment; and judges used it for pretrial release and sentencing. Civilians were also able to purchase information from the CCH database, including the fingerprints, name, race, sex, and birthdate of convicted persons.

The CCH database was unveiled around the same time as the state's first digitized booking, monitoring, and security database. Both were built in the first instance to help manage Illinois's expanding carceral population. Between 1974 and 1983, the number of imprisoned persons in Illinois doubled, triggering an overcrowding crisis whose effects rippled across state agencies. And as carceral conditions grew more brutalistic, Illinois found itself ranking fourth in jail suicides.[28] Many technocrats in the Illinois Criminal Justice Information Authority (ICJIA) believed that updating and adding several new features to the CCH database would allow for more efficient management of overcrowded facilities. The ICJIA

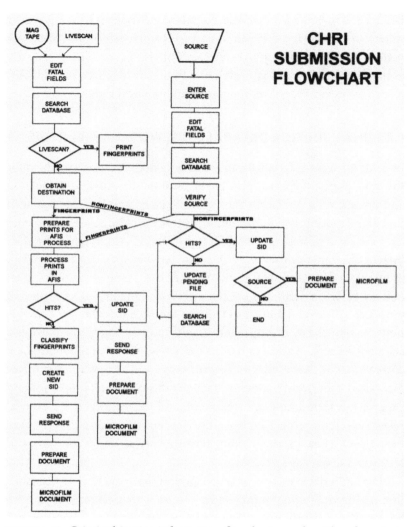

FIGURE 18. Criminal justice information flowchart: an algorithm for criminal justice data flow. The chart considers multiple information sources, as it is predicated on the network function. From Illinois Criminal Justice Information Authority, *An Overview of the Illinois Criminal History Records Information (CHRI) System: Part I of the 1993–94 Criminal History Records Audit* (Chicago: State of Illinois, 1994), 15.

was established in 1983. Its overriding objective was to optimize criminal justice administration through digital technologies. With the carceral crisis rising, the ICJIA embarked on a project to update the state's correctional database systems and eventually linked them across the web. The first step was to clean data throughout criminal justice agencies. Auditors found that CCH records were not up to date, lacked adequate security, and were missing disposition and racial information.[29] But technocrats assured that "technology in [criminal justice] seems to come in waves, and a very big wave is about to break."[30] Interoperable databases were at the head of this latest wave. With database networks, believed technocrats, state authorities would be able to receive all types of information about each individual prisoner, which would allow for more effective cell assignments, disciplinary techniques, medical attention, and more. And so the Criminal History Records Information Act was unanimously approved by the Illinois House in 1983. The act stipulated that all criminal justice agencies would have to submit charges, convictions, dispositions, and fingerprints to the CCH database network in a uniform manner.[31] This, experts held, would aid correctional officials in classifying inmates, judges in categorizing offenders, law enforcement in investigations, probation officers with presentence investigations, and state attorneys in deciding upon charges. Over the course of the decade, all circuit court counties, correctional facilities, sheriffs, state's attorneys, and police departments were eventually made to submit arrest, charge, custodial, disposition, and fingerprint data to the CCH network.

Before CCH was upgraded, human operators arranged this information into different categories—arrests, dispositions, custodial receipts, and status changes—and then sent them to the state's criminal justice database. The information was sent through computer tapes, electronic submission, and paper submission. The database included information on inmate arrivals, appeals, releases, sentence commutations, and deaths, in addition to circuit court and state's attorney depositions. During the early 1980s, police departments throughout the state began adopting network principles of the internet to optimize its data pipelines. Police began linking into the Police Information Management System (PIMS), one of the country's first systems allowing police to share information through a common network. PIMS established a statewide network in which departments exchanged arrest, fingerprint, home address, incident, property, and vehicle information.[32] It also hosted physical descriptions of convicts and suspects. Just one year after launch, the Information Authority turned to supercomputing to accommodate the rapidly increasing number of agencies in the PIMS network. Toward the end of the decade, patrol vehicles were outfitted with mobile data terminals so that officers could enter information directly into databases. One of this system's most innovative features was that it enabled patrol officers to check license plates, which allowed police to check for warrants on motorists. Thus the patrol unit became a mobile node in the punitive state's information network.

This increase in "police productivity" put considerable pressure on courts, resulting in a backlog of caseloads.[33] The Information Authority determined that the rapid growth in the court backlog would triple the average time it took to process criminal cases. To rectify this, the Information Authority developed a case management database network that scheduled, tracked, and kept records of trials, decisions, and sentences.[34] It also retained information on court costs, child support, fines, fees, and victim/witness information. The authority's new database included a jury selection application and an application for public defenders to access files. By 1993, the Information Authority had articulated a vision of "judicial automation," which revolved around linking court databases into the burgeoning network to streamline sentencing procedures.[35] Data centralization posed unique difficulties for the courts at this point in time, as courts are reliant on information from a greater number of sources than corrections and law enforcement. Courts also depend on a greater variety of documents (e.g., decisions, filings, motions, stenographic transcriptions, tickets). The Information Authority thus looked to automated judicial databases in California and proposed a multifunctional, internet-based database for Illinois's court system. Once implemented, the authority claimed, lawyers could use the newfound interoperability to transmit filings in both criminal and civil cases. The public could access the database through public terminals to view and pay traffic violations. The new database was to work in conjunction with the Criminal History

Record Improvement Program, an initiative to set up an internet-based, interstate network of disposition and felon reporting. The goal of the program was to create a statewide criminal justice telecommunications system that would defray line charges accrued from the profusion of information.

The more punitive the city's administration became, the more information its criminal justice system churned out. This was especially evident where indigent populations were criminalized. In 1996, the Department of Housing and Urban Development adopted its "one strike and you're out" rule that banned many people with criminal records from public housing. About twenty-one thousand people reentered Chicago from prison, and half of the individuals in the city's emergency centers had felony convictions.[36] The Information Authority found that felonies reduced callbacks to job applications by 40 percent. The American Bar Association found that 1,449 Illinois statutes constricted felons' rights, entitlements, and opportunities.[37] The subsequent mass production of criminal justice data made data management the largest challenge to the Information Authority.[38] Indeed, between 1984 and 1994, the total number of criminal records increased by 51 percent, which made the state's criminal justice database system the fifth largest in the country.[39] About two decades after launch, the total number of annual arrests entered into the database was 93 percent greater than the number entered in its first year. In its initial phase, about 60 percent of records in the CCH database came from Cook County, the county in which Chicago is located. By the end of the 1980s, this figure increased to 70 percent.[40]

In mitigating this data eruption, the Illinois Sentencing Policy Advisory Council implemented a cost–benefit model that calculated recidivism probabilities to help determine candidates for early release. Database management systems in prisons were also linked to other databases throughout the state apparatus to speed up prisoner processing. Correctional Institution Management Information System (CIMIS) was one such example.[41] One of the more striking features of CIMIS was its exploitation of the network form. Carceral technocrats declared that linking the database with the Information Authority's wider network would cut the amount of time it took to book inmates in half. Such a network, they declared, would transmit data between correctional facilities and courts, medical institutions, police departments, and public and housing authorities for each inmate. This ability was said to enable administrators to cross-check inmate files with public aid files to determine eligibility for benefits while imprisoned. The database was also equipped with an accounting application to manage all money inmates possessed upon prison entry, the funds they received while incarcerated, and records of commissary transactions. CIMIS was also linked into the state's Automated Fingerprint Identification System (AFIS), which processed between five hundred and six hundred characteristics per second.[42] This was attributed to speeding up inmate processing and reducing fingerprint backlogs by nearly 60 percent.[43] From 1993 to 1999, the number of fingerprints submitted to the database increased by 53 percent.[44] To organize the profusion of biometric data, authorities turned to optical scanners and imaging software that took fingerprints directly from central booking or crime scenes, stored them in computer files, and transmitted them via the internet to CIMIS. It also matched fingerprints with state identification numbers, year of birth, and sex. Furthermore, AFIS afforded access to the Department of State Police's fingerprint database, which stores fingerprint data taken from background checks on applications for certain purchases, licenses, and jobs.

What the Information Authority envisioned was a wirelessly connected punitive apparatus that could move the criminalized subject from point to point without interruption. This goal, untenable as it might be, led the state to take on massive projects to consolidate its criminal justice information via the web. Near the end of the century, the Information Authority teamed with the University of Illinois at Chicago faculty to upgrade criminal justice websites so that users could retrieve statistics from the state's 102 counties. The authority produced and distributed its *Criminal Justice Internet Applications Online Handbook* to ensure that criminal justice websites followed standardized formats. Specifically, the handbook set the standards of CJHTM-L, an online discussion list for criminal justice webmasters; PoliceNet, a free web space for public safety agencies; and Spider Net, a law enforcement webmaster discussion list. The Automated Disposition Reporting Users Group—a committee of staff members from circuit court clerks' offices, the Illinois Courts' Administrative Office, the ISP, and the Secretary of State's Office—also created a standardized data dictionary and electronic transmission format for exchanging information about court activities on the web.

CROWDSOURCING THE PATROL FUNCTION IN CHICAGO

Inasmuch as the internet allows for the "extension of life as is,"[45] it allows for the extension of racialized policing. The internet has been especially effective in dispersing modes of racialized profiling and control through the web and the public sphere. Of course, incident reporting phone lines have long existed and saw considerable expansion in the 1980s. Unlike emergency phone lines, however, the meshing of penal management and the web allows the state to mobilize large segments of the public sphere in real time.

In 1984, the state of Illinois's Information Authority released its first proposal to make all criminal convict records publicly available. It was called the Criminal History Records Information (CHRI) Act. The proposal revisited many of the debates that surrounded the Freedom of Information Act (1977). Specifically, it explored the prospects of establishing statewide rules concerning public access to information about convictions. The CHRI Act made some of this information publicly available for a fee. Though arrest records that did not result in convictions were sealed by the act, information about people in custody or wanted persons was available for purchase. The final version of the bill was the product of contradictory objectives. For the Information Authority, "what we are debating is whether the government is going to do it . . . or whether private industry is going to do it."[46] For some representatives, the act was intended to establish control over the publicization of criminal justice statistics. For the Department of Law Enforcement, the CHRI Act did not revolve around the question of whether criminal history record information would become public. For law enforcement, the bill was an instrument to provide ways for civilians to offer information through mobile phones. Cellular phones were part of a new community-based strategy, Cellular Watch, organized by the National Crime Prevention

Council and the electronics retailer Radio Shack. Cellular Watch was meant to provide channels for civilians to report crimes and suspicious behaviors. In addition to data entry, Illinois authorities moved to increase the public's ability to retrieve criminal justice information. The Uniform Conviction Information Act (1991) mandated that all conviction information be made publicly available. Employers, landlords, private citizens, and licensing and investigative agencies were the presumed consumers of the information. The act precipitated a wave of public requests for criminal identification information. The same year the act passed, the ISP received 4,140 name requests and 499 fingerprint requests.[47] In the span of just two years, the number of name requests rose by over 120 percent, and fingerprint requests increased by nearly 40 percent. Custodial care facilities, employers, rental agencies, and the U.S. Postal Service were among the most frequent customers.

"Information," the CPD confidently declared a few years after passage of the Uniform Conviction Information Act, "is power. To support our new, decentralized approach to decisionmaking, the Department must establish a new, decentralized approach to data collection and analysis . . . to give officers the information they need, when and where they need it."[48] The CPD unveiled the first publicly accessible police database using Esri in 1995, the Information Collection for Automated Mapping (ICAM). Touted as a user-friendly digital mapping program for patrol officers and the public, it generated maps of CPD data according to beat, district, and sector. City officials held high-profile press conferences in police station houses to showcase police personnel and residents using the interface to plot buildings, churches, bars, liquor stores, pay phones, and schools identified as criminogenic by the machine. Much like CompStat, ICAM was presented to the public as a resource to cultivate networks of community patrols. It was developed alongside the Community Alternative Policing Strategy initiative, which designated civilians as a "new weapon in the fight against crime" and encouraged them to use ICAM to help police identify targets for patrol forces (see Figure 19).[49] Thus, while ICAM was originally restricted to computer terminals in precinct stationhouses, it was extended to public kiosks and the web in 1996. ICAM was in many ways the technical expression of the city's drive to revitalize and extend

FIGURE 19. Fusion warfare training data. Fusion was viewed as a way not only of bolstering surveillance but also of coordinating action between branches of the armed forces. Whether for the Air Force or urban police, the core functions of these datacenters are target identification and suppression. From "Persistent Engagement: Maj. Gen. Skinner Leads Cyberwarriors of 24th Air Force," *Airman Magazine*, December 3, 2018, https://airman.dodlive.mil/2018/12/03/persistent -engagement/. Photograph by Jesse A. Hyatt for the U.S. Navy.

community policing earlier in the decade. For authorities in the 1990s, the success of community-based policing hinged on the efficient storage, retrieval, and utilization of publicly assessable information systems. Turning the public into an information source was also viewed as a means of diversifying department datasets and mobilizing local knowledge.

Despite ICAM's arrival, the CPD remained far behind the curve in terms of capitalizing on the organizational opportunities afforded by internet technology. One such opportunity pertains to networking—the ability to continuously integrate additional nodes into the system. This inclusionist ideal of the internet, in which information flows freely, has a storied history that begins in earnest with the bulletin board system (BBS) movements in the late 1970s. These movements established the basic principles for social media networks, namely, the dream of a space where unfettered communication reigns. The radical implications of the

BBS movement wouldn't truly hit the CPD for three and a half decades. In 2005, the CPD and Local Initiatives Support Corporation undertook a ten-year program to create an online module for CLEAR.[50] The program marked the first time a municipal police project was funded by the MacArthur Foundation. It was modeled after a statewide project a year prior to build an interdepartmental database network accessible to police throughout the state. Dubbed I-CLEAR, the network was the product of the combined labors of the CPD, ISP, and federal government. In Chicago, the CPD's Information Services Division, consultants from Oracle Corporation, and faculty from the University of Illinois's Department of Criminal Justice took lessons from I-CLEAR to design a similar network on the urban scale. City officials maintained that in making CLEAR publicly accessible, the new system, named CLEARpath, would breathe new life into community-based policing.

Initiatives to crowdsource CPD surveillance began to coalesce on the national scale during the time of CLEARpath's arrival. In 2006, the governor of Texas awarded the Texas Border Sheriffs' Coalition funds to build what turned out to be a network of military-grade surveillance cameras erected along the Rio Grande Valley section of the southern border. The network, which streamed video footage to the web in real time, was built by a tech firm that specializes in virtual community watch services. Users from around the planet are able to register as "virtual Texas deputies" and monitor the border, write reports, and send alerts to Border Patrol with the click of a button. This web-based surveillance apparatus, which introduced its own topology of administrative power, reached Chicago when CLEARpath was released five years later. Anyone with an internet connection could register to access CLEARpath, which enabled users to chart twenty-five blue-collar crimes and three white-collar crimes (forgery, fraud, embezzlement). It also came with tabs for mapping city services, gun offenders, narcotics activity, sex offenders, sex workers, troubled buildings, and civilian anticrime groups. It sent crime alerts, reports on gangs, and terrorist threat levels to its users. Registering for CLEARpath also gained users access to regular crime reports through emails, landlines, and text messages. It conveyed information on beat meetings, police districts, and police-sponsored events and allowed civilians to interact with the superintendent. CLEARpath also came equipped with a Crime Stoppers module that contained a gallery of wanted persons. Each photograph was formatted to be easily downloaded and converted into posters. Business, civilians, and community organizations can subscribe to receive posters of wanted persons. Crime Stoppers was linked to a phone line through which anonymous tippers could offer information to police for cash rewards. Another aspect of CLEARpath centered on giving the public opportunities to assist police in open cases. The public could assist police using CLEARpath through its anonymous Online Crime Reporting module. The module enabled the public to offer information on graffiti, harassment, lost property, property damage, simple assault, theft, and trespassing. Moreover, CLEARpath had a module for organizing, informing, and registering neighborhood watch groups to augment the surveillance of illicit markets.

The CPD's networking capacity was given a veritable boost in 2014 by the Department of Homeland Security Office for Interoperability and Compatibility. The office coordinated efforts by the CPD, the Office of Emergency Management and Communications, and Purdue University's Visual Analytics Center in a citywide program called Chicago Long-Term Evolution. Part of the program was dedicated to ensuring that the city could receive video data from the Nationwide Public Safety Broadband Network (NPSBN). Plans for NPSBN had been incubating since the onset of the War on Terror but gained considerable momentum through the Middle Class Tax Relief and Job Creation Act (2012). The act ultimately provided funding for FirstNet, a First Responder Network Authority housed in the Department of Commerce, which forged a public–private partnership with AT&T, General Dynamics, Inmarsat Government, Motorola Solutions, and Sapient Consulting to build and manage a $40 billion wireless broadband network.

From the perspective of the police apparatus, wireless networks were seen as a means of *human dronification*, the transformation of civic subjects into a flexible configuration of sentinels. The extension of police surveillance through wireless networks echoes Foucault's analysis of the police surveillance's tendency toward generalization, as the police apparatus had to be given the instrument of "permanent, exhaustive, omnipresent surveillance" and fueled by "unceasing observation . . . accumulated in a series of report and registers."[51] However, it is important to stress the fact that police surveillance and its network of human drones are tools of social management designed explicitly for minorities who are cast to the margins of the civic sphere.

SEEING LIKE A POLICE STATE

The democratization of police data allows for the democratization of racialized policing. While New York City trailed Chicago in exploring the full potential of making police datasets available on the internet, it quickly realized what could be gained. Much like the community policing ideology that helped bring ICAM into existence in Chicago, the NYPD's online crime mapping application, CompStat 2.0, was touted by officials as an instrument of community-based policing. In point of fact, the NYPD's move to create an online portal to its incident report system was catalyzed by mounting antagonisms between the police and black and latinx communities. The relations grew especially explosive following the 2014 murder of Eric Garner, an unarmed man killed for selling cigarettes without tax stamps. Mayor Bill de Blasio (2014–) presented the act of putting the department's incident information online as an olive branch of sorts. The mayor insisted that the online database would improve governmental transparency. Unveiled on CompStat's twenty-first birthday, version 2.0 gave the public access to unprecedented amounts of information from NYPD databases. It came equipped with a data visualization engine that enabled users to make charts, graphs, and maps of reported incidents by date and time of day. Whereas the first installment of CompStat geocoded crime events at the scale of the precinct, version 2.0 geocoded them at the scale of the street address.

One of CompStat 2.0's less apparent functions was creating a virtual community to extend the NYPD's environmental awareness. In some ways, forging community groups to augment NYPD surveillance was nothing new. Since the early 1940s, the NYPD has organized precinct community councils (originally called precinct coordinating councils) to give civilians opportunities to express local concerns and provide police with local insights. But with CompStat 2.0, the NYPD took the concept of councils to cyberspace. Like precinct community counsel meetings, CompStat 2.0 provided the public with opportunities to transmit information to police. And like these councils, CompStat 2.0 was designed to perform a community-building function. But whereas precinct community councils forged local networks, CompStat 2.0 forged citywide networks. In fact, CompStat 2.0 was viewed more than seventy-five thousand times in its opening week.[52] It was regarded by the city as a smashing success. Online magazines lauded the application that "looks a little like Yelp, but for grand larceny" and provides a "weirdly fun way of poking around the city."[53] CompStat 2.0 was effectively created to fuse police subjectivity with public subjectivity. Its ultimate product would be a digitized intersubjectivity[54] that monitored, interpreted, articulated, and even experienced urban space from the tactical viewpoint of police. CompStat 2.0 was like a virtual reality headset that enabled the public to see like a police state.

This process, where administrative power wields wireless networks to reinforce its exclusionary practices, was captured in an episode of the anthology film series Black Mirror titled *Men against Fire*. The episode centers on a military organization in Denmark tasked with liquidating a group of untouchables. The organization gives each soldier a neural implant called MASS, which enables the former to control the latter's sensory inputs and situational awareness. The implant enhanced soldier conditioning, communication, firearm accuracy, and intelligence by augmenting their cognition with ballistics data, drone feeds, suspect profiles, simulated memories, and three-dimensional maps. But its most important attribute was that it suppressed empathy by blocking each soldier's ability to properly hear, see, or smell the untouchable population. In the end, we learn the true identities of the untouchables: they are people identified to be at higher risks of cancer, criminal tendencies, low intelligence quotient scores, multiple sclerosis, muscular dystrophy, sexual deviances, and Sjogren–Larsson syndrome. MASS implants did not only help soldiers identify these untouchables but also inflict violence upon them with good conscience. Similar to *Men against Fire*, then, CompStat 2.0 involves racialized administrative power operating under a pretext of public safety. CompStat 2.0

digitally represents the most heavily stigmatized populations of New York City as objects of differential supervision and punishment. CompStat 2.0 reflects how the state attempts to administer what American studies theorist Chandan Reddy terms subjectivity practices.[55] These practices, which have been intensified following the explosive social contradictions of the late 1960s, are characterized by increased efforts on behalf of the state to mobilize racially heterogeneous populations to defray costs of the racialized violence required of capital accumulation. With CompStat 2.0, minorities from the most heavily marginalized communities are enjoined to aid the police apparatus in crime-reduction initiatives. In the end, the CompStat 2.0 website is a technology developed with latent ambitions to convert the diverse public into a homogenous appendage of the NYPD. Practically speaking, it was designed to cultivate virtual communities of additional eyes and ears for the police.

The democratization of criminal justice data went hand in hand with the antidemocratic essence of mass criminalization. The spread of the data across the web brought penal populism into the internet age. In 2013, the city launched its Data Analytics Recidivism Tool (DART), the first web-based application to track and analyze the seventy-five thousand individuals rearrested each year. The first of its kind in the country, DART compiles data on rearrests for criminal, felony, and violent offenses. It stores the age, arraignment recommendations, borough, charges, desk appearance tickets, dispositions, gender, open cases, prior convictions, and sentences of these recidivists. DART was launched under the pretenses of data democratization and governmental transparency and was said to empower civic groups, journalists, and researchers. Perhaps the most perverse permutation of NYPD networking was initiated by the police union, the Sergeant's Benevolent Association.[56] Two years after DART was launched, the union's president issued an antihomeless open letter to the public in reaction to gains made by police reform activists and the City Council. The letter called the reform demands following Eric Garner's murder the work of "inept and spineless public officials" engaged in self-interest, self-promotion, and self-aggrandizement. The letter implored New Yorkers to photograph homeless people, panhandlers, and quality-of-life offenders and email the photographs to the union, which it posted on a Flickr account. The vitriolic focus on homeless people reflected the extent to which the police had morphed into an apparatus whose prime objective was to manage the collateral damage of urban restructuring. So entrenched in this hateful enterprise was the union that it sought to mobilize the public to spread the stigma of poverty via the web.

WEAVING THE PENAL WEB

In Neal Stephenson's novel *Diamond Age*, the primary technology of urban security consisted of airborne pods the size of ping-pong balls that floated throughout the city.[57] The pods were programmed to "hang in space in a hexagonal grid pattern, about ten centimeters apart near the ground . . . and spaced wider as they got higher. . . . When the wind gusted, the pods swung into it like weather vanes, a grid deformed for a bit as the pods were shoved around; but all of them eventually worked their way back into place, swimming upstream like minnows, propelling the air turbines."[58] One of the core functions of the pod grid was to maintain territorial order. They were deployed to establish borders and monitor the sights and sounds on the street. Individuals could walk through the floating grid simply by pushing some pods out of the way—that is, "*unless* Royal Authority had told the pods to electrocute you or blast you." This established a mobile meshwork of surveillance and capture, which maintained sociospatial divisions within and around the city.

The faintly visible yet profound extension of penal web technology is making Stephenson's description appear more realistic. While today's mobile smart devices allow the penal state to mobilize ordinary civilians as its eyes and ears, future web technologies such as intelligent agents, the Internet of Things (IoT), and semantic tagging establish conditions for something different. In 2014, the National Institute of Justice and RAND Corporation convened an expert panel to explore how new web technologies could be harnessed by the penal state. Part of the panel revolved around brainstorming how Web 2.0 technologies could be used. Whereas Web 1.0 technologies are designed primarily for linking documents over the internet (e.g., hypertextual protocol or TCP/IP), Web 2.0 technologies are designed for social networking and crowdsourcing. Social network analysis is one methodology to grow out of Web 2.0. In criminal justice, this methodology manifested in algorithms sent to probe the web for signs of future criminal activity. More than four hundred law enforcement agencies conduct social media surveillance in some way or another. The NYPD began monitoring the social media activity of hundreds of youths in "proto-gangs," some of whom were as young as ten years of age. A variety of social media intelligence platforms have been developed by technology corporations to find criminogenic signals in online activity. The corporations are numerous: for instance, Dataminr in New York; Digital Stakeout in Atlanta, Georgia; Media Sonar Technologies in Ontario; Snaptrends in Austin, Texas; or TransVoyant in Alexandria, Virginia. Geofeedia, a firm whose social media surveillance software was partially funded by the Central Intelligence Agency, mines geolocation data, images, and screen names from Periscope, YouTube, Twitter, and other common social media apps. In Baltimore, demonstrators protesting police officers Caesar R. Goodson, Garrett E. Miller, Edward M. Nero, William G. Porter, and Lieutenant Brian W. Rice's merciless killing of Freddie Gray were identified through social media surveillance through search terms including basic Arabic words, #BlackLivesMatter, #MuslimLivesMatter, and "protest."

The apparatchiks of the American penal state have also shown interest in consolidating criminal justice information through cloud computing. "If the commercial model holds true in the law enforcement world," Integrated Justice Information Systems Institute researchers concluded in 2012, "then it is reasonable to expect that the largest agencies might be attracted to the construction of their own private cloud."[59] Cloud computing is delivered through various service models characterized by varying levels of user control over applications, operating systems, servers, storage, and systems platforms. The key advantage of these services is that they dramatically lower the cost of data storage and retrieval. As they became more prevalent in the private sector, the Bureau of Justice Assistance stressed that cloud services were becoming necessary due to the rapid growth of criminal justice data generated by networks of audio sensors, body cameras, environmental sensors, and surveillance cameras. The IACP similarly recognized cloud computing as a means to respond to increased demands on storage prompted by the implementation of body cameras and other sensory devices.

Technologists of mass punishment have also promoted cloud computing as a means to manage the strain on data storage. For instance, as the Illinois Department of Corrections found its facilities were overpopulated by nearly fifteen thousand people, it was forced to increase parole programs that took in data from counselors, psychiatrists, medical doctors, and supervisors. The state's chief of information technology policy and planning implored lawmakers to provide data storage upgrades, which arrived in the form of Microsoft Dynamics Customer Relation Management Online cloud service. In 2010, the National Archives and Records Administration mandated that all federal agencies begin to adopt cloud computing services. The National Institute of Standards and Technology established standards and guidelines for the project. Shortly thereafter, the FBI mandated that all cloud technologies sold to U.S. law enforcement agencies comply with CJIS standards. The CJIS Group, which was bought by Curran Companies, was pivotal in facilitating the transition in state agencies and the IT sector. This grand standardization project created new opportunities for IT businesses. Amazon Web Services (AWS) announced its compliance with CJIS standards and nestled its way into this emerging market niche. In fact, the AWS Cloud is now used in a wide spectrum of enforcement services for everything from storing data on citations, incidents, and reports in real time to boost officer productivity, to forensic data for evidence-tracking systems, to "situational awareness video" data from body camera feeds.

Penal experts have scouted Web 3.0 technologies, where data can be searched using natural language. This enables digital devices to "understand" the content of data and information and communicate it to humans in spoken and written language. The NIJ and RAND Corporation has proposed exploiting this technology to automate the surveillance of former offenders' activities and social connections, inmate phone calls, offender locational data, and online money exchanges. Penal bureaucrats have also sought to supplement semantic technologies with Web 4.0 and the IoT, which links erstwhile "dumb" objects into the web so that they can be monitored and manipulated continuously and from afar. IoT also makes objects and surfaces interfaces for web browsers, which renders material environments conduits for information flows. In the criminal justice field, one possible application of IoT technology is wearable biomedical sensors to monitor alcohol and drug use of people under supervision. Another involves virtual police badges with proximity sensors to enhance patrol units' awareness of where other units are located to synchronize their movements. The federal government and technology firms have explored the feasibility of IoT-enabled aerial drones and driverless vehicles to keep watch over roads, public squares, and targeted communities; facial recognition systems capable of searching though all mug shot databases; tools capable of extracting structured data from narrative descriptions in incident reports; and virtual courtroom video teleconferencing kits that could eliminate court visits in some cases.

But what does all this mean for penal governance? What might such potentially radical levels of decentralization mean for the punitive management of criminalized populations? As 2015 rolled around, almost 20 million people had felony records, and up to 100 million people had criminal records of some sort.[60] The American Bar Association's National Inventory of the Collateral Consequences of Conviction lists more than forty-eight thousand administrative penalties, laws, and regulations that constrain the mobility of people with felony records. These records restrain access to housing markets, labor markets, and public welfare agencies. The meshing of the penal state and the web means that these records can be automatically retrieved in any official dealings with private and public institutions that use computers. This state of affairs establishes conditions for a truly millennial mode of punishment, characterized by extreme shaming, ostracism, and embarrassment, which are all backed by the administrative state's apparatuses of violence. Perhaps more frighteningly, the penal state's embrace of the network form through the web gives rise to new vectors of penal populism. Networks are decentralized, relatively centerless. They flourish by devolving and/or subtracting power centers and replacing them with provisional command posts. They cannot be identified with reference to any single point.[61] Insofar as we can identify a "system" to emerge from network logics, it is a *swarm system,* consisting of local actors communicating in global networks. During ordinary times, each node's capacity to contribute to networks lies dormant. But it can be instantly activated by another node in close proximity or a command post from afar. The rise of punitive web technology maintains the situation in which the negatively racialized poor can remain in cities, but they must remain apart from their centers of conspicuous consumption, labor markets, leisure, residences, and wealth. The web-based networks of punishment ensnare criminalized subjects in something like a low-intensity form of Agamben's state of exception, where violence and legal authority meet and mesh to strip away the subject's civic persona. Indeed, digitized penal stigma facilitates differential access to capital, labor markets, and physical liberty on the part of criminalized populations. However, what today's networks of racial punishment demonstrate is that this state is anything but exceptional.

5

HOW TO PROGRAM
A CARCERAL CITY

The state's management of racial categories is analogous to the management of highways or ports or telecommunication: racist ideological
and material practices are infrastructure that needs to be updated,
upgraded, and modernized periodically.

    —RUTH WILSON GILMORE and CRAIG GILMORE, *Restating*
    the Obvious

"The most effective technology," observes urban theorist Nigel Thrift, "is
what becomes adopted as infrastructure."[1] Writer Tsutomu Nihei takes
this assertion to the extreme in a manga where urban governance is fully
automated, performed by a computer program designed to optimize the
city's core functions. The program ultimately decided that in maximiz-
ing the use of city resources, it was best to remove humans from the
equation. It achieved this through massive machines that were originally
designed to manage infrastructure. The machines were reprogrammed
to banish humans from the urban core, which they achieved by digging
an artificial canyon, forcing people into the canyon, and then encasing
them with an impenetrable dome called the megastructure. The human
underground was also patrolled by drones that could instantly materialize
almost anywhere through futuristic three-dimensional printers located
across the territory.

    The criminal justice system's burgeoning network of smart machines
makes Nihei's vision appear less and less fictional. The past decade and
a half has watched a mounting assortment of smart cameras, monitors,

and sensors make their way into urban infrastructure. What is more, many cities have taken to building digital infrastructures exclusively for criminalized populations. These systems operate according to what geographers Clyde Woods and Katherine McKittrick call plantation logics, as their objective is "physically fencing [places] off, and condemning their sociospatial difference."[2] Contrary to Nihei's account, the spread of the carceral state's digital architecture is not the result of unchecked automation. One of the first major waves of smart infrastructure was prompted by national security initiatives at the beginning of the War on Terror. At this point, the Department of Homeland Security (DHS) worked with the private sector to fortify areas of high economic importance. But eventually, urban police departments became vectors of smart securitization, which resulted in ensembles of smart machines slowly materializing in areas of low economic importance for very distinct purposes.

The idea that digital computers could manage urban processes traces back to the 1960s. During the decade, companies like Control Corporation, General Electric, North Electric Company, and Westinghouse began to build minicomputer-based systems that could autonomously and remotely regulate energy grids. It was these industrial powerhouses that planted seeds for the notion that city infrastructure could be administered by dead labor. The idea that these machines could administer poor minorities was conjured by the informational powerhouses that rose toward the end of the century. It is worth noting that this idea formed during a time when public infrastructure development, ownership, and operation in cities had become driven heavily by the private sector.[3] The carceral state's infrastructure was not immune to this, as it became increasingly common for prison construction to be financed through lease revenue bonds and exchange-traded funds bundled into larger public projects.[4] By the time cities began exploring ways to modernize public safety infrastructures, IT companies had also become formidable actors in the infrastructure sector. The firms stridently introduced their own vision of urban society anchored in the Internet of Things (IoT), or networks of smart machines that autonomously communicate and interact with each other. Giants like the International Data Corporation, IBM, Motorola Solutions, and Siemens began to work diligently to transfer as many public services and facilities as possible into their ecosystems of smart machines.[5] In doing so, they offered a utopian vision to public officials of cities where economic transactions, energy provision, street lights, subway systems, traffic lights, and, eventually, criminal justice would be managed by machines talking to one another behind the scenes.[6]

On one hand, smart urbanization has established previously undreamed of amenities for privileged "users" of urban space. Machines communicating across airports, public transportation systems, and mobile transportation platforms make travel between global cities increasingly frictionless for professional elites. Telematics systems connect businesses, consumers, and city officials into a global network of ceaseless interaction and exchange. But on the other hand, at the same time, smart infrastructures engender new forms of exclusion and enclosure. Cities have erected special architectures of surveillance around public housing, public schools, and street intersections. Small tech companies like MorphoTrak and Nomad Global Communications Solutions help police make mobile booking units that allow officers to identify, photograph, and fingerprint suspects while they are still in the street. Criminalized communities are thus finding themselves slowly enveloped by the carceral state's infrastructural landscape.

The ceaseless documentation, analysis, spatiotemporal prediction, online monitoring, and surveillance of criminalized neighborhoods is what one gets when information capital penetrates the criminal justice apparatus. While the industrial capitalists no longer find these areas exploitable, the information capitalists do. For three decades, IT companies have proposed a steady stream of new technologies they claim will make managing high-crime neighborhoods frictionless and efficient. The result has been the slow buildup of smart technology in what are for the most part disinvested communities. From the view of information capitalists, these communities represent a new accumulation frontier. In fact, they have sold so much data processing technology to urban police departments that a new branch of the carceral state has emerged: the real-time crime center. These datacenters are the panoptic towers that preside over an elaborate network of smart surveillance devices. What is more, the datacenters have been indispensable in exporting carceral power to the living spaces of the urban castaways.

THE ORIGINS OF CRIME DATACENTERS

Crime datacenters have their origins in War on Terror securitization. The turn of the twentieth century quickly brought federal, state, and city officials together to look for ways to modernize urban security infrastructure. One of the primary objectives, according to a Congressional Service Report, was to protect nodes of economic activity from terrorist attacks.[7] In achieving this, IT and telecom companies turned to their well-established organizational logic, the network. Internet companies already had a model for developing infrastructure working closely with the government. Major companies received a considerable boost from Vice President Al Gore's High Performance Computing Act (1991). The bill tapped private companies, including Ameritech, Delaware River, Pacific Bell, and Sprint, to bring together erstwhile disconnected internet networks on a national "information superhighway." This was done in part by building facilities called *network access points,* which functioned as relays for the disparate networks. On the urban scale, telecommunication operation facilities, such as 60 Hudson and 32 Avenue of the Americas, routed internet networks from hundreds of carriers.

The War on Terror's surveillance infrastructure was built according to these topological principles. Such infrastructure consisted of sprawling webs of devices that fed into central facilities. In achieving a state-of-the-art national security apparatus, the DHS and companies established network access points called *fusion centers.* The DHS also created the National Fusion Center Association, an eighty-member consortium of datacenters that connected data flows from the Coast Guard, departments of corrections, Customs and Border Protection, DHS, the Drug Enforcement Administration, the Highway Patrol, the National Guard, police departments, and private entities. The anatomy of these datacenters was at once decentralized and centralized. On one hand, they were made up of formerly dispersed networks of audio detection devices, environmental sensors, CCTVs, ground sensors, human patrols, and surveillance drones. On the other hand, the sprawling infrastructures condensed in centralized control rooms garnished with video walls that visualized data flows in maps, live video feeds, and statistical charts, graphs, and tables

FIGURE 20. Mayor Michael Bloomberg and police commissioner Raymond Kelly introduce a real-time crime datacenter in New York City, 2006. The datacenter marks the arrival of a new branch of the carceral state, which allows patrol units to monitor and quickly descend on criminalized individuals, places, and populations. Photograph by Bryan Smith. Courtesy of ZUMA Press Inc./Alamy Stock Photo.

(Figure 20). The ultimate goal was to achieve full-spectrum dominance, or the ability to preempt unauthorized behavior through digital supremacy.[8]

It was not long before public officials and corporations attempted to adopt similar surveillance systems to serve alternative purposes. In 2005, the George W. Bush administration revealed designs for a data fusion center for the Immigration and Naturalization Service's Integrated Surveillance Intelligence System.[9] DHS officials contracted the Boeing Corporation for the project, the Secure Border Initiative.[10] The Bureau of Justice Assistance, Department of Justice, and Office of Justice Programs also began funding cities to establish datacenters for criminal justice. The result was a nationwide proliferation of real-time crime centers,[11] or datacenters that processed data from a wide spectrum of sources, including audio sensors, dispatch systems, environmental sensors, license plate readers, precinct databases, service calls, and surveillance cameras. From an infrastructural standpoint, the goal of crime centers was to centralize the rapidly expanding surveillance infrastructures built during the War on Terror. From the standpoint of social management, crime datacenters were meant to function somewhat like information age equivalents to panopticon towers. But instead of prisons, entire neighborhoods were their analytical space. Motorola Solutions avowed that the analytical power of its real-time technology would make the need to respond to incidents a thing of the past,[12] because, the company asserted matter-of-factly, the technology would prevent crime from happening in the first place. Active Solutions marketed cameras on grounds that they drastically reduced everything from violent crime to littering. RAND Corporation researchers argued that predictive analytics could be harnessed in these datacenters to control "deviant places" as different as U.S.-occupied parts of Iraq and high-crime parts of Minneapolis.[13]

The ability to generate, circulate, and analyze vast aggregates of surveillance data from police departments, private businesses, and transportation authorities owed much to the emergence of long-term evolution (LTE) wireless networks. Pioneered by Nokia Networks, Ericsson, and NTT Docomo, these networks allowed for the unprecedentedly high-speed transfer of large quantities of data. In terms of surveillance infrastructure, one of the key benefits of LTEs was the ability to continuously stream high-resolution audio and video data. The resultant deluge of data created new opportunities for companies like ABM American, CineMassive, and Esri, and other vendors of data visualization tools. In some ways, William Gibson anticipated this meshing of corporate power, virtualization, and surveillance in his Sprawl trilogy. Gibson wove stories of a future in which someone who was linked into cyberspace could program a map to display all data exchanges. He emphasized that these exchanges were particularly intense in cities. As such, cyberspace attracted its share of industrial saboteurs, spies, and thieves, which compelled corporations to upload security programs called Intrusion Countermeasures Electronics (aptly abbreviated as ICE). Crime datacenters similarly create datafied models of urban space. Unlike Gibson's Intrusion Countermeasures Electronics, city administrators and police patrols plugged into digital representations of urban space to probe for unauthorized behaviors in the real world. By abstracting urban terrain into data for the sole purpose of scanning, identifying, and capturing humans, crime datacenters simulate criminalized neighborhoods as if they were objects of continuous carceral management. This intrinsically millennial perspective was made possible by the availability of a widely diverse constellation of digital media. The datacenters structured the data and came to constitute a new node of carceral power.

Police in New York, Chicago, and Baltimore first explored designs for crime datacenters in the mid-aughts. In 2008, the Memphis Police Department introduced a $3.5 million surveillance network. Provided by SkyCop Inc., it was designed to be conspicuous with its "imposing towers, lights and cameras [that] signal police presence in a commanding way." It was selectively deployed in neighborhoods such as Shelby Forest–Frayser (84 percent black), Parkway Village–Oakhaven (76 percent black), and White Haven–Coro Lake (94 percent black).[14] The following year saw the city of Los Angeles launch its Real-Time Analysis and Critical Response (RACR) Division, which synthesized the surveillance operations of the Los Angeles Police Department's Department Operations Center Unit, Department Operations Support Unit, Crime Analysis Section, Detective Support Section, and Incident Command Post Unit. Spectrum Integrated Technology Consulting Group helped design the LAPD's control room, which is covered by video walls that display continuously updating incident maps, live video feeds, news feeds, seismic activity, service calls, and satellite imagery. The RACR provided a technical basis for the Los Angeles Smart Policing Initiative and the city's Strategic Extraction and Restoration program to "extract" chronic offenders in the predominately latinx and black Newton Division, Southeast Division, Southwest Division, and 77th Street Division. As the decade turned, the Boston Police Department introduced a half-million-dollar datacenter that monitors the city's emergency dispatch system, CCTVs, gunshot detective system, and radio communications. Its control room is embedded in the Boston Regional Information Center, which was designed to enhance coordination between federal agencies, police, and the private sector through a "net of surveillance over everyone in the Boston metropolitan region."[15] About 270 miles south of Boston, in Philadelphia, police introduced what eventually became the Delaware Valley Intelligence Center. Its control room accesses more than two thousand surveillance cameras and license plate readers, the majority of which are also used by the transportation authority.[16] Around the same time, the Houston Police Department collaborated with Information Builders, a New York City–based software company, to design a $3 million digital surveillance infrastructure.[17] The goal, according to the police chief, was to establish a "CompStat on steroids" by generating and crunching larger quantities of data than the celebrated NYPD.[18] Similar projects cropped up across cities of variable sizes and regions: the Charlotte–Mecklenburg Police Department (CMPD) boasts 1,000 cameras operated by the area transit system, department of transportation, and police plus 140 license plate readers that perform 1.5 million scans per week; Detroit's crime datacenter, the Public Safety Headquarters, includes a hidden network of cameras designed specifically to monitor homeless people.

By 2015, companies including AT&T, Cisco Systems, General Electric, IBM, Infineon Technologies, Intel Corporation, Verizon Enterprise Solutions, and Symantec AG found themselves in an IoT security industry reportedly worth almost $10 billion.[19] The market overflowed with a diverse range of digital tools and services: Constant Technologies Inc. provides police with audiovisual connectivity and source routing and control; Motorola's Real-Time Crime Solution Starter Kit integrates alarm, computer-aided dispatch, record keeping, sensors, and video systems; SkyCop's Security Enclosure System offers intelligent video systems with analytic video monitoring, environmental monitoring, high compression digital recording, license plate recognition, and thermal image monitoring. The promiscuous entanglement of the IT sector and the security state had grown such that in 2015, the DHS opened its Silicon Valley office to fund market-based projects to securitize smart infrastructures across the country. For the private sector, the office was set up to communicate the needs of homeland security to start-up tech companies, fund research and development, and help firms accelerate the transition of security technologies to the marketplace. Such funding initiatives were enacted through the DHS's Science and Technology Directorate's Silicon Valley Innovation Program, which awarded more than $3 million to small tech companies around the country to build technology for border control, critical infrastructure, and cybersecurity. The same year the DHS opened its Silicon Valley office, police in Fresno, California, introduced a privately funded surveillance infrastructure made up of 140 traffic cameras, 180 police surveillance cameras, 400 officer body cameras, 750 public school cameras, and license plate readers that record 25,000 plates a month.[20] The following year, the CMPD introduced its surveillance infrastructure. A large part of the CMPD's acoustic detection infrastructure was paid for by federal grants originally awarded for the Democratic National Convention four years prior. The department used the surplus funds to upgrade its surveillance infrastructure in low-income areas with high crime indexes. It was yet another instance where the expansive thrust of the IoT security economy infiltrated marginal communities and hinted toward a digitally native mode of carceral management.

THE EMERGENCE OF DOMAIN AWARENESS IN NEW YORK CITY

The potential of carceral power to be projected through digital infrastructure can be gleaned from New York City. From a global standpoint, IoT-based surveillance arrived somewhat belatedly in New York City. In fact, the great surveillance networks in London and Shanghai were objects of envy for New York City officials. The city's lag was partially due to the fact that by the time the NYPD launched its first datacenter, the city was trending toward its lowest rates of serious crime in half a century. As such, data fusion first arrived amid counterterrorist initiatives in the downtown and financial districts.

Shortly after the War on Terror was declared, the NYPD unveiled its Office of Information Technology to upgrade its entire digital infrastructure. Part of the project involved establishing an NYPD-managed datacenter that had access to the city's security systems. Its first order of business was converting NYPD record-keeping functions into database management systems. At the time, the department was using more carbon paper than any other agency in the city.[21] To digitize the datasets scattered across the department's seventy-six precincts, the police hired Dimension Data, a South African–based technology corporation. Together they developed hardware, digital forms and worksheets, and an entirely new and proprietary fiber-optic cable network. This laid the groundwork for a state-of-the-art surveillance infrastructure. About four years after the cabling was completed, the NYPD's Counterterrorism Bureau approached Microsoft to assist the bureau with developing a smart surveillance network in the southern part of Manhattan. This was part of what was called the Lower Manhattan Security Initiative. The initiative gave rise to the Lower Manhattan Security Coordination Center, which oversaw three thousand cameras owned by the city and Wall Street firms.[22] It processed data from more than 1.7 miles of biological, chemical, and nuclear detectors spread out across the southern part of Manhattan. Some of the cameras were capable of autonomous movement recognition; tagging physical objects, such as clothes or bags; and notifying the NYPD, Mass Transit Authority, Port Authority, and private institutions.[23] The Coordination Center brought together a galaxy of data on arrests, crime suspects, ex-convicts, precinct crime rates, reported incidents, and warrants from city, state, and federal databases using IBM's software.[24] It ran pilot tests in the subway on video analytics software designed to identify hair color, facial hair, and skin tone.[25] Five years following the launch of the center, a similar surveillance project commenced in midtown Manhattan. This extension of the city's surveillance infrastructure materialized through a network of five hundred CCTVs in Grand Central Station, Penn Station, and Times Square. It was dubbed the Midtown Manhattan Security Initiative. The mayor explained that this datacenter was designed with intentions of establishing a supervisory infrastructure over "major centers of finance, commerce and government, transportation hubs and iconic landmarks."[26] In this phase of securitization, the city increased its total number of public- and private-sector cameras linked into fusion centers by nearly 160 percent.

While New York City's surveillance complex was originally designed for counterterrorist operations, it was adapted to supervise the city's surplus populations following the recession of 2007–9. The Great Recession and its detonation of impoverishment compelled city officials to securitize public housing complexes. Unemployment in the city increased an astounding 3 percent between 2008 and 2009. The Department of Labor reported that during this period, private-sector employment decreased by more than 2 percent, with great losses in the lower levels of the service industry.[27] It was the steepest decline in employment in history of the city's monthly unemployment data, totaling the highest number of unemployed persons (four hundred thousand) ever recorded. The racial structure of the recession was crystal clear. While unemployment hovered around 10 percent at the city level, it was higher in negatively racialized communities. The Russell Sage Foundation and Stanford Center on Poverty and Equality calculated that black unemployment was nearly twice that of white unemployment in Queens and more than twice that in Brooklyn and Manhattan.[28] In 2010, black unemployment reached 16 percent, Hispanic unemployment about 12 percent, white unemployment nearly 8 percent, and Asian unemployment 7 percent. Whereas the highest-income neighborhoods had an average unemployment rate of 7 percent, the lowest-income neighborhoods averaged more than double that.[29] These figures reached a median of 17 percent in the deteriorating public housing structures in black and latinx East New York, Central Bronx, and South Bronx. These dislocations, along with their attendant social problems, were met by the city in part by extending its digital disciplinary apparatus. If the city was to dedicate substantial revenues to these communities, it would be for disciplinary purposes.

Between 2006 and 2010, the city spent roughly $100 million to expand its fiber-optic network into the New York City Housing Authority (NYCHA).[30] The goal was to bring some eighty-five public housing units into the orbit of the NYPD's surveillance complex. With the cabling in place, the city's technocrats proclaimed, public housing complexes could be placed under permanent supervision. The cables provided the necessary technical conditions for installing automated dispatch systems, criminal identification systems, high-resolution cameras, and shot-detection sensors in targeted sections of the Bronx and Brooklyn.

The Domain Awareness System (DAS) was the name of the datacenter that was made to manage the extensive web of digital surveillance. DAS was rolled out by city officials, IBM, and police personnel under the pretense of replacing the NYPD's declining communications systems. The deputy commissioner of information technology estimated the project would require upward of $350 million. One of the first orders of business was grafting a webwork of cables that connected every NYPD facility underneath the city. Although the department traditionally relied on leasing its network services to telecommunications companies, its new cabling complex, FINEST 2.0, established a networked architecture exclusively for the police apparatus. FINEST 2.0 boasted hundreds of miles of cabling, increased precinct bandwidth by a factor of 100, and constituted a material foundation to expand the number of smart cameras throughout criminalized territories. For instance, in 2012, Domain Awareness added three thousand surveillance cameras.[31] The number tripled within five years. Around this time, NYCHA estimated that the NYPD alone had installed 1,140 automated surveillance cameras in about 220 public housing facilities across the city.[32] The perimeters of these facilities were also fortified by Mobile Utility Surveillance Towers and twenty-five-foot-tall SkyWatch towers. By 2016, NYPD officials had revealed plans to extend its fiber network into every NYCHA development in the city.[33] One of the obstacles in achieving this, however, has been a lack of energy, cooling equipment, and physical space in the department's existing datacenters. To rectify this, the NYPD secured a twenty-year lease on three floors in a skyscraper located at 375 Pearl Street, more commonly known as the Verizon Building.

This tremendous expansion of Domain Awareness in many ways echoes general theories of surveillance society.[34] The system has automated databases as technical centerpieces and consists of a variegated infrastructure that continuously generates, retrieves, stores, analyzes, and transmits information about the public body. It is also by all accounts in a state of continuous diffusion and mutation. But its permeation in no way signals that the city will "effectively dispense with traditional methods like brutal public punishment [and] external controls and constraints."[35] There are, to be sure, at least two parallel surveillances: one that calcifies around centers of political economic power and consumerism, which erodes the civil rights of fully constituted citizens, and one that calcifies around devalued areas to erode the human rights of second-class citizens and noncitizens. Domain Awareness cross-fertilizes the territorial logics of the War on Terror, disciplinary logics of the War on Crime and War on Drugs, and infrastructural logics of IoT into a tactical grid of supervision. The system was in many ways organized to generate what Simone Browne describes as racializing surveillance, as it establishes an antagonistic relation between racial minorities and their surrounding environments.[36] The absurdly large datasets created through Domain Awareness infrastructure also created new opportunities for accumulating information capital. Tech companies eagerly lined up to address the department's new need for data management and storage. The NYPD's assistant commissioner of data analytics, deputy commissioner for information technology, and Strategic Technology Division officers estimated that a combined $600 million worth of funding from the DHS and federal forfeitures went into DAS's information management architecture.[37] This money was funneled into the IT sector through contracts for services for network administration, software and hardware maintenance, systems integration services, and video data wall services.[38] Data processing emerged over the decade as one of the NYPD's most dedicated tasks. The patrol officer does not simply administer sanctions but also plays bookkeeper for population management. By 2017, city officials reported that DAS held information on more than 100 million summonses, 54 million 911 calls, 15 million complaints, 12 million detective reports, 11 million arrests, 2 million warrants, and a month's worth of video footage from nine thousand CCTV cameras.[39] Within five years of operation, DAS was collecting, mining, and disseminating data from more than 5 million New York State criminal records, parole, and probation files; 20 million criminal complaints, emergency calls, and summonses; 31 million national crime records; and 33 billion public records.[40] By 2013, the *New York Times* reported that the NYPD's database housed 16 million data points on license plates.[41] Only a couple years later, the number of data points had increased to 2 billion.[42]

DATA FUSION, DATA EXPLOSION IN CHICAGO

Much like it did for New York City, the DHS catapulted Chicago's crime datacenter and surveillance infrastructure. By the end of the 2000s, the secretary of homeland security had declared that no other U.S. city had a more extensive or integrated network of cameras than Chicago.[43] Fusion centers first arrived in Chicago's host state of Illinois in 2003. It was the same year that the Illinois State Police (ISP) opened its Statewide Terrorism and Intelligence Center in the state's capital of Springfield.[44] The center was linked into databases from the DHS, Federal Bureau of Investigation, Transportation Security Administration, Secret Service, and Treasury Department. It was also linked into the Chicago Police Department's (CPD) Citizen and Law Enforcement Analysis and Reporting database, the Illinois Department of Corrections' Offender Tracking System, and various other administrative databases. To manage the profusion of interdepartmental data flows, the state enrolled private data mining corporations, including Dun and Bradstreet, Experian, LexisNexis, and ISO ClaimSearch. Like DAS, the ISP's intelligence center was characterized by the state using public revenue to pay IT companies to manage their surveillance data. And like DAS, the IT sector was eager to assist. The Black Belt provided the ideal site in which to do so.

Chicago's digital surveillance apparatus expanded substantially as the new millennium moved forward. Midway through 2003, the CPD began to deploy surveillance pods "in areas where they're needed and [that] enable us to increase the number of arrests in those areas."[45] Three years later, the city launched the Deployment Operations Center (DOC) (see chapter 3). The DOC began relatively small, comprising a commander and a dozen analysts who specialized in gangs and narcotics to generate target zones. The DOC also monitored feeds from field microphones, handheld devices, local area networks, patrol cars, and surveillance pod cameras. In 2007, the CPD opened another datacenter in the Crime Prevention Information Center (CPIC), which mined data from databases throughout state agencies, publicly and privately operated cameras, and the city's gunshot detection sensors.[46] The center also accesses some 1,260 cameras in "trouble spots" and 4,500 in public schools.[47] CPIC cost $1 million to build, which was provided through the CPD's operation budget, DHS grants, and seized drug money.

The city's first major program to get a hold on the proliferating surveillance infrastructure was Operation Virtual Shield, which involved collaboration with IBM and its partners Firetide and Genetec.[48] In addition to establishing a central command point over Chicago's surveillance complex, the initiative involved dispersing more surveillance pods throughout the city. The pods were first introduced in the DHS under the pretext of securitizing potential terrorist targets. But another wave of pods occurred in majority black South Side and West Side communities shortly after. The city claimed that each camera in Virtual Shield was equipped with pan-tilt-zoom capability that allowed police to remotely rotate each camera and magnify its images. At five hundred feet, beamed the city and companies, such cameras could capture an object less than one inch thick. Virtual Shield cameras were also claimed to have the ability to act autonomously, courtesy of facial recognition software made by the NEC Corporation.[49] Moreover, the smart cameras could be linked into the city's mugshot database, which stored 4.5 million criminal booking photos. Such a unison of video analytics and interoperable databases gave rise to a radically new condition: machines could now track the movements of former offenders as they maneuvered through public space. Virtual Shield's most cutting-edge component, the chief emergency officer declared, was its network of cameras that could "follow" machine-identified individuals and vehicles from camera to camera as they moved about the city.[50]

Virtual Shield was largely responsible for bringing Chicago's public transportation system into the CPD's digital landscape. With more than $22 million from the DHS grants in hand, the city installed so many surveillance devices throughout the transportation system that it doubled its total number of cameras.[51] In 2011, the city was operating an estimated ten thousand cameras. In a couple of years, the grants saw the appearance of some twenty-two thousand high-definition cameras across Chicago Transit Authority (CTA) buses, trains, and public transit stations. Anywhere from one to ten surveillance cameras were mounted in each of the eighteen hundred buses in the CTA's fleet, some of which could be rotated 360 degrees by remote operators. The CTA also embarked upon a $14 million program to retrofit 850 older-model railcars with high-definition cameras. Many of the CPD's squadron vehicles were also equipped with automated advanced license plate recognition, which matched plates with those stored in city, regional, state-level, and national databases in real time and notified patrol units of vehicles of interest.

Surveillance pods slowly began to saturate City Housing Authority facilities. The most conspicuous of these were attached on posts in public housing and lit up with flashing blue lights. Installing cameras was a typical solution by the city when responding to social problems either engendered or exacerbated by the Great Recession. Between 2008 and

2009, the Department of Labor and Bureau of Labor Statistics calculated that the monthly average unemployment rate for all residents of Chicago's metropolitan region increased from 6 percent to 9 percent. It was nearly 16 percent and 12 percent for black and Hispanic residents, respectively (compared to 3 percent for residents classified as white).[52] From 2007 to 2010, the percentage of people out of work for twenty-seven weeks or more rose from almost 23 percent to nearly 49 percent in Illinois.[53] By 2012, almost a full third of residents classified as black lived below the poverty line, compared to 24 percent of those classified as Hispanic and nearly 15 percent of those classified as white.[54] The same year witnessed a 27 percent decrease in Illinois teen employment, which reached the lowest in the state's recorded history. Approximately 92 percent of males aged sixteen to nineteen categorized as black and 80 percent of those categorized as Hispanic in the city of Chicago were jobless during the year.[55] Illicit markets propagated, and the rate of drug killings increased by 38 percent.

Police violence was the crudest of the city's responses to deteriorating conditions in the Black Belt. A report by the city found that from 2007 to 2015, more than fifteen hundred CPD officers acquired ten or more complaint registers, sixty-five of whom received thirty or more.[56] Approximately 40 percent of the complaints were not investigated by the Bureau of Internal Affairs or the Independent Police Review Authority. The violences inherent in Chicago's approach to handling negatively racialized poverty were punctuated by the video of Officer Jason Van Dyke shooting seventeen-year-old Laquan McDonald sixteen times in 2014 for walking away from him during questioning. This triggered a storm of protest, which achieved its most potent expression the following November, when hundreds of people marched into Chicago's downtown retail district, the Magnificent Mile, at the apex of the shopping season. The spectacle of Chicago's quarantined black and latinx subjects seizing urban centers of conspicuous consumption revealed the city's racially binarized structure. Human antivalue came face-to-face with centers of valorization, the explosive implications of which prompted Mayor Rahm Emanuel to assemble a task force on policing and racism. The task force report concluded that several normalized CPD practices gave "validity to the widely held belief the police have no regard for the sanctity of life when it comes to people of color."[57] The report paid special attention to the fact that about 75 percent of CPD shootings, 72 percent of street stops, and 76 percent of taserings involve black or latinx subjects, though these groups make up 60 percent of the city's population. The same spectacle opened space for the ACLU, Black Lives Matter Chicago, and the NAACP to pressure the city to devise a consent decree. Black Lives Matter also mobilized protests at City Hall in response to plans to open a new $95 million police academy in 2018. The city's agreement to the decree, which established new rules for use of force, hiring and retention, and transparency, was in many ways an armistice meant to defuse demands to defund the CPD and criminally prosecute Mayor Emanuel for concealing police murders.

While organized resistance to police terror was mounting, the city established six Strategic Decision Support Centers, or "hyperlocal intelligence centers," to orchestrate patrol deployments in Englewood and Harrison. Less than a year after launch, the CPD's Bureau of Technical Services announced plans to create an additional four centers at a consumer electronics show in Las Vegas. A year later, the city announced plans to open eleven more centers. The centers were staffed with CPD intelligence officers and University of Chicago Crime Lab analysts. The expansion was to take place alongside the hiring of one thousand additional officers and a tenfold increase in the CPD's automated gunshot detection system that spans 110 square miles.[58]

HYPERCARCERALIZATION

Crime datacenters are powerful tools for invisibilizing and normalizing the methods by which cities administer racial criminalization. It is no coincidence that the influx of formerly incarcerated persons into peripheral urban communities has proceeded alongside the rise of digital architectures of police supervision. At present, there are 5 million formerly convicted people in the United States, 27 percent of whom are unemployed, a figure comparable to the Great Depression.[59] These individuals are structurally locked out of contemporary urban economies, which revolve around consumption, finance, real estate, and technical knowledge production. Such are the conditions in which carceral power merges with smart urbanization.

In some city, someone on probation is wearing a GPS monitor while he walks to an automated kiosk to check in with his probationer officer. In that same city, a child passes through a metal detector to enter a school that was targeted by geographic information software for heightened policing. An employer is running a background check on an ex offender, while a gentrifier scrolls through neighborhood crime rates to decide where to live. A police officer uploads a suspect's fingerprints into a mobile device, while a security camera notifies another officer about a person of interest. The vast nexus of smart machines that branches out from these centers forms the backbone of *hypercarceralization,* a digitally native carceral power that is hyperrealist in its preoccupation with computer simulation; hypertextual with its boundless web of documents; hypermediated with its profusion of audio, graphics, and video; and hyperactive in its inexorable surveillance and assessment. At the core of this monstrosity is the power fantasy of city administrators, corporations, and large parts of the public to establish a human filtration system. While this is only an aspiration, and a latent one at that, it is an aspiration immanent to smart urbanization. In fact, the determination to quarantine criminalized populations from these cities is so intense that it has birthed its own unique carceral apparatus, the crime datacenter—the warden of criminalized communities.

All of this is made possible by the convergence of the carceral state and IoT. The result is an actual material network of cabling, cellular towers, energy sources, sensors, and smart devices. Such an achievement is not being assembled out of concern for the well-being of those who inhabit places overlain by the network. For the IT sector, the mad rush to invest in criminal justice infrastructure is an innovative way of finding value in devalued urban populations and places. For cities, the infrastructure provides a new medium to execute an old form of racial management. Domain Awareness is programmed to look for the same demographic groups and neighborhoods that were besieged by mass incarceration. This is certainly true of the surveillance technology grafted into public housing facilities, which lies like carceral carapaces around the lifeworlds of devalued populations.

CONCLUSION
Viral Abolition

It was stones yesterday; it will be hand grenades tomorrow and whatever else is available the next day.

—MALCOLM X, *The Ballot or the Bullet*

In a stunning passage written in 1971, Huey P. Newton points out the limitations of applying formal logic to social control.[1] In it he invokes the geometric law that the parts of a figure cannot amount to more than its totality. "But a prisoner," reminded Newton, "is not a geometrical figure, and an approach which is successful in mathematics, is wholly unsuccessful when dealing with human beings." According to Newton, the increasing number of dissenting individuals forced into prisons reflected the expansion of abolitionist perspective. Newton's observation resonates in the age of computerized criminalization, which is characterized by individuals whose life chances are warehoused in database management systems.

The struggle against the spread of policing and punishing machines is entangled with the struggle to abolish the prison. Just as the prison abolitionists discovered the historical precedents and diverse institutions that underpinned mass imprisonment, the time has come to unveil the carceral state's sociotechnical basis. The abolitionist view makes the ways in which criminalized subjects and computers interact across community spaces, detention centers, jails, living quarters, prisons, hospitals, and workplaces recognizable as a distinct power apparatus. Abolitionism also makes it clear that this apparatus is a reflection of the wider society.

Indeed, opposition to digitized criminalization requires creating the conditions where more body cameras, more CCTVs, more data storage facilities, more electronic bracelets, more environmental sensors, and more software applications are no longer commonsense solutions to social problems. Opposition also requires decommodifying the criminal justice system's institutional landscape. The state is a mere consumer of these technologies; let us not lose sight of the producers. So long as criminal justice technology is produced for profit, newer technologies are bound to make their way to the market.

The abolition of the digital branch of criminal justice requires political solutions, not technical ones. The pitfalls of technical solutions to criminal justice racism were laid bare in the state's response to the Ferguson uprising. The Obama administration's reaction to Ferguson was a more technophiliac version of Lyndon Johnson's response to the urban uprisings a half century prior. Both technocratic approaches only deepened the administrative state's presence in marginalized black and latinx communities—and both provided economic stimulus to technology corporations. In the case of Ferguson, the president's office responded by authorizing the national Task Force on 21st Century Policing to explore technical solutions to the escalation of revolts against racialized police violence.[2] Its recommendations hit all the familiar points of liberal-technocratic policing discourse. In the end, the Department of Justice and the National Institute of Justice were to develop national standards for police audio, biometric, and visual IT infrastructures and work with local police departments and communities to design and implement them. The task force also emphasized developing body-worn cameras for the dual purposes of police transparency and community surveillance, less-than-lethal technologies such as conductive energy devices, and a closed public safety broadband network. The report served as a foundation for the Police Data Initiative, a national program involving police working in tandem with data scientists, design experts, researchers, and tech corporations.

Alternative approaches to abolishing digitized forms of criminalization have already begun to manifest, and they have been most successful by exploiting the viral form. These confrontations have revolved around invading the criminal justice system's data infrastructure and turning its embarrassment of documents into a liability. Grassroots actors have found success in producing and circulating knowledge, images, and videos through the same media that extend the carceral state. This book would not have been possible without the wealth of resources compiled and distributed by these unsung activists. Both aspects, constant invasion of the administrative state's data infrastructure and new social forms of data production, have prepared grounds for ways of thinking about escaping the long and cold embrace of digitized criminalization. Against this type of political maneuvering, writes Baudrillard, which is "viral in structure—as though every machinery of domination secreted its own counterapparatus, the agent of its own disappearance—against this form of almost automatic reversion of its own power, the system can do nothing."[3]

In the case of New York, the city's police database and surveillance infrastructure emerged as sites of confrontation by civilian libertarians and grassroots organizations. In the early days of NYPD restructuring in the 1990s, a coalition of nearly forty civil liberties and grassroots organizations formed Communities united for Police Reform (CuPR). The group's goals revolved around finding ways to increase media coverage of police brutality; reform the Civilian Complaint Review Board; end the controversial stop, question, and frisk tactic; and establish independent prosecutors for cases related to police misconduct. CuPR's steering committee first came together at a Coalition for Community Safety summit in Puerto Rico in 2008. The summit involved a series of workshops to revitalize police accountability activism in New York City. It was the first time such a diverse set of New York–based police activists had come together since September 11, 2001, which was seized upon by city officials and the police union to stigmatize anyone who criticized racial police violence.

The group formally launched CuPR in autumn 2010. Its legal team focused on bolstering public oversight of the police through, among other things, access to the NYPD's unreleased data. This tactic was inspired by group member Center for Constitutional Right's 1999 landmark class action suit *Daniels, et al. v. the City of New York*, filed after NYPD officers Sean Carroll, Richard Murphy, Edward McMellon, and Kenneth Boss viciously murdered Guinean immigrant Amadou Diallo. One of the settlements required that the NYPD allow audits of stop-and-frisk data. The center followed *Daniels* with a 2003 federal class action suit, *Floyd, et al. v. the City of New York,* which was filed upon finding massive racial disparities in the data. In a twist, the racial patterns in the data worked against the legitimacy of the state. In fact, the governor endorsed a bill that would relieve officers from having to record a race in instances that did not lead to arrests. *Floyd* blocked this and won a provision requiring the NYPD's quarterly dissemination of stop-and-frisk data with racial tabulations. The New York Civil Liberties Union (NYCLU), also a CuPR member, made efforts to make the NYPD's hidden data publicly accessible as well. NYCLU drew on an influential 2006 report by the American Civil Liberties Union on pedestrian and motor stops in southern California. The *Ayres Report,* as it was called, chronicled disproportionate stops and arrests of blacks and latinx persons in Los Angeles. It prompted national discussion about the importance of recording and releasing the racial and ethnic backgrounds of civilians stopped.[4] A year later in New York City, NYCLU sued the NYPD in the New York State Supreme Court to disclose its database with stop-and-frisk statistical data. NYCLU has since released quarterly stop-and-frisk reports and analyses, with breakdowns on stops by precinct, reason for stop, stops resulting in frisks, stops involving use of force, gun recoveries, and innocent stops—all with reference to race, ethnicity, and age. The contradictions between the racial state and the liberal state condensed in these data. It was as if the NYPD's own data turned against it.

In contrast to civil libertarian organizations, CuPR's grassroots contingent saw countersurveillance in the streets as the most important tool for mitigating racialized police harassment. As such, producing and circulating its own data was of primary importance. Its tactics were productive as compared to those of the civil libertarians, as they gave rise to new networks, knowledges, and practices. Multiple grassroots groups collaborated to form a protean network of "copwatches" that deposited footage of police–civilian encounters in a central location. The grassroots copwatches were inspired by the Malcolm X Grassroots Movement (MXG) People's Self-Defense campaign. Organized with the Medgar Evers Center for Law and Social Justice, National Conference of Black Lawyers, the campaign modeled itself after the Black Panther Party for Self-Defense's emphasis on armed patrols. The campaign launched alongside three copwatch countersurveillance teams that monitored NYPD interactions with residents throughout central Brooklyn. MXG regarded copwatches as informal means of identifying and preventing police misconduct while at the same time radicalizing participants. Copwatches continued to grow through the early part of the 2000s, which led MXG to team with the Justice Committee to form the People's Justice Coalition. The coalition trained and organized neighborhood watch teams in a citywide network. It maintained a cache of video equipment and hand-held radios, which it loaned on fixed schedules, and publicized when members got arrested or issued a summons through LISTSERVs. Moreover, it transferred all footage of police transgression online on the network's website, on YouTube, and through blast emails. To join People's Justice, teams needed to agree to guidelines including, among other things, sharing data and footage, making sure to highlight the experiences of trans and immigrant communities in all transmissions, and documenting incidents of police abuse regardless of the victim's social identifiers.

The countersurveillance apparatus continued to spread alongside burgeoning protests against the NYPD's rising use of the stop-and-frisk tactic. The populations who were targeted by the police were made crystal clear in the NYPD's own databases. The data had a magnetic effect across the city's diverse landscape of antiracist, antihomophobic, immigrants rights, and homeless rights activists. Headlines described this:

A diverse group of people came out to the rally including demonstrators from immigrant, Muslim, homeless and LGBT communities. While stop-and-frisk has been labeled a problem affecting Black and Latinos in the city, other groups said they too have been victims of the practice.[5]

Demonstrators mostly adhered to the organizers' call to march in silence, hushing talkers along the route. Members of labor unions and the N.A.A.C.P. appeared to predominate, but there were also student groups, Occupy Wall Street, Common Cause, the Universal Zulu Nation and the Answer Coalition. A group of Quakers carried a banner criticizing the stop-and-frisk practice.... As of Friday, 299 organizations had endorsed the march, including unions, religious groups and Japanese, Chinese, Korean, Arab, and Jewish groups. The turnout reflected the growing alliance between civil rights groups and gay and lesbian activists, who in past years have often kept each other at arm's length.[6]

Gay men of color, along with women and transgender people of color, are among the black and Latina/os disproportionately subjected to more than 685,000 stops and frisks by the NYPD last year.... Along with other members of communities of color, LGBTQ youth of color seek the freedom that has been denied to hundreds of thousands of people of color through around the clock police patrols, police violence, racial, gender, homophobic profiling and stop and frisk.[7]

Whether it's the abusive use of stop-and-frisk, quotas or systemic abuses of power, our city needs the reforms and accountability provided by the Community Safety Act. New Yorkers shouldn't be policed different based on the color of their skin, their sexual orientation or any other characteristics that have nothing to do with criminal behavior. The City Council is moving in the right direction to address these protracted issues and our communities support efforts to improve the NYPD.[8]

This transformation of social difference into social equivalence was placed at the center of the CuPR's flagship legislative proposal, the Community Safety Act. Its first provision mandated that age, sex, gender identity/expression, housing status, immigration status, occupation, and sexual orientation be considered "protected categories" in court. It was deliberately intended to transform public discourse surrounding police discrimination by broadening who is included when talking about victims of police abuse. It was also intended to affect how discrimination is assessed in courts. CuPR emphasized that heightening the visibility and voices of peripheral social groups is their overall strategy for NYPD reform. CuPR organizations published interviews with impacted citizens in forty-one media outlets, including BET.com, Caribbean Life, Chelsea Now, Colorlines, DNAinfo.com, *Ebony* magazine, *Epoch Times,* Foxnews.com, *Gay City News,* Local10.com, the *New York Times, Hudson Valley Press,* the *Huffington Post,* the *Village Voice,* the *Nation, New Amsterdam News,*

Norwood News, Reuters, and *WNYC News Blog.* The act also mandated that criteria for determining police bias be changed from establishing intent to proving differential harm to a particular community. In 2012, the NYPD deactivated its stop, question, and frisk apparatus. After one year of abandoning it as a policy, the NYPD reported that stops decreased by nearly 95 percent. The Community Safety Act was signed into law shortly thereafter. In the end, these strategies, whether litigative or grassroots, revolved around capturing, producing, and circulating information about how the criminal justice system operates. They turned the medium by which mass criminalization is expanding into a site of social struggle.

Information-based struggles against racial criminalization have also crystallized in Chicago. In these cases, the goals of activists included not only capturing, producing, and circulating data relevant to the criminal justice apparatus but also destroying data. In terms of generating data, an independent association of journalists called the Invisible Institute offers an informative case. In 2015, it launched its Citizens Data Project, which publicized a massive database of Chicago Police Department (CPD) disciplinary information. The institute stressed that its origins were rooted in principles of guerilla journalism, most notably the ideal of a horizontally run organization free from corporate capital. One of the institute's more formative cases involved Diane Bond, onetime resident of public housing on South State Street. Bond was repeatedly sexually and verbally abused by the CPD's notorious "Skullcap Crew," an anti-gang tactical unit that was stationed in public housing in the South Side. Members of the crew, including Christ Savickas, Joe Seinitz, Andrew Schoeff, Robert Stegmiller, and Edwin Utreras, received 128 known allegations, 60 citizen-filed complaints, and 20 federal lawsuits in 15 years of operation.[9] In 2007, the institute partnered with civil rights attorneys at the Edwin F. Mandel Legal Aid Clinic at the University of Chicago's Law School. One of the legal team's requests to the court involved lifting protective orders on CPD databases with information on disciplinary histories of officers and "complaint registers" with information on internal investigations of complaints.

While the access to the data was originally overruled in 2009, the opinion left the door open for obtaining the data through the bureaucratic channels established by the Freedom of Information Act. This led to a seven-year campaign by the Invisible Institute, Loevy and Loevy, the People's Law Office, and the Mandel Clinic, which came to a head in the *Kalven v. Chicago* decision in the Illinois Court of Appeals in 2014. The Fraternal Order of Police quickly appealed on the grounds that its contracts stipulated disciplinary information would be destroyed after five years. While waiting on the appellate, the Invisible Institute launched a limited preview of the data on a website titled the Citizens Police Data Project in 2015. This was near the same time that then officer Jason Van Dyke murdered Laquan McDonald, which triggered five months of antiracist struggle on Michigan Avenue and in City Hall, which ultimately established conditions for making the rest of the CPD's disciplinary data public.

The result was the largest public police misconduct database in the country. It gave birth to a universe of data that exposed the racist brutalism endemic to policing in Chicago's Black Belt communities. From 2007 to 2016, only 1.5 percent of excessive force complaints, 75 percent of which were filed by black Chicagoans, were sustained by CPD investigators. The database also revealed that 20 percent of CPD officers employed for at least a year received ten or more complaints between 2000 and 2016. Of about 112,000 complaints filed during this time, only 2 percent were sustained, and 1 percent led to meaningful action on the part of the police. Moreover, the data showed that the 6 percent of officers accused of physical domestic abuse were twice as likely to have received use-of-force complaints. In 2018, this universe expanded with Citizens Police Data Project 2.0. The updated version quadrupled the size of the original databases and included the disciplinary histories of officers going back to the 1960s and information on nearly a quarter million allegations. Citizens Police Data Project 2.0 allows users to rank officers, à la CompStat, according to the number of complaints they have received, among other statistical values.

Political mobilization around administrative data is not only about producing new data but sometimes also about destroying data. Pressures from the Black Youth Project 100 Chicago, Blocks Together, Brighton Park Neighborhood Council, Chicagoans for an End to the Gang Database, Mijente, the Office of Inspector General (OIG), and Organized

Communities against Deportations eventually compelled the CPD to abolish its gang database network. Moreover, the Coalition to Expand Sanctuary formed in opposition to the CPD's gang database network as it was discovered that the U.S. Immigration and Customs Enforcement, U.S. Customs and Border Protection, and U.S. Citizenship and Immigration Services used the database to track, capture, and, in many instances, deport immigrants mostly from Mexico and South America.

A report by the OIG illustrated the arbitrary yet instrumental nature of the database for managing poor black and latinx men and immigrants. For one, it demonstrated the capriciousness endemic to how the CPD identified individual subjects and areas as gang related in its databases. Individuals were classified as gang related according to various, unverifiable criteria. Being arrested in the company of a registered gang member, identifying oneself as a gang member, and having tattoos recognized by gang specialists in the police department were all grounds for being classified as a gang member. Just under 60 percent of people in the network were registered by police for residing in or frequenting a gang's area; affecting their "style of dress, use of hand signs, symbols"; or maintaining an ongoing relationship with a known gang member.[10] Over 11 percent of people registered in the network as gang members were not even associated with a specific gang. What is more, the CPD did not notify individuals that they were registered as gang members and had no process for appealing the gang member designation. For geographic areas, the gang-related classification can be a function of the density of individuals classified as gang related or local graffiti, spatial statistical analysis, or the discretion of elected officials, community members, or gang units. The Inspector General's report calculated that some 95 percent of the 134,242 cataloged throughout the gang database network were categorized as African American, black, or Hispanic.

The data in the CPD's database were astonishingly inaccurate. The OIG found that CPD officers had entered "BLACK," "BUM," "CRIMINAL," "DORK," "LOOSER" [sic], "SCUM BAG," and "TURD" as occupations on gang member profiles. Nevertheless, the consequences of being included in the gang catalog could be severe. Such was the case with Wilmer Catalan-Ramirez, an undocumented immigrant who was falsely identified as a gang member. Catalan-Ramirez was severely injured during an ICE raid and locked in an ICE-approved detention center for a little under a year. He was only released after protracted efforts by Organized Communities against Deportation, the Roderick and Solange MacArthur Justice Center, and the National Immigration Project of the National Lawyers Guild.

In 2018, Chicagoans for an End to the Gang Database filed a class action complaint against the City of Chicago, the police superintendent, and CPD officers. Its core complaints were that the gang databases were arbitrary, discriminatory, over inclusive, and error-ridden. The coalition also argued that individuals categorized as gang members were denied due process protections, and were subjected to harassment, false arrests, and false imprisonment. The coalition calculated that 128,000 people were included in the database, 95 percent of whom were classified as black or Hispanic. Early in 2019, the coalition passed an ordinance prohibiting the Cook County Sheriff's Office from adding new information into the Regional Gang Intelligence Database and from sharing information from the database and outlining steps to destroy it.

The struggle against digitized criminalization points to the need to politicize our understanding of data production. These struggles establish the basis for a truly political digital theory. The many coalitions formed in opposition to this development have shown quite clearly how racial governance has adapted to the era of big data. Their labors also illustrate the need to pursue decarceration and decriminalization through viral tactics, among others. So far, effective resistance has been a matter of turning the digital infrastructure of the racial state against itself, turning its tendency to document everything into a vulnerability, scrutinizing its datasets, producing data on the practices it seeks to hide, destroying the databases that abet its necropolitical functions, circulating abolitionist content with an eye toward intergroup coalition building, and replicating the process ad nauseam.

If opposition to digitized modes of criminalization is to gain momentum, it cannot be only defensive; it must also be abolitionist. This is to say that it must question the very society that incentivizes the production of technologies for racialized social management. It must consider who the beneficiaries are, be they in the government, the university, or the IT sector. This is to say that the conflict must come face-to-face with the wider political economy of criminal justice technoscience that has quietly expanded for half a century. This type of critique, which is the hallmark of critical theory, will be needed to produce alternative ways of addressing the social problems specific to the cities chronicled herein. For we have seen how massive amounts of revenue and collective energies have gone into producing IT to manage everything from drug violence to homelessness, unemployment, and truancy. It is worth asking how we might capture these resources and use them for life-affirming solutions to the problems engendered by our distinct social system. It is also worth asking how the public might seize the means of digital communication and use them toward abolitionist ends.

Such discourse is desperately needed. The infrastructure that supports digitized criminalization has been laid for the most part outside public debate or even awareness. This book is at least three decades late, and there is no doubt that many of the technologies it chronicles have already been replaced by newer ones. Nevertheless, a growing number of people are mobilizing in opposition to the digitization of the War on Crime. It can hide in secrecy no longer. The state officials, technology corporations, and university professors who have helped build this computer-aged edifice are already on the defensive. In 2014, the Oakland Privacy Working Group and other organizations blocked the extension of the Port of Oakland's real-time crime center. The Stop LAPD Spying Coalition successfully pressured the Los Angeles Police Department to abolish its predictive policing program five years later. In spring 2019, San Francisco became the first city to ban facial recognition surveillance technology. And market bubbles haunt the criminal justice technology industry just like any other. These factors serve as a reminder that no matter how daunting it appears, mass criminalization in the digital age is not all-powerful. In fact, the expanding number of challenges to criminal justice technology might be a sign that it has run up against a threshold and will be tolerated no longer. Maybe it will be scaled back to avert deepening the crisis. We will see.

ACKNOWLEDGMENTS

This manuscript began as a two-page chapter and has been cultivated into a book by friends, family, and colleagues over the better part of a decade. First, I am indebted beyond measure to my sister for sparking my interests in histories and theories of science—make it so. Many of the core ideas in this book were developed at the New School for Social Research, where I had the extraordinary fortune to have Nancy Fraser's advisement. I am also thankful for the wealth of challenging and memorable conversations at New School with Melissa Amezcua Yepiz, Nathan J. Angelo, Banu Bargu, Jane Carey, Navid Hassanevedah, Fanon Howell, Andreas Kalyvas, Daniel Kato, Carlos Wolfgang Lozano, Darya Marchenkova, Atlee McFellin, Timothy Pachirat, David Plotke, Hannah Rappleye, Emilio Travieso, and Margarita Velasco. I am also appreciative to the Departments of Political Science and Sociology at Brooklyn College CUNY for their selfless support during my graduate studies. I am especially grateful for Paisley Currah, Zeynep Gülrü Göker, Lynn Horridge, Lawrence Johnson, Namita Manohar, Gregory Smithsimon, Celina Su, and, last but not least, Alex S. Vitale.

I am grateful to many people across the University of Illinois Urbana–Champaign. First and foremost, I thank the Department of Geography and Geographic Information Science for its uncanny support, which was essential in the execution of this book: Tom Basset, Trevor Birkenholtz, Julie Cidell, Matt Cohn, Susan Etter, Ezekiel Kalipeni, Mei-Po Kwan, Sara McLafferty, Yoo Min Park, Bruce Rhoads, Jesse Ribot, Murugesu Sivapalan, Shaowen Wang, and, with a huge thank-you, David Wilson. The book also benefited immeasurably from the friendships and minds of Tariq Omar

Ali, Irvin J. Hunt, Kai James, Ghassan Moussawi, Mauro Nobili, Chelsey Norman, James Pascaleff, and Charles Roseman. I am also grateful for the stimulating discussions across campus with Shay Akil, Asif Ali, Teresa Barnes, Angelica Camacho, M. Alex Evans, Shawn Fields, Kadeem Fuller, Behrooz Ghamari-Tabrizi, Maria Gillombardo, Rebecca Ginsburg, Jessica Greenberg, Andrew Greenlee, Jaime Jones, Maryam Kashani, James Kilgore, Jeffery T. Martin, Faranak Miriftab, Cynthia Oliver, Karen Olowu, A. Naomi Paik, Junaid Rana, Gilberto Rosas, Ken Salo, Carol Spindel, and Angel L. Veles. The book also owes part of its existence to the Unit for Criticism and Interpretative Theory. I am especially thankful for my manuscript workshop at the Unit in spring 2019, where I gained invaluable insights and candor from Lisa Marie Cacho, Jonathan X. Inda, Karrie Karahalios, Susan Koshy, and a visiting Virginia Eubanks.

This book would not have been possible without several sources of support. I thank the Campus Research Board at the University of Illinois Urbana–Champaign for its generous support through the Funding Initiative for Multiracial Democracy; the Unit for Criticism and Interpretative Theory for the Junior Scholar Fellowship; the Relational Poverty Network; the O'Connell Scholarship at the University of Illinois Urbana–Champaign; and the Carceral Studies Workshop with Daniel Gonzalez, Anna Kotova, Ruby Mendenhall, Dominique Moran, and Simon Pemberton (and Daniel, Jonathan, and Naomi) in summer 2018. I am also grateful for the generous feedback of Sarah Elwood, Steve K. Herbert, and Jodi Melamed on different parts of this manuscript. Numerous people across the academic and publishing worlds helped me complete this book in some way, shape, or form: Arvis Averette, Anne Bonds, David Chandler, Charmaine Chua, Deborah Cowen, Kate Driscoll Derickson, Roberta Engleman, Harriet Evans, Walter Jacobs, Peggy James, Pieter Martin, Holly Monteith, Chantal Mouffe, Natalie Oswin, and Rashad Shabbaz. Moreover, this book would not have been possible without the help of several organizations that aided me in research, including the ACLU, the Bronx Defenders, the Center for Constitutional Rights, Communities united for Police Reform, the Malcolm X Grassroots Initiative, Make the Road, the NYCLU, Picture the Homeless, and Streetwise and Safe. The book also benefited greatly from the thought-provoking friendships of Alex Bass,

Ryan F. Bradley, Christos Chatziionnou, Peter de la Cruz, Faye R. Gleisser, Fatima Hassan, Laura Jo Hess, Bryan Huber, Miguel Jiron, Julie Miller, Nana Yaw Osei, Jerome Ruban, Alex Salgado, Andrew Sanni, and Jordan Yearsley. A special thank-you to Daniel and Molly McCormack Moody at UCM. Completing this project would have been unthinkable without Sydney, whom I met one morning in Evanston, Illinois, while working on what eventually became this book. Your ideas, patience, and love resonate in its every sentence. Last, I thank my mother, whose companionship means something that I will not attempt to capture with words.

NOTES

INTRODUCTION

1 Bureau of Justice Statistics, *Survey of State Criminal History Information Systems, 2012* (Washington, D.C.: U.S. Department of Justice, 2014).

2 Michelle Alexander, *The New Jim Crow: Mass Incarceration in the Age of Colorblindness* (New York: New Press, 2012).

3 Theo Douglas, "Chicago Police Cut Crime with Major Upgrades to Analytics and Field Technology," *Government Technology,* January 23, 2018.

4 FBI, "National Crime Information Center," http://www.fbi.gov/services /cjis/ncic.

5 For half a century, law enforcement has been the fastest rising expenditure in most state budgets in the United States, increasing by more than 1,000 percent (compared to nearly 450 percent in state and local spending on education during this period). Amanda Petteruti and Nastassia Walsh, *Moving Target: A Decade of Resistance to the Prison Industrial Complex* (Washington, DC: Justice Policy Institute, 2008).

6 Information capitalists are understood in this book in relation what is commonly called *informational economy*, an economy characterized by agents who depend on the ability to generate, process, and efficiently apply information bits. This definition is taken from Castells. The present book understands information technology companies, telecommunications firms, engineers, programmers, professional researchers, and many others to operate in this fraction's orbit. Manuel Castells, *The Rise of Network Society: The Information Age: Economy, Society, and Culture,* vol. 1 (1996; repr., Malden, Mass.: Blackwell, 2000).

7 I use *digitization* in a general sense to mean the implementation of computer software and hardware into extant social practices, and the practices that arise as a result. This is not meant to suggest that these practices are ever fully automated.

8 Robinson Meyer, "The Big Money in Police Body Cameras," *Atlantic*, April 30, 2015.

9 Alain Touraine, *The Post-industrial Society: Tomorrow's Social History— Classes, Conflicts and Culture in the Programmed Society* (New York: Random House, 1971). Daniel Bell, *The Coming of Post-industrial Society: A Venture in Social Forecasting* (New York: Basic Books, 1973). Castells, *Rise of Network Society*.

10 "Dark Side of the Boom," *Wired*, November 1, 1998; Manuel Castells, *End of Millennium: The Information Age—Economy, Society, and Culture* (Malden, Mass.: Wiley-Blackwell, 2010).

11 See, e.g., Julia Angwin et al., "Machine Bias," *Pro Publica*, May 23, 2016. Cathy O'Neil, *Weapons of Math Destruction: How Big Data Increases Inequality and Threatens Democracy* (New York: Crown, 2016). Andrew Gunthrie Ferguson, *The Rise of Big Data Policing: Surveillance, Race, and the Future of Law Enforcement* (New York: New York University Press, 2017).

12 W. E. B. Du Bois, "Die Negerfrage in Den Vereinigten Staaten," *New Centennial Review* 6, no. 3 (1906); *Black Reconstruction in America: 1860–1880* (1935; repr., New York: Free Press, 1998).

13 Cedric Robinson, *Black Marxism: The Making of the Black Radical Tradition* (Chapel Hill: University of North Carolina Press, 2000). This book also draws on Theodore Allen, *The Invention of the White Race* (London: Verso, 1994); Clyde Woods, *Development Arrested: The Blues and Plantation Power in the Mississippi Delta* (London: Verso, 2000). Stuart Hall, *Representation: Cultural Representations and Signifying Practices* (London: Sage, 1997). Angela Y. Davis, *Women, Race, and Class* (London: Women's Press, 1982). Eric Williams, *Capitalism and Slavery* (1944; repr., Chapel Hill: University of North Carolina Press, 1994).

14 There are too many influential works to enumerate here. Some key texts in conceptualization of this book include Ruth Wilson Gilmore, "Fatal Couplings of Power and Difference: Notes on Racism and Geography," *Professional Geographer* 54, no. 1 (2002): 15–24; Joy James, *Resisting State Violence: Radicalism, Gender, and Race in U.S. Culture* (Minneapolis: University of Minnesota Press, 1996); Jodi Melamed, *Represent and Destroy: Rationalizing Violence in the New Racial Capitalism* (Minneapolis: University of Minnesota Press, 2011); Melamed, "Racial Capitalism," *Journal of the Critical Ethnic Studies Association* 1, no. 1 (2015): 76–85; Alexander G. Weheliye, *Habeas Viscus: Racializing Assemblages, Biopolitics, and Black Feminist Theories of the Human* (Durham, N.C.: Duke University Press, 2014); Lisa Marie Cacho, *Social Death: Racialized Rightlessness and the Criminalization of the Unprotected* (New York: New York University Press, 2012); A. Naomi Paik, *Rightlessness: Testimony and Redress in U.S.*

Prison Camps since World War II (Chapel Hill: University of North Carolina Press, 2016); Nada Elia et al., eds., *Critical Ethnic Studies: A Reader* (Durham, N.C.: Duke University Press, 2016); Achille Mbembe, "Necropolitics," *Public Culture* 15, no. 1 (2003): 11–40; Iyko Day, *Alien Capital: Asian Racialization and the Logic of Settler Colonial Capitalism* (Durham, N.C.: Duke University Press, 2016); Alyosha Goldstein, *Formations of United States Colonialism* (Durham, N.C.: Duke University Press, 2014); and Denise Ferreira da Silva, *Toward a Global Idea of Race* (Minneapolis: University of Minnesota Press, 2007).

15 Alexander Galloway and Eugene Thacker, *The Exploit: A Theory of Networks* (Minneapolis: University of Minnesota Press, 2007). Gilles Deleuze, "Postscript on the Societies of Control," *October* 59 (1992); Jean Baudrillard, *Simulacra and Simulation* (Ann Arbor: University of Michigan Press, 1995); Alexander Galloway, *Protocol: How Control Exists after Decentralization* (Cambridge, Mass.: MIT Press, 2006). McKenzie Wark, *A Hacker Manifesto* (Cambridge, Mass.: Harvard University Press, 2004). Seb Franklin, *Control: Digitality as Cultural Logic* (Cambridge, Mass.: MIT Press, 2015).

16 Department of Justice, *State and Federal Corrections Information Systems: An Inventory of Data Elements and an Assessment of Reporting Capabilities* (Washington, D.C.: U.S. Department of Justice, 1998).

17 The Black Codes were a series of laws passed in former slave states in the U.S. South in the mid-1860s. Typical laws deprived the suffrage of blacks, prohibited them from owning land, and authorized their forced unpaid labor for vagrancy. The book draws from Lawrence Lessig's discussion of code as law. Lessig's study argues that code regulates not only cyberspace but also space, time, and human subjects. See Lessig, *Code: And Other Laws of Cyberspace* (New York: Basic Books, 1999).

18 See David Theo Goldberg, *The Racial State* (Malden, Mass.: Wiley-Blackwell, 2001). Michael Omi and Howard Winant, *Racial Formation in the United States: From the 1960s to the 1990s* (New York: Routledge, 1994).

19 For a comprehensive study of racialized criminalization in the United States, see Coramae Richey Mann, *Unequal Justice: A Question of Color* (Bloomington: Indiana University Press, 1993).

20 The Court of Indian Offenses criminalized indigenous social and medical practices to invalidate native land uses and privatize indigenous lands by force. The country's first drug prohibition law, the Opium Exclusion Act (1909), was devised to manage Chinese immigrants who were perceived as threats to white workforces. Rising levels of white unemployment during the Great Depression sparked the passage of the Marihuana

202 NOTES TO INTRODUCTION

Tax Act (1937) to criminalize Mexican farmworkers and brought new border technologies into existence, such as observation towers, radio transmitters, and radio-equipped gyrocopters.

21 The book's conceptualization of the administrative state is drawn from the strategic relational theory developed by Nicos Poulantzas. Apparatuses of the state, such as the police, educational system, or social welfare agencies, expose the constant conflict between social classes. Poulantzas, *State, Power, Socialism* (London: Verso, 2000). Bob Jessop, *State Power* (Cambridge: Polity Press, 2008).

22 Giorgio Agamben, *What Is an Apparatus?* (Stanford, Calif.: Stanford University Press, 2009), 14.

23 For instance, political scientist Virginia Eubanks has demonstrated how the introduction of data analytics to the welfare apparatus was prompted by reactionaries against the welfare rights movement. Eubanks, *Automating Inequality: How High-Tech Tools Profile, Police, and Punish the Poor* (New York: St. Martin's Press, 2018).

24 This phase of modern policing was also central to the construction of *homo economicus* in continental Europe, as it involved documenting the circulation and consumption of commodities, enumerating populations, measuring their productivity, and rating their quality of life. Mark Neocleous, *The Fabrication of Social Order: A Critical Theory of Police Power* (London: Pluto Press, 2000). Michel Foucault, *Security, Territory, Population: Lectures at the Collège de France 1977–1978* (New York: Picador, 2009).

25 From the seventeenth century onward, statistics have been instrumental in the nation form's social management techniques: *Statistiken* were indispensable to German cameralism, *les statistiques* were a core theme in the rise of Napoleonic France and the moral sciences of André-Michel Guerry and Antoine Destutt de Tracy, *statistica* were crucial to the unification and liberalization of the Italian state, and statistical methods drawn from mercantilist and Malthusian population studies were key in the creation of Britain's Poor Union Board and Board of Trade. See, e.g., R. S. N. Pillai and V. Bagavathi, *Statistics (Theory and Practice)* (New Delhi: S Chand, 2008).

26 Robert Nichols, "The Colonialism of Incarceration," *Radical Philosophy Review* 17, no. 2 (2014): 435–55.

27 The Posse Comitatus Act (1878) was passed to limit the deployment of national military forces in domestic affairs. Many critical criminologists point to the Regan administration's War on Drugs as a watershed moment in the corrosion of the bill.

28 Rashad Shabazz, *Spatializing Blackness: The Architectures of Confinement*

and Black Masculinity in Chicago (Urbana: University of Illinois Press, 2015). Katherine McKittrick, *Demonic Grounds: Black Women and the Cartographies of Struggle* (Minnesota: University of Minnesota Press, 2006). Woods, *Development Arrested.*

29 Francesca Musiani, "La Gouvernance Des Algorithmes," *Internet Policy Review* 2, no. 3 (2013): 1–8.

30 It is worth noting that PredPol is based in a city where blacks are thirteen times more likely to be arrested than whites. P. Jeffrey Brantingham, "The Logic of Data Bias and Its Impact on Place-Based Predictive Policing," *Ohio State Journal of Criminal Law* 15 (2018): 473–86; P. Jeffrey Brantingham, Matthew Valasik, and George Mohler, "Does Predictive Policing Lead to Biased Arrests? Results from a Randomized Controlled Trial," *Statistics and Public Policy* 5, no. 1 (2018): 1–6.

31 No data produced by the police apparatus, not even emergency call or victim data, obviate the policies and practices that presuppose their existence. In fact, the Bureau of Justice Statistics's 1973 introduction of the National Crime Victimization Survey (NCVS) was the result of political efforts to mobilize the public against an unquestionably racialized "public enemy number one." And insofar as the NCVS defined victimization to legitimize Nixon's catastrophic War on Drugs, it also helped reinforce the notion that victimhood is an individual, rather than social, phenomenon. See Brian Jordan Jefferson, "Digitize and Punish: Computerized Crime Mapping and Racialized Carceral Power in Chicago," *Environment and Planning D: Society and Space* 35, no. 5 (2017): 775–96; Jefferson, "Predictable Policing: Predictive Crime Mapping and Geographies of Policing and Race," *Annals of Association of American Geographers* 1, no. 108 (2018): 1–16.

32 Andrew Gunthrie Ferguson, *The Rise of Big Data Policing: Surveillance, Race, and the Future of Law Enforcement* (New York: New York University Press, 2017). Ric Simmons, "Quantifying Criminal Procedure: How to Unlock the Potential of Big Data in Our Criminal Justice System," *Michigan State Review* 2016 (2016): 947.

33 Norbert Weiner defined information as a function of organization, structure, and functionality; Russell Ackoff postulated data as the cell form of information, knowledge, and ultimately wisdom; and Luciano Floridi theorized information as an abstract entity endowed with its own structured data and program logic. Weiner, *Cybernetics; or, Control and Communication in the Animal and the Machine* (New Orleans, La.: Quid Pro, 2015). Ackoff, "From Data to Wisdom," *Journal of Applied Systems Analysis* 16, no. 1 (1989)3–9. Floridi, "What Is the Philosophy of Information?," *Metaphilosophy* 33, no. 1/2 (2002): 123–45.

34 Ian Hacking, "Styles of Scientific Thinking or Reasoning: A New Analytical Tool for Historians and Philosophers of the Sciences," in *Trends
in the Historiography of Science,* ed. Kostas Gavroglu, Y. Christianidis,
and Efthymios Nicolaidis, 31–48 (Boston: Springer, 1994). Rob Kitchin,
*The Data Revolution: Big Data, Open Data, Data Infrastructures and
Their Consequences* (London: Sage, 2014). Lisa Gitelman, *"Raw Data"
Is an Oxymoron* (Cambridge, Mass.: MIT Press, 2013). Andrew Iliadis
and Federica Russo, "Critical Data Studies: An Introduction," *Big Data
and Society* 3, no. 2 (2016): 1–7.

35 Data scientist Doug Laney's definition, often referred to as the three Vs
(volume, velocity, variety) of big data, is the most widespread definition
in data sciences. More recently, a fourth *V,* veracity, has been added to
this increasingly common definition of big data. Of course, the opportunities for misinformation afforded by big data run against this addition.
Recognizing the effect of commodity logics on data production lends
depth to Laney's definition of big data as being churned out in extraordinary volumes, circulated at extraordinary velocities, and produced
with extraordinary variety. In terms of volume, the surplus taken from
the production and sale of hardware and software is inserted into the
next round of production, which results in reproduction on an extended
scale. The more hardware and software that is sold (and used), the more
digital data that will exist. Big data travel with incredible velocity, but
technical explanations only tell part of the story. From the perspective
of companies, the time hardware and software spends circulating from
manufacturer to retailer to consumer is wasteful, as the products yield
no value during these intervals. Companies overcome this by constantly
bombarding us with a variety of products on staggered cycles to decrease
such unproductive intervals. Faster devices are constantly presented as
reasons to discard older, slower ones. Laney's three Vs are thus partially
determined by another *V,* the *valorization* of capital. Laney, "3d Data
Management: Controlling Data Volume, Velocity, and Variety," META
Group, http://blogs.gartner.com/doug-laney/files/2012/01/ad949-3D
-Data-Management-Controlling-Data-Volume-Velocity-and-Variety
.pdf.

36 See Kitchin's discussion of "data ontologies" in *Data Revolution.*

37 Specifically, this book builds on the work of Ida B. Wells, W. E. B. Du Bois,
Stuart Hall et al., Khalil Gibran Muhammad, and Simone Browne's recent
pathbreaking work; all explore relations between the production and
interpretation of racial differentiation. Wells, *Southern Horrors: Lynch
Law in All Its Phases* (Scotts Valley, Calif., 2017); Du Bois, "Race Traits
and Tendencies of the American Negro. By Frederick L. Hoffman, F.S.S.,"

Annals of the American Academy of Political and Social Science 9 (1897). Hall et al., *Policing the Crisis: Mugging, the State, and Law and Order* (London: Palgrave, 1978). Muhammad, *The Condemnation of Blackness: Race, Crime, and the Making of Modern Urban America* (Cambridge, Mass.: Harvard University Press, 2011). Browne, "Digital Epidermalization: Race, Identity and Biometrics," *Critical Sociology* 36, no. 1 (2009): 131–50.

38 Patricia Hill Collins, *Black Feminist Thought: Knowledge, Consciousness, and the Politics of Empowerment* (New York: Routledge, 2000).

39 Lisa Lowe, *The Intimacies of Four Continents* (Durham, N.C.: Duke University Press, 2015).

40 Such databases not only abnormalize nonwhite subjects but also help produce white subjects. For instance, in the United States, historian Mae M. Ngai illustrates how a similar Registry Act in 1929 served as a medium of rendering thousands of illegal Eastern and Southern Europeans full rights-bearing "whites." The act legalized the status of "law-abiding aliens" and allowed them to register as permanent residents for a fee. The Registry Act, Ngai observes, was a technology for differentiating "white" permanent residents from Mexican "illegal aliens." Ngai, *Impossible Subjects: Illegal Aliens and the Making of Modern America* (Princeton, N.J.: Princeton University Press, 2004).

41 Kim TallBear, "Narratives of Race and Indigeneity in the Genographic Project," *Journal of Law, Medicine, and Ethics* 35, no. 3 (2007): 412–24.

42 Karl Marx, *Capital, Volume 2: A Critique of Political Economy* (New York: Penguin, 1993). David Harvey, "Globalization and the 'Spatial Fix,'" *Geographische revue* 3, no. 2 (2001): 22–30.

43 Ruth Wilson Gilmore, *Golden Gulag: Prisons, Surplus, Crisis, and Oppression in Globalizing California* (Berkeley: University of California Press, 2007). Loïc Wacquant, "From Slavery to Mass Incarceration: Rethinking the 'Race Question' in the US," *New Left Review* 13 (2002): 41–60; Bruce Western and Katherine Beckett, "How Unregulated Is the U.S. Labor Market? The Penal System as a Labor Market Institution," *American Journal of Sociology* 104 (1999): 1030–60.

44 Stephen Graham and Simon Marvin, *Splintering Urbanism: Networked Infrastructures, Technological Mobilities and the Urban Condition* (London: Routledge, 2001).

45 The book draws heavily from carceral geographers, including Brett Story, *Prison Land: Mapping Carceral Power across Neoliberal America* (Minneapolis: University of Minnesota Press, 2019); Anne Bonds, "'Profit from Punishment'? The Politics of Prisons, Poverty and Neoliberal Restructuring in the Rural American Northwest," *Antipode* 38, no. 1

(2006): 174–77; Dominique Moran, "Leaving Behind the 'Total Institution'? Teeth, Transcarceral Spaces and (Re)Inscription of the Formerly Incarcerated Body," *Gender, Place, and Culture: A Journal of Feminist Geography* 21, no. 1 (2014): 35–51; Gilmore, *Golden Gulag*; Dominique Moran, Nick Gill, and Deirdre Conlon, eds., *Carceral Spaces: Mobility and Agency in Imprisonment and Migrant Detention* (Farnham, U.K.: Ashgate, 2013); Shabazz, *Spatializing Blackness*; and Jack Norton, "Little Siberia, Star of the North: The Political Economy of Prison Dreams in the Adirondacks," in *Historical Geographies of Prisons: Unlocking the Usable Carceral Past*, ed. Karen Morin and Dominique Moran, 168–84 (New York: Routledge, 2015).

46 Laura Kurgan, Sarah Williams, David Reinfurt, and Eric Cadora, *The Pattern* (New York: Spatial Information Design Lab, 2008).

47 Katherine Beckett and Noami Murakawa, "Mapping the Shadow Carceral State: Toward an Institutionally Capacious Approach to Punishment," *Theoretical Criminology* 16, no. 2 (2012): 221–44.

48 Political economy is used throughout this book to mean the production, distribution, and consumption of the material *and* symbolic means required for social reproduction. These means include basic life necessities, cultural practice, housing, medical access, wages, social status, and an endless list of others. For a review of intersectional analysis, see Patricia Hill Collins, *Black Feminist Thought* (2000; repr., London: Routledge, 2009), and Patricia Hill Collins and Sirma Bilge, *Intersectionality* (Cambridge: Polity Press, 2016).

49 For instance, the subject's experience with discrimination cannot be fully understood only by considering racism. One would have also to consider how national citizenship, gender, and socioeconomic status come into play, among other factors.

50 Joel A. Tarr, Thomas Finholt, and David Goodman, "The City and the Telegraph: Urban Telecommunications in the Pre-telephone Era," *Urban History* 14, no. 1 (1987): 5–18.

51 Bernard Harcourt, *Against Prediction: Profiling, Policing, and Punishing in an Acturial Age* (Chicago: University of Chicago Press, 2007).

1. COMPUTATION AND CRIMINALIZATION

1 Louis S. Robinson, "History of Criminal Statistics (1908–1933)," *Journal of Criminal Law and Criminology* 24, no. 1 (1933): 125–39. Michael D. Maltz, "Crime Statistics: A Historical Perspective " *Crime and Delinquency* 21, no. 3 (1977): 32–40.

2 Robinson, "History of Criminal Statistics."

3 Daniel L. Cork and Janet L. Lauritsen, *Modernizing Crime Statistics:*

Report 1—Defining and Classifying Crime (Washington, D.C.: National Academies Press, 2016).

4 Quotation from Cork and Lauritsen, 13.

5 See, e.g., Jed Handelsman Shugerman, "The Creation of the Department of Justice: Professionalization without Civil Rights of Civil Service," *Stanford Law Review* 66, no. 121 (2014).

6 Herman Hollerith, "An Electrical Tabulating System," *The Quarterly* 10, no. 16 (1889). Hollerith, "The Electrical Tabulating Machine," *Journal of the Royal Statistical Society* (1894): 678–89.

7 Edwin Black, *IBM and the Holocaust: The Strategic Alliance between Nazi Germany and America's Most Powerful Corporation* (New York: Crown, 2001). Eubanks, *Automating Inequality.*

8 Frederick L. Hoffman, *Race Traits and Tendencies of the American Negro* (New York: Macmillan, 1896), 2.

9 Khalil Gibran Muhammad, *The Condemnation of Blackness: Race, Crime, and the Making of Modern Urban America* (Cambridge, Mass.: Harvard University Press, 2011).

10 Muhammad.

11 John Koren, "Criminal Statistics Report of Committee No. 3 of the Institute," *Journal of Criminal Law and Criminology* 5, no. 5 (1915): 653–59. Edwin Sutherland and C. C. Van Vechten Jr., "Reliability of Criminal Statistics," *Journal of Criminal Law and Criminology* 25, no. 2 (1934): 10–20.

12 Maltz, "Crime Statistics."

13 See Craig Uchida, Carol Bridgeforth, and Charles Wellford, *Law Enforcement Statistics: The State of the Art* (College Park, Md.: U.S. Department of Justice, 1984).

14 Samuel Walker, *A Critical History of Police Reform* (Lexington, Mass.: Lexington Books, 1977).

15 International Association of Chiefs of Police (IACP), ed., *Uniform Crime Reporting* (New York: J. J. Little and Ives, 1929).

16 Lawrence Rosen, "The Creation of the Uniform Crime Report: The Role of Social Science," *Social Science History* 19, no. 2 (1995): 215–38.

17 IACP, *Uniform Crime Reporting,* 118.

18 IACP.

19 See Walker, *A Critical History of Police Reform.*

20 Wickersham Commission, *National Commission on Law Observance and Enforcement: Report on the Cost of Crime* (Washington, D.C.: Wickersham Commission, 1931).

21 Quotation from Gerda W. Ray, "From Cossack to Trooper: Manliness, Police Reform, and the State," *Journal of Social History* 28, no. 3 (1995): 570.

22   Charles Jaret, "Troubled by Newcomers: Anti-immigrant Attitudes and Action during Two Eras of Mass Immigration to the United States," *Journal of American Ethnic History* 18, no. 3 (1999): 9–39.

23   Hans Vought, "Division and Reunion: Woodrow Wilson, Immigration, and the Myth of American Unity," *Journal of American Ethnic History* 13, no. 3 (1994): 24–50.

24   Wickersham Commission, *Report on the Cost of Crime.*

25   Kenneth J. Peak and Tamara D. Madensen-Herold, *Introduction to Criminal Justice: Practice and Process* (Thousand Oaks, Calif.: Sage, 2018).

26   William Bopp, *O. W. Wilson and the Search for a Police Profession* (Port Washington, N.Y.: Kennikat Press, 1977).

27   Federal Bureau of Investigation, *Uniform Crime Reporting Statistics: Their Proper Use* (Washington, D.C.: FBI, 2011).

28   Loomis Mayfield, Maureen Hellwig, and Brian Banks, *The Chicago Response to Urban Problems: Building University/Community Collaborations* (Chicago: Great Cities Institute, 1998).

29   Zaragosa Vargas, *Crucible of Struggle: A History of Mexican Americans from the Colonial Period to the Present Era* (Oxford: Oxford University Press, 2010).

30   About 90 percent of Chicagoans in the Black Belt were black in the 1920s and 1930s. St. Clair Drake and Horace R. Cayton, *Black Metropolis: A Study of Negro Life in a Northern City* (New York: Harcourt, 1945). These enclaves exceeded the city's recommended residential capacity by 87,300. Ninety thousand people were living per square mile in the Black Belt, compared to only twenty thousand per square mile in majority white neighborhoods. The mortality rate of the former was twice that of the latter. About 60 percent of the white workforce was employed in skilled sectors, compared to 19 percent of the black male workforce and 9 percent of the black female workforce; 90 percent of black female workers and 73 percent of black male workers were in semi- and low-skilled sectors, compared to 35 percent of white female workers and 34 percent of white male workers. Drake and Cayton.

31   Robert Park, "The Concept of Position in Sociology," *Papers and Proceedings of the American Sociological Society* 20 (1926): 1–14.

32   Michael Friendly and Nicolas de Sainte Agathe, "André-Michel Guerry's Ordonnateur Statistique: The First Statistical Calculator?," *The American Statistician* 66, no. 3 (2012): 195–200. Guerry's cartographical approach reached its apex in 1864 with his wide-spanning study on crime and "moral statistics," which represented data from some 226,000 crime cases in England and France and 85,000 suicide records using 17 statistical maps.

33   Renowned sociologist Robert Sampson identified work by Clifford Shaw and Henry McKay as the "most fundamental sociological approaches

to the study of crime and delinquency." Robert Sampson and W. Byron Groves, "Community Structure and Crime: Testing Social Disorganization Theory," *American Journal of Sociology* 94 (1989): 774–802.

34 Robert Park, "The City: Suggestions for the Investigation of Human Behaviour in an Urban Environment," *American Journal of Sociology* 20 (1915): 577–612.

35 Robert Park, Ernest Burgess, and Roderick McKenzie, *The City* (Chicago: University of Chicago Press, 1925).

36 Ernest Burgess, "The Growth of the City," in Park et al., *The City*, 47–62.

37 Martin Bulmer, "The Early Institutional Establishment of Social Science Research: The Local Community Research Committee at the University of Chicago, 1923–30," *Minerva* 18, no. 1 (1980): 51–110. *Chicago School of Sociology: Institutionalization, Diversity and the Rise of Sociological Research* (Chicago: University of Chicago Press, 1985).

38 Namely Frye v. United States, 293 F. 1013 (D.C. Cir 1923).

39 See John F. Fox Jr., *The Birth of the FBI's Technical Laboratory—1924 to 1935* (Washington, D.C.: FBI, n.d.).

40 Allan Sekula, "The Body and the Archive," *October* 39 (1986): 3–64.

41 "Washington Develops a World Clearing House for Identifying Criminals by Fingerprints," *New York Times*, August 10, 1932. Ralph Ioimo, *Introduction to Criminal Justice Information Systems* (Boca Raton, Fla.: CRC Press, 2016).

42 U.S. Commission on Civil Rights, *The Economic Progress of Black Men in America* (Washington, D.C.: CCR, 1986).

43 Daniel Patrick Moynihan, *The Negro Family: The Case for National Action* (Washington, D.C.: U.S. Department of Labor, 1965).

44 In fact, in 1950, none of the major cities in the United States were classified as majority black. By 1990, fourteen cities fit this profile, and another ten were on the cusp. In terms of smaller cities, two were classified as majority black in 1950, compared to forty in 1990. See David Wilson, *Inventing Black-on-Black Violence: Discourse, Space, and Representation* (New York: Syracuse University Press, 2005).

45 Elizabeth Hinton, *From the War on Poverty to the War on Crime: The Making of Mass Incarceration in America* (Cambridge, Mass.: Harvard University Press, 2017).

46 Jerome H. Skolnick, *The Politics of Protest: A Report Submitted by Jerome H. Skolnick, Director Task Force on Violent Aspects of Protest and Confrontation of the National Commission on the Causes and Prevention of Violence* (New York: Ballantine Books, 1969).

47 Richard Nixon, "What Has Happened to America?," *Reader's Digest*, October 1967.

48 Melvin Conway, *Datamation* 14, no. 2831 (1968).

49 Alexander Joseph, "A Progress Report: A Study of Needs and the Development of Curricula in the Field of Forensic Science," in *Law Enforcement Science and Technology*, ed. S. A. Yefsky, 251–56 (London: Academic Press, 1967).

50 O. W. Wilson, *Police Administration* (New York: McGraw-Hill, 1963).

51 *The Challenge of Crime in a Free Society: A Report by the President's Commission on Law Enforcement and Administration of Justice* (Washington, D.C.: U.S. Government Printing Office, 1967).

52 Law Enforcement Assistance Act of 1965, 89th Cong., s. 1792 and s. 1825 (1965).

53 Yefsky, *Law Enforcement Science and Technology*, preface.

54 Don M. Gottfredsen and Kelley B. Ballard Jr., "A National Uniform Parole Reporting System," in Yefsky, *Law Enforcement Science and Technology*, 221–28. E. M. Butler, "The Examination of Paint with the Electron Microbe," in Yefsky, 347–52.

55 Niklas Luhmann's fetishization of "the system" manifested in his notion that social systems were operationally bounded off from their surrounding environments. Luhmann, "The World Society as a Social System," *International Journal of General Systems* 8, no. 3 (1982): 131–38. Eric Paras offers an illuminating account of Foucault's preoccupation with "systematicity," albeit without fully exploring how the rise of systems theory influenced Left Bank intellectuals during the 1960s. Paras, *Foucault 2.0: Beyond Power and Knowledge* (New York: Other Press, 2006).

56 Daniel Glaser, "The Assessment of Correctional Effectiveness," in Yefsky, *Law Enforcement Science and Technology*, 181.

57 Larry P. Polansky, Computer Use in the Court: Planning, Procurement and Implementation Consideration (Washington, D.C.: American University Law Institute, 1978), 112.

58 Paul M. Whisenand, "Automated Police Information Systems: An Argument for Vertical and Horizontal Integration," *Journal of Criminal Law and Criminology* 62, no. 3 (1972): 422–29.

59 Ioimo, *Introduction to Criminal Justice Information Systems*, for instance, traces the rise of communication centers throughout urban police departments to the development of CAD systems.

60 Yefsky, *Law Enforcement Science and Technology*.

61 Edward Comber, "Activation of the California Criminal Justice Information Design Study," in Yefsky, *Law Enforcement Science and Technology*, 555.

62 E. Ray Knickel, "Car Locator Uses and the Patrol Car Emitter-Call Box Sensor Technique," in Yefsky, *Law Enforcement of Science and Technology*, 904.

63 Maureen Brown, "Criminal Justice Discovers Information Technology," in *Criminal Justice 2000*, ed. Winnie Reed and Laura Winterfield, 219–59 (Washington, D.C.: National Institute of Justice, 2000).

64 J. H. Wegstein and J. Rafferty, "Machine Oriented Fingerprint Classification System," in Yefsky, *Law Enforcement Science and Technology*, 459–66.

65 E. F. Codd, "A Relational Model of Data for Large Shared Data Banks," *Communications of the ACM* 13, no. 6 (1970): 377–87.

66 See Ioimo, *Introduction to Criminal Justice Information Systems*.

67 Glaser, "Assessment of Correctional Effectiveness."

68 Marguerite Q. Warren, "The Community Treatment Project: History and Prospects," in Yefsky, *Law Enforcement Science and Technology*, 193.

69 Harland Hill, "Some Proposals for the Development of Information Systems in the Field of Corrections," in Yefsky, *Law Enforcement Science and Technology*.

70 Hill, 211.

71 This gravitation toward the micro scale crystallized in Jane Jacobs, who postulated that increases in urban crime indexes were due to an erosion of "intricate, almost unconscious, network[s] of voluntary controls and standards" on city sidewalks. Jacobs, *The Death and Life of Great American Cities* (New York: Vintage Books, 1961), 32.

72 Specifically, it analyzed assault, auto theft, business burglary, daytime residence burglary, nighttime residence burglary, purse snatching, robbery, and theft from auto. Phillip S. Mitchell, "Optimal Selection of Police Patrol Beats," *Journal of Criminal Law and Criminology* 63, no. 4 (1973): 577–84.

73 Stan Openshaw, *The Modifiable Areal Unit Problem* (Norwich, England: Geo Books, 1983).

74 Lawrence W. Sherman, "Police Crackdowns: Initial and Residual Deterrence," *Crime and Justice* 12 (1990): 1–48. David Weisburd and Lorraine Green Mazerolle, "Measuring Immediate Spatial Displacement: Methodological Issues and Problems," in *Crime and Place: Crime Prevention Studies*, ed. David Weisburd and John Eck, 349–61 (Monsey, N.Y.: Criminal Justice Press, 1995).

75 Ronald V. Clark. "Technology, Criminology and Crime Science," *European Journal on Criminal Policy and Research* 10, no. 1 (2004): 55–63.

76 By the dawn of Nixon's War on Drugs, some sociologists were calculating how magnetic certain microspaces were to potential offenders. For some criminologists, certain nodes and pathways in urban networks were believed to radiate cues that signaled opportune conditions for lawbreakers.

Crime events were understood as surface effects of convergences between potential offenders and microspaces that transmit their vulnerability to criminal invaders. Paul Brantingham and Patricia Brantingham, "The Spatial Patterning of Burglary," *Howard Journal of Penology and Crime Prevention* 14, no. 2 (1975): 11–23. P. Jeffrey Brantingham and Patricia Brantingham, *Environmental Criminology* (Beverly Hills, Calif.: Sage, 1981). Paul Brantingham and Patricia Brantingham, "Mobility, Notoriety, and Crime: A Study of Crime Patterns in Urban Nodal Points," *Journal of Environmental Studies* 11 (1982): 89. Paul Brantingham and Patricia Brantingham, "How Public Transit Feeds Private Crime: Notes on the Vancouver 'Sky Train' Experience," *Security Journal* 2, no. 2 (1991): 91–95.

77 Patricia Brantingham and P. Jeffrey Brantingham, "Criminality of Place: Crime Generators and Crime Attractors," *European Journal on Criminal Policy and Research* 3, no. 3 (1995): 5–26. Lawrence W. Sherman, Patrick R. Gartin, and Michael E. Buerger, "Hot Spots of Predatory Crime: Routine Activities and the Criminology of Place," *Criminology* 27, no. 1 (1989): 27–56.

78 Richard Frank, Vahid Dabbaghian, Andrew Reid, Suraj Singh, Jonathan Cinnamon, and Patricia Brantingham, "Power of Criminal Attractors: Modeling the Pull of Activity Nodes," *Journal of Artificial Societies and Social Simulation* 14, no. 1 (2011): Article 6.

79 Barry Fosberg, "Ripeness and Hot Spots in Time: Possible Futures in Micro Place-Based Policing," *Crime Mapping and Analysis News*, no. 3 (2015). Metaphors of comets (crime patterns that trail across space in a linear manner), pulsars (single areas that oscillate between high and low crime rates), binaries (a pair of locations that alternate between high and low crime indexes in a synchronous fashion), and constellations (wider areas that cycle between crime indexes in a synchronous fashion) were deployed to explain why crime rates are higher in some areas than in others.

80 See Nadine Schuurman, "Formalization Matters: Critical GIS and Ontology Research," *Annals of the Association of American Geographers* 96, no. 4 (2006): 726–39.

81 Max Horkheimer and Theodor W. Adorno, *Dialectic of Enlightenment* (Stanford, Calif.: Stanford University Press, 2002), 4, 12.

82 Herbert Marcuse, *One-Dimensional Man* (1964; repr., Boston: Beacon Press, 1991), 97.

83 Loïc Wacquant, *Prisons of Poverty* (Minneapolis: University of Minnesota Press, 2009).

84 Marc Mauer and Ryan S. King, *A 25-Year Quagmire: The War on Drugs*

and Its Impact on American Society (Washington, D.C.: Sentencing Project, 2007).

85 Noami Murakawa, *The First Civil Right: How Liberals Built Prison America* (New York: Oxford University Press, 2014).

86 Sentencing Project, "Racial Disparities," https://www.sentencingproject .org/issues/racial-disparity/.

87 Muhammad, *Condemnation of Blackness.*

2. DREAMS OF DIGITAL CARCERAL POWER

1 Engineer Gordon E. Moore's law states that the number of components, that is, transistors, in integrated electronics such as microchips would double annually, thereby increasing memory capacity at exponential rates. Electrical engineer Mark Kryder found that the storage capacity on magnetic disks increased at an even faster rate than the integrated electronics discussed by Moore.

2 Manuel Castells, *The Rise of Network Society: The Information Age: Economy, Society, and Culture,* vol. 1 (1996; repr., Malden, Mass.: Blackwell, 2000), 411.

3 William Julius Wilson, *The Truly Disadvantaged: The Inner City, the Underclass, and Public Policy* (Chicago: University of Chicago Press, 1987).

4 Loïc Wacquant, *Urban Outcasts: A Comparative Sociology of Advanced Marginality* (London: Polity, 2008). Wilson, *Truly Disadvantaged.*

5 See Gilmore, *Golden Gulag.* Bruce Western and Katherine Beckett, "How Unregulated Is the U.S. Labor Market? The Penal System as a Labor Market Institution," *American Journal of Sociology* 104 (1999): 1030–60. Noami Murakawa, *The First Civil Right: How Liberals Built Prison America* (New York: Oxford University Press, 2014). Michael Tonry, *Malign Neglect: Race, Crime, and Punishment in America* (Oxford: Oxford University Press, 1996).

6 Malcolm X, *Malcolm X Speaks: Selected Speeches and Statements* (New York: Grove Press, 1994).

7 Malcom X, 66.

8 Federal Bureau of Investigation, *(COINTELPRO) Black Extremist* (Washington, D.C.: U.S. Government Printing Office, 1967).

9 In 1971, Nixon's National Advisory Commission on Criminal Justice Standards and Goals recommended standardized criminal justice information systems to rectify the situation. These databases proceeded to slowly spread through large departments in the mid-1980s before exploding throughout departments in the following decade. NACCJSG,

The Criminal Justice Standards and Goals of the National Advisory Commission Digested from a National Strategy to Reduce Crime (Harrisburg: Pennsylvania Joint Council of the Criminal Justice System, n.d.). Christopher J. Harris, "Police and Soft Technology: How Information Technology Contributes to Police Decision Making," in *From the New Technology of Crime, Law and Social Control,* ed. John Byrne and Donald J. Rebovich, 153–84 (Monsey, N.Y.: Criminal Justice Press/Willow Tree Press, 2007).

10   Mitchell, "Optimal Selection."

11   David Weisburd and J. Thomas McEwen, "Introduction: Crime Mapping and Crime Prevention," in *Crime Mapping and Crime Prevention,* ed. David Weisburd and J. Thomas McEwen, 1–26 (Monsey, N.Y.: Criminal Justice Press, 1998).

12   Wacquant, *Urban Outcasts.*

13   See Darnell F. Hawkins, Samuel Myers, and Randolph Stone, eds., *Crime Control and Social Justice: The Delicate Balance* (Westport, Conn.: Praeger, 2003).

14   Julie Barrows and C. Ronald Huff, "Gangs and Public Policy: Constructing and Deconstructing Gang Databases," *Criminology and Public Policy* 8, no. 4 (2009): 675–703.

15   Claire M. Johnson, Barbara A. Webster, Edward F. Connors, and Diana J. Saenz, "Gang Enforcement Problems and Strategies: National Survey Findings," *Journal of Gang Research* 3, no. 1 (1995): 1–18.

16   Richard V. Ericson and Kevin D. Haggerty, *The New Politics of Surveillance and Visibility* (Toronto: University of Toronto Press, 2006).

17   Peter Kraska, ed., *Militarizing the American Criminal Justice System: The Changing Roles of the Armed Forces and the Police* (Boston: Northeastern University Press, 2001).

18   Thomas J. Cowper and Michael E. Buerger, *Improving Our View of the World: Police and Augmented Reality Technology* (Washington, D.C.: Federal Bureau of Investigation, 2003).

19   Susan C. Hammen (Smith), "IACA Welcomes the New Crime Analysis and Mapping News," *Crime Mapping and Analysis News* 1, no. 15 (2014).

20   Charles Pinderhughes, "Toward a New Theory of Internal Colonialism," *Socialism and Democracy* 25 (2011): 235–56.

21   Sentencing Project, "Racial Disparities."

22   See David Wilson, *Inventing Black-on-Black Violence: Discourse, Space, and Representation* (New York: Syracuse University Press, 2005).

23   Amnesty International, *Not Part of My Sentence: Violations of the Human Rights of Women in Custody* (London: Amnesty International, 1999).

24   Ted S. Storey, "When Intervention Works: Judge Morris E. Lasker and New York City Jails," in *Courts, Corrections, and the Constitution: The*

Impact of Judicial Intervention on Prisons and Jails, ed. John J. Di Iulio, 138–72 (Oxford: Oxford University Press, 1990).

25 Attica ended with state troopers putting nearly three dozen inmates to death. Moreover, the increasingly organized and politicized nature of the prison revolts precipitated a shift from medicalized penal models devised to "correct" prisoners to sociologist Robert Martinson's punitive models devised to break them. This dual movement of penology and politics crystallized in the anti–Black Panther Party (BPP) doctrine of Ronald Reagan during his gubernatorial campaign in California. Reagan mocked the BPP's Ten-Point Platform for being "provoked by a social philosophy that saw man as primarily a creature of his material environment [and] criminals as the unfortunate products of poor socioeconomic conditions or an underprivileged upbringing." Reagan countered structural interpretations of his domestic policy through an explosive cocktail of market fundamentalism mixed with weaponized criminal justice. Angela Y. Davis—herself imprisoned for sixteen months as a result of these charades—described the inherent contradictions in this colonial administrative configuration. One one hand, the War on Crime buried those who challenged state-organized repression in "America's dungeons," but on the other hand, these dungeons were fertile ground for radicalization. See Robert Martinson, "What Works?—Questions and Answers about Prison Reform," *The Public Interest,* Spring 1974. Ronald Reagan, *Public Papers of the Presidents of the United States, Ronald Reagan: Containing the Public Messages, Speeches, and Statements of the President: Book II—July 3 to December 31, 1982* (Washington, D.C.: U.S. Government Printing Office, 1982). Angela Y. Davis, "Political Prisoners, Prisons and Black Liberation," in *If They Come in the Morning . . . : Voices of Resistance* (New York: Verso, 2016).

26 Search Group Inc., *CIMIS National Contact List* (Sacramento, Calif.: National Consortium for Justice Information and Statistics, 1980).

27 Brant Serxner and James R. Coldren Jr., *CIMIS Operations Report: Cook County Department of Corrections* (Chicago: City of Chicago, 1982).

28 Donice Neal, "Technology and the Supermax Prison," in *Supermax Prisons: Beyond the Rock,* ed. Donice Neal, 53–66 (Lanham, Md.: American Correctional Association, 2003).

29 Neal.

30 Brian A. Jackson, Joe Russo, John S. Hollywood, Dulani Woods, Richard Silberglitt, George B. Drake, John S. Shaffer, Mikhail Zaydman, and Brian G. Chow, "Fostering Innovation in Community and Institutional Corrections: Identifying High-Priority Technology and Other Needs for the U.S. Corrections Sector," in *Priority Criminal Justice Needs Initiative* (Santa Monica, Calif.: RAND Corporation, 2015).

31 Allan Turner and Duane Blackburn, "Biometrics: Separating Myth from Reality," *Corrections Today* 64, no. 7 (2002): 110–11.

32 Association of State Correctional Administrators, Corrections Program Office, Bureau of Justice Statistics, National Institute of Justice, *State and Federal Corrections Information Systems: An Inventory of Data Elements and an Assessment of Reporting Capabilities* (Washington, D.C.: U.S. Department of Justice, 1998).

33 Stan Stojkovic, David Kalinich, and John Klofas, *Criminal Justice Organizations: Administration and Management* (Belmont, Calif.: Wadsworth, 2014).

34 Keith Harries, *Mapping Crime: Principle and Practice* (Washington, D.C.: National Institute of Justice, 1999).

35 Sarah V. Hart, "Making Prisons Safer through Technology," *Corrections Today* 65, no. 2 (2003): 26.

36 TechBeat, *CORMAP It* (Washington, D.C.: National Institute of Justice, 2002).

37 Jesse Jannetta, *CompStat for Corrections* (Irvine, Calif.: Center for Evidence-Based Corrections, 2006).

38 Thomas G. Blomberg, Jim Clark, Leslie Hill, Bill Bales, and Karen Mann, *Correctional Operations Trend Analysis System (COTAS): An Independent Validation* (Tallahassee, Fla.: Florida State University College of Criminology and Criminal Justice and Center for Criminology and Public Policy Research, 2011).

39 Harries, *Mapping Crime*. April Pattavina, *Information Technology and the Criminal Justice System* (London: Sage, 2005).

40 Gorge A. Jouganatos and Reginald A. H. Goodfellow, *An Inventory Study of the State of California's Land Holdings* (Sacramento: California State University, 2001).

41 Bernard Harcourt, *Against Prediction: Profiling, Policing, and Punishing in an Actuarial Age* (Chicago: University of Chicago Press, 2006).

42 Susan Turner, James Hess, and Jesse Jannetta, *Development of the California Static Risk Assessment Instrument (CSRA)* (Irvine: University of California, Irvine Center for Evidence-Based Corrections, 2009). Elyse J. Revere and Mari Curbelo, *Alternative-to-Incarceration Information Services End of Year Report: Fiscal Year 2001* (New York: New York City Criminal Justice Agency, 2001).

43 The Youth Level of Service/Case Management Inventory from Multi-Health Systems; the Positive Achievement Change Tool (PACT) from Assessment.com; the Correctional Offender Management Profiling and Alternative Sanctions (COMPAS) from Northpointe Institute of Management; and the Youth Assessment and Screening Instrument from Orbis Partners Inc. are but a few examples.

44 U.S. Bureau of Labor Statistics, *Geographic Profile of Employment and Unemployment, 2009* (Washington, D.C.: U.S. Bureau of Labor Statistics, 2009).

45 Harries, *Mapping Crime*.

46 Erin L. Bauer, Carol A. Hagen, Angela D. Greene, Scott Crosse, Michele A. Harmon, and Ronald E. Claus, *Kiosk Supervision: A Guidebook for Community Corrections Professionals* (Washington, D.C.: U.S. Department of Justice, 2016).

47 Quote from R. K. Schwitzgebel, R. L. Schwitzgebel, W. N. Pahnke, and W. S. Hurd, "A Program of Research in Behavioral Electronics," *Behavioral Science* 9 (1964): 233–38.

48 Chris Mai and Ram Subramanian, *The Price of Prisons: Examining State Spending Trends, 2010–2015* (New York: Vera Institute of Justice, 2017).

49 James Kilgore, Emmett Sanders, and Myaisha Hayes, *No More Shackles: Why We Must End the Use of Electronic Monitors for People on Parole* (Urbana, Ill.: Center for Media Justice, n.d.).

50 James Kilgore, "Repackaging Mass Incarceration: The Rise of Carceral Humanism and Non-alternative Alternatives," *Counterpunch,* June 6, 2014, https://www.counterpunch.org/2014/06/06/repackaging-mass-incarceration/.

51 Ryken Grattet, Joan Petersilia, and Jeffrey Lin, *Parole Violations and Revocations in California* (Irvine: University of California, Davis, 2008).

52 Rachel Porter, Sophia Lee, and Mary Lutz, *Balancing Punishment and Treatment: Alternatives to Incarceration in New York City* (New York: Vera Institute of Justice, 2002).

53 Douglas Young, Rachel Porter, and Gail A. Caputo, *Alternative to Incarceration Programs for Felony Offenders in New York City* (New York: Vera Institute of Justice, 1999).

54 William D. Burrell and Robert S. Gable, "From B. F. Skinner to Spiderman to Martha Stewart: The Past, Present, and Future of Electronic Monitoring of Offenders," *Journal of Offender Rehabilitation* 46, no. 3/4 (2008): 101–18.

55 Pew Research Center, *Use of Electronic Offender-Tracking Devices Expands Sharply* (Washington, D.C.: Pew Research Center, 2016).

56 Mirko Bagaric, Dan Hunter, and Gabrielle Wolf, "Technological Incarceration and the End of the Prison Crisis," *Journal of Criminal Law and Criminology* (forthcoming).

57 ACLU, *War Comes Home: The Excessive Militarization of American Policing* (New York: ACLU, 2014). ACLU, *Alternatives to Immigration Detention: Less Costly and More Humane Than Federal Lock-Up* (Washington, D.C.: ACLU, 2014).

58 Steve Polilli, "The High-Tech Court of the Future," *The Compiler* 13, no. 1 (1993): 12.

59 Polilli.

60 Human Rights Watch, *Decades of Disparity: Drug Arrests and Race in the United States* (New York: Human Rights Watch, 2009).

61 Eric C. Johnson, "Court Automation and Integration: Issues and Technologies," *Technical Bulletin,* no. 2 (1997).

62 Ioimo, *Introduction to Criminal Justice Information Systems.*

63 Colin Reilly and Victor Goldsmith, *Rackets: Case Tracking and Mapping System* (New York: National Institute of Justice, 1999).

64 Robin Davis, Billie Jo Matlevich, Alexandra Barton, Sara Debus-Sherill, and Emily Niedzwiecki, *Research on Videoconferencing at Post-arraignment Release Hearings: Phase I Final Report* (Fairfax, Va.: ICF International, 2015).

65 Elizabeth C. Wiggins, Meghan A. Dunn, and George Cort, *Federal Judicial Center Survey on Courtroom Technology* (Washington, D.C.: Federal Justice Center, 2003).

66 Bureau of Justice Assistance, *Report of the National Task Force on Court Automation and Integration* (Washington, D.C.: Bureau of Justice Assistance, 1999).

67 Laura and John Arnold Foundation, *Public Safety Assessment: Risk Factors and Formula* (Washington, D.C.: Laura and John Arnold Foundation, 2013–16).

68 In many instances, variables such as alienation, anomie, anger, low education, and unemployment are identified as indicators of criminality. See Stojkovic et al., *Criminal Justice Organizations.*

69 Danielle Kehl, Priscilla Guo, and Samuel Kessler, "Algorithms in the Criminal Justice System: Assessing the Use of Risk Assessments in Sentencing," in *Responsive Communities Initiative* (Cambridge, Mass.: Harvard Law School, 2017).

70 Ioimo, *Introduction to Criminal Justice Information Systems.*

71 Julia Angwin, Jeff Larson, Surya Mattu, and Lauren Kirchner, "Machine Bias," *Pro Publica,* May 23, 2016.

72 James Bonta and D. A. Andrews, *The Psychology of Criminal Conduct* (London: Routledge, 2016).

73 Jennifer L. Skeem and Jillian K. Peterson, "Major Risk Factors for Recidivism among Offenders with Mental Illness," unpublished report, Council of State Governments Report, St. Paul, Minn.

3. A FULLY AUTOMATED POLICE APPARATUS

1 Lee Brown, *Blueprint for the Future: Information and Technology for Community Policing into the 21st Century* (New York: NYPD, 1992).

2 See, e.g., Eli B. Silverman, *NYPD Battles Crime: Innovative Strategies in Policing* (Boston: Northeastern University Press, 1999). William Bratton, *The Turnaround: How America's Top Cop Reversed the Crime Epidemic* (New York: Random House, 1998). Jack Maple and Chris Mitchell, *The Crime Fighter: Putting the Bad Guys Out of Business* (New York: Doubleday, 2000).

3 Peter K. Manning, *The Technology of Policing: Crime Mapping, Information Technology, and the Rationality of Crime Control* (New York: NYU Press, 2011).

4 Rashad Shabazz, *Spatializing Blackness: The Architectures of Confinement and Black Masculinity in Chicago* (Urbana: University of Illinois Press, 2015).

5 David Harvey, *The New Imperialism* (Oxford: Oxford University Press, 2005).

6 For instance, in 1980, the municipal bond market was worth about $400 billion; by 2014, it was approximately $3.5 trillion. Mark Davidson and Kevin Ward, "Introduction," in *Cities under Austerity: Restructuring the US Metropolis,* ed. Mark Davidson and Kevin Ward, 1–26 (New York: SUNY Press, 2018).

7 Moshe Adler, "Why Did New York Workers Loose Ground in the 1990s?," *The Regional Labor Review* 5, no. 1 (2002).

8 U.S. Census, *Unemployment Rate, by Race and Hispanic Origin: 1980 to 1998* (Washington, D.C.: U.S. Census Bureau, 1999).

9 This deviated from trends at the national scale, where 71 percent of people living below the poverty line were categorized as white, 17 percent as black, and nearly 12 percent as latinx that same year. Justine Calcagno, *Trends in Poverty Rates among Latinos in New York City and the United States, 1990–2011* (New York: Center for Latin American, Caribbean, and Latino Studies, 2013).

10 Nancy Wackstein, "Memo to Democrats: Housing Won't Solve Homelessness," *New York Times,* July 12, 1992. Dennis Culhane et al., "Public Shelter Admission Rates in Philadelphia and New York City: The Implication of Turnover for Sheltered Population Counts," *Housing Policy Debate* 5, no. 2 (1998): 107–40.

11 Manuel Castells, *The Informational City: Economic Restructuring and Urban Development* (New York: Wiley-Blackwell, 1992).

12 Stephen Graham and Simon Marvin, *Splintering Urbanism: Networked*

Infrastructures, Technological Mobilities, and the Urban Condition (London: Routledge, 2001).

13 Jason Bram, "New York City's Economy before and after September 11," *Current Issues in Economics and Finance* 9, no. 2 (2003).

14 Larry Orr, Judith Feins, Robin Jacob, Erik Beecroft, Lisa Sanbonmatsu, Lawrence F. Katz, Jeffrey B. Liebman, and Jeffrey R. Kling, *Moving to Opportunity Interim Impacts Evaluation* (Washington, D.C.: Office of Policy Development and Research, 2003).

15 U.S. Census, *Unemployment Rate.*

16 Calcagno, *Trends in Poverty Rates.*

17 Bram, "New York City's Economy."

18 Alex Vitale, "Innovation and Institutionalization: Factors in the Development of 'Quality of Life' Policing in New York City," *Policing and Society* 15, no. 2 (2005): 99–124.

19 Saskia Sassen, *The Global City: New York, London, Tokyo* (Princeton, N.J.: Princeton University Press, 2001).

20 Chicago Police Department [CPD], *1994 Annual Report: A Year in Review* (Chicago: CPD, 1995). CPD, *1995 Annual Report: A Year in Review* (Chicago: CPD, 1996). CPD, *2008 Annual Report: A Year in Review* (Chicago: CPD, 2009). CPD, *2009 Annual Report: A Year in Review* (Chicago: CPD, 2010). CPD, *2010 Annual Report: A Year in Review* (Chicago: CPD, 2011).

21 Larry Weintraub, "Daley, Martin Disagree on Suspension of Rights," *Chicago Sun-Times,* July 13, 1991.

22 The technological basis of the much-studied Social Credit System of policing in Chinese cities is mostly of American origin. In fact, the Communist Party refers to its system as a "marketized solution to punishment." See Martin Chorzempa, Paul Triolo, and Samm Sacks, *China's Social Credit System: A Mark of Progress or a Threat to Privacy?* (Washington, D.C.: Peterson Institute for International Economics, 2018).

23 Brown, *Blueprint for the Future.*

24 Brown.

25 Manning Marable, *Beyond Boundaries: The Manning Marable Reader* (London: Routledge, 2011).

26 Lee Brown, *Policing New York City in the 1990s: The Strategy for Community Policing* (New York: NYPD, 1991).

27 Bureau of Justice Assistance, *CompStat: Its Origins, Evolution, and Future in Law Enforcement Agencies* (Washington, D.C.: Police Executive Research Forum, 2013). Vincent Henry, "CompStat Management in the NYPD: Reducing Crime and Improving Quality of Life in New York City," paper presented at the 129th International Senior Seminar Visiting Experts' Papers, Tokyo, 2006.

28 Brown, *Blueprint for the Future*, ix.
29 Brown, vi.
30 Dan Higgins, "Stac Version 4.0 Released," *Compiler* 15, no. 1 (1995/1996). Brown, *Blueprint for the Future*.
31 Michael D. Maltz, Andrew C. Gordon, and Warren Friedman, *Mapping Crime in Its Community Setting: Event Geography Analysis* (New York: Springer, 2000).
32 Maltz et al., xi.
33 Fran Spielman, "Daley Praises School Bust—Detectors Net Tilden Weapons," *Chicago Sun-Times*, March 27, 1991.
34 Matt L. Rodriguez, *Together We Can* (Chicago: City of Chicago, 1993).
35 Sal Perri, "Law Enforcement and the Information Highway," *Compiler* 15, no. 1 (1995/1996).
36 Thomas F. Rich, *The Chicago Police Department's Information Collection for Automated Mapping (ICAM) Program* (Washington, D.C.: National Institute of Justice, 1996).
37 Richard M. Daley and Matt L. Rodriguez, *Fact Sheet: Information Collection for Automated Mapping (ICAM)* (Chicago: City of Chicago, 1995). Richard M. Daley, "Talking Points for Mayor Richard M. Daley: ICAM Demonstration in the 14th District," Chicago, 1995.
38 Richard Pastore, "Chicago Police Department Uses It to Fight Crime, Wins Grand CIO Enterprise Value Award 2004," *CIO*, February 15, 2004.
39 Wesley Skogan, Susan M. Hartnett, Jill DuBois, Jason Bennis, and So Young Kim, *Policing Smarter through It: Learning from Chicago's Citizen and Law Enforcement Analysis and Reporting (CLEAR) System* (Washington, D.C.: U.S. Department of Justice, 2003).
40 Skogan et al.
41 Wesley Skogan, Dennis P. Rosenbaum, Susan M. Hartnett, Jill DuBois, Lisa Graziano, and Cody Stephens, *CLEAR and I-CLEAR: A Status Report on New Information Technology and Its Impact on Management, the Organization and Crime-Fighting Strategies* (Chicago: Chicago Community Policing Evaluation Consortium, 2005).
42 Jonathan Walters, "Clear Connection: A High-Tech Partnership Is Driving Down Crime in Chicago," *Governing*, August 2007. With AIRA, pieces of evidence and personal property taken by police were also queriable. CPD personnel working in evidence, forensics, and recovered property can locate items and trace their movement through chains of custody, while also sending and receiving relevant information about those items to the Illinois State Police Laboratory.
43 Dennis P. Rosenbaum and Cody Stephens, *Reducing Public Violence and Homicide in Chicago: Strategies and Tactics of the Chicago Police*

Department (Chicago: Center for Research in Law and Justice, 2005).

44 Sean D. Hamill, "Residents, Police Band Together in Crime Battle," *Chicago Tribune*, December 23, 2002.

45 Fran Spielman, "Again, Gang Gunfire Is Answered by Silence from City's Political Leaders," *Chicago Sun-Times*, April 29, 2003. "Daley: Cops Will Go Where Crime Is—Indirect Reference to Patrol Issue Pleases Concerned Aldermen," *Chicago Sun-Times*, May 6, 2003.

46 Skogan et al., *CLEAR and I-CLEAR*.

47 Megan A. Alderden, Amy Schuck, Cody Stephens, Timothy A. Lavery, Rachel M. Johnston, and Dennis P. Rosenbaum, *Gang Hot Spots Policing in Chicago: An Evaluation of the Deployment Operations Center Process* (Washington, D.C.: U.S. Department of Justice, 2012).

48 Alderden et al.

49 CPD, *2006 Annual Report: A Year in Review* (Chicago: CPD, 2007).

50 CPD, *2010 Annual Report: A Year in Review.*

51 Alderden et al. 2012.

52 Tom Diaz, *No Boundaries: Transnational Latino Gangs and American Law Enforcement* (Ann Arbor: University of Michigan Press, 2009).

53 CPD, *2006 Annual Report: A Year in Review.*

54 George L. Kelling and W. H. Sousa, *Do Police Matter? An Analysis of the Impact of New York City's Police Reforms* (New York: Manhattan Institute, 2001). Vincent Henry, *The CompStat Paradigm: Management Accountability in Policing, Business and the Public Sector* (Flushing, N.Y.: Looseleaf Law Publications, 2003).

55 Neil Smith, "Giuliani Time: The Revanchist 1990s," *Social Text* 57 (1998): 1–20.

56 Rudolph Giuliani, "The New Mayor; Transcript of Inaugural Speech: Giuliani Urges Change and Unity," *New York Times*, January 3, 1994.

57 Citizen's Crime Commission, *A Report by the Citizens Crime Commission of New York City, Inc.* (New York: CCC, 1990); Vitale, "Innovation and Institutionalization."

58 Rudolph Giuliani and William Bratton, *Police Strategy No. 5: Reclaiming the Public Spaces of New York* (New York, 1994).

59 Here unchecked physical disorders (graffiti, dilapidated buildings) and social disorders (intoxication, rowdiness) were said to be causally related to criminal activity. George L. Kelling and William Bratton, "Declining Crime Rates: Insiders' Views of the New York City Story," *The Journal of Criminal Law and Criminology* 88, no. 4 (1998): 1217–32. Daniel Patrick Moynihan, "Defining Deviancy Down," *The American Scholar* 62, no. 1 (1993).

60 George L. Kelling and James Q. Wilson, "Broken Windows: The Police and Neighborhood Safety," *Atlantic*, March, 29–38.

61 For a comprehensive argument, see Bernard Harcourt, *Illusion of Order: The False Promise of Broken Windows Policing* (Cambridge, Mass.: Harvard University Press, 2005).

62 Brian Jordan Jefferson, "Broken Windows Policing and Constructions of Space and Crime: Flatbush, Brooklyn," *Antipode* 48, no. 5 (2016): 1270–91.

63 Silverman, *NYPD Battles Crime.* Henry, *CompStat Paradigm.* Kathleen Gilsinan and Adam Stepan, *From CompStat to Gov 2.0 Big Data in New York City Management* (New York: Columbia University School of Internation and Public Affairs, 2014). Maple and Mitchell, *Crime Fighter.*

64 Victor Goldsmith, Arthur Langer, and Robert Graff, *Innovative Crime Mapping Techniques and Spatial Analysis* (1997; repr., Washington, D.C.: Research Foundation of the City University of New York, 2004). John Mollenkopf, Victor Goldsmith, Philip McGuire, and Sara McLafferty, *Identification, Development and Implementation of Innovative Crime Mapping Techniques and Spatial Analysis* (Washington, D.C.: National Institute of Justice, 2000).

65 Alex Hirschfield and Kate Bowers, *Mapping and Analysing Crime Data: Lessons from Research and Practice* (London: CRC Press, 2001). Mollenkopf et al., *Identification, Development and Implementation.*

66 Quotation from Thomas J. Lueck, "From Database to Crime Scene: Network Is Potent Police Weapon," *New York Times,* June 7, 2007.

67 See Christian Parenti, *Lockdown America: Police and Prisons in the Age of Crisis* (London: Verso, 2008).

68 See, e.g., the documentary *Crime by the Numbers,* directed by Don Argott.

69 Bratton, *Turnaround.*

70 See, e.g., Edwin E. Ghiselli and Jacob P. Siegel, "Leadership and Managerial Success in Tall and Flat Organization Structures," *Personnel Psychology* 25, no. 4 (1972): 617–24.

71 Henry, *CompStat Paradigm.*

72 James J. Willis, Stephen D. Mastrofski, and David Weisburd, *CompStat in Practice: An In-Depth Analysis of Three Cities* (Washington, D.C.: Police Foundation, 2003).

73 Giuliani and Bratton, *Police Strategy No. 5.*

74 Larry E. Sullivan and Marie Simonetti Rosen, *Encyclopedia of Law Enforcement* (London: Sage, 2004).

75 Giuliani and Bratton, *Police Strategy No. 5.*

76 "Mayor Bloomberg Discusses Crime Reduction Strategies at Citizen's Crime Commission Breakfast," press release, 2005.

77 "Archives of Michael R. Bloomberg," press release, 2002–13.

78 Center for Constitutional Rights, *Stop and Frisk: The Human Impact* (New York: CCR, 2012).

79 Jefferson, "Broken Windows Policing."
80 New York Civil Liberties Union, *NYPD Quarterly Reports* (New York: New York Civil Liberties Union, 2015).
81 "Mayor Michael R. Bloomberg Announces Operation Silent Night," press release, Mayor's Office, 2002. "Mayor Michael R. Bloomberg Announces Operation Spotlight," press release, Mayor's Office, New York, 2002. "Archives of Michael R. Bloomberg."
82 "Mayor Bloomberg Discusses Crime Reduction Strategies."
83 "Mayor Bloomberg Discusses Crime Reduction Strategies."
84 School Safety Agents, *NYPD School Safety Agent Duties and Responsibilities: A Guide for DOE and NYPD Personnel* (New York: NYPD, n.d.).
85 Brian Jordan Jefferson, "From Prisons to Hyperpolicing: Neoliberalism, Carcerality, and Regulative Geographies," in *Historical Geographies of Prisons: Unlocking the Usable Carceral Past,* ed. Karen Morin and Dominique Moran, 185–204 (London: Routledge, 2015).
86 New York City School–Justice Partnership Task Force, *Keeping Kids in School and out of Court: Report and Recommendations* (New York: New York City School–Justice Partnership Task Force, 2013).
87 New York Civil Liberties Union, *Education Interrupted: The Growing Use of Suspensions in New York City's Public Schools* (New York: New York Civil Liberties Union, 2011).
88 Rocco Parascandola, "NYPD Readies for Scan-and-Frisk," *NY Daily News,* January 23, 2013. Rashida Richardson and Jay Stanley, "TSA Tests See-Through Scanners on Public in New York's Penn Station," ACLU, 2018.
89 Craig Uchida, *A National Discussion on Predictive Policing: Defining Our Terms and Mapping Successful Implementation Strategies* (Los Angeles, Calif.: National Institute of Justice, 2009). Ingrid Burrington, "What Amazon Taught the Cops," *Nation,* May 27, 2015.
90 Uchida, *A National Discussion.*
91 John McCarthy et al., "A Proposal for the Dartmouth Summer Research Project on Artificial Intelligence, August 31, 1955," *AI Magazine* 27, no. 4 (2006).
92 Charlie Beck and Colleen McCue, "Predictive Policing: What Can We Learn from Wal-Mart and Amazon about Fighting Crime in a Recession?," *The Police Chief* 76, no. 11 (2009). Kalee Thompson, "The Santa Cruz Experiment," *Popular Science,* November 2011.
93 Elizabeth Flock, "Alum Marshals Data to Fight Chicago Crime," *University of Chicago Magazine,* June 27, 2011, https://www.uchicago.edu/features/20110627_byte_cop/.
94 See, e.g., Priscillia Hunt, Jessica Saunders, and John S. Hollywood, *Evalu-*

ation of the Shreveport Predictive Policing Experiment (Santa Monica, Calif.: RAND Corporation, 2014).

95 D. Kim Rossmo, "Place, Space, and Police Investigations: Hunting Serial Violent Criminals," in *Crime and Place*, ed. John Eck and David Weisburd, 217–36 (Monsey, N.Y.: Criminal Justice Press, 1995).

96 Brian Jordan Jefferson, "Predictable Policing: Predictive Crime Mapping and Geographies of Policing and Race," *Annals of Association of American Geographers* 108, no. 1 (2018): 1–16.

97 Manning, *The Technology of Policing*. Luis Garicano and Paul Heaton, "Information Technology, Organization, and Productivity in the Public Sector: Evidence from Police Departments," *Journal of Labor Economics* 28, no. 1 (2010): 167–201. Jessica Saunders, Priscillia Hunt, and John S. Hollywood, "Predictions Put into Practice: A Quasi-Experimental Evaluation of Chicago's Predictive Policing Pilot," *Journal of Experimental Criminology* 12 (2016): 347–71.

98 Whether measured through dissimilarity, isolation, or interaction indexes, urbanized racial segregation is generally most intense in the very cities that employ predictive law enforcement. John Iceland, Daniel H. Weinberg, and Erika Steinmetz, *Racial and Ethnic Residential Segregation in the United States: 1980–2000* (Washington, D.C.: U.S. Census Bureau, 2002). Milwaukee, Baltimore, and St. Louis have the widest spatial distributions of majoritized and minoritized populations; Baltimore, Chicago, and Milwaukee have the least degree of potential contact between the populations; and in Baltimore, Chicago, and Milwaukee, minorities have the least exposure to majorities.

99 Jerry Ratcliffe and George F. Rentgert, "Near Repeat Patterns in Philadelphia Shootings," *Security Journal* 21 (2008).

100 U.S. Bureau of Labor Statistics, "Local Area Unemployment Statistics 2007–2016," in *Databases, Tables, and Calculators by Subject* (Washington, D.C.: U.S. Bureau of Labor Statistics, 2016).

101 U.S. Department of Labor, *Geographic Profile of Employment and Unemployment, 2008* (Washington, D.C.: U.S. Bureau of Labor Statistics, 2010). U.S. Department of Labor, *Geographic Profile of Employment and Unemployment, 2009* (Washington, D.C.: U.S. Bureau of Labor Statistics, 2010). U.S. Bureau of Labor Statistics, "BLS Spotlight on Statistics: The Recession of 2007–2009," in *Unemployment Demographics* (Washington, D.C.: U.S. Bureau of Labor Statistics, 2012).

102 Kevin Hoffman, "Level of Long-Term Unemployment in Illinois among Highest in Us," *Reboot Illinois*, August 5, 2015.

103 U.S. Census, "Poverty Status in the Past 12 Months," in *American Community Survey* (Washington, D.C.: U.S. Census Bureau, 2012).

104 Teresa L. Córdova, Matthew D. Wilson, and Jackson C. Morsey, *Lost: The Crisis of Jobless and Out of School Teens and Young Adults in Chicago, Illinois and the U.S.* (Chicago: Great Cities Institute, University of Illinois at Chicago, 2014).

105 John Byrne, "Rahm Emanuel Pivots from Disadvantaged Youth to Tech Talk," *Chicago Tribune*, May 19, 2015.

106 Flock, "Alum Marshals Data to Fight Chicago Crime."

107 Bernard Harcourt, *Against Prediction: Profiling, Policing, and Punishing in an Actuarial Age* (Chicago: University of Chicago Press, 2006).

108 Jefferson, "Predictable Policing."

109 By the end of 2012, the rate of long-term (at least twenty-four months) residential housing vacancies per residential address was exponentially higher in Black Belt neighborhoods when compared to the rest of Chicago. West Englewood's rate was 155 percent higher than the city average (2.86 percent), Woodlawn's rate was 180 percent higher, Washington Park's was 246 percent higher, Englewood's was 256 percent higher, and Riverdale's was a perplexing 711 percent higher than the city average. To compound matters, community areas with exorbitant residential vacancies were targeted for disinvestments in an array of public services, including garbage disposal and road repair. The physical disorder stemming from abandonment and disinvestment is particularly acute across South Side neighborhoods, where more than 50 percent of residents reported graffiti and trash as a problem in 2010 (compared to city averages of 21 percent and 27 percent, respectively). See Caterina G. Roman and Carly Knight, *Physical Environment of Public Housing Residents in Two Chicago Developments in Transition* (Washington, D.C.: Urban Institute 2010).

110 U.S. Bureau of Justice Statistics, *Arrest Data Analysis Tool: Offense by Age and Race 1990 to 1999* (Washington, D.C.: U.S. Bureau of Justice Statistics, 2016).

111 CPD, "2009 Annual Report: A Year in Review."

112 Elizabeth E. Joh, "The New Surveillance Discretion: Automated Suspicion, Big Data, and Policing," *Harvard Law and Policy Review* 10 (2016).

113 Saunders et al., "Predictions Put into Practice."

114 David Robinson, "Chicago Police Have Tripled Their Use of a Secret, Computerized 'Heat List,'" *Equal Future*, May 26, 2016.

115 Matt Stroud, "The Minority Report: Chicago's New Police Computer Predicts Crimes, but Is It Racist?," *The Verge*, February 19, 2014.

116 Dick briefly suggests in the story that the mutants were in fact hydrocephalics.

117 Philip K. Dick, *The Minority Report* (New York: Citadel Press Books, 1987), 73.

118 Specifically, the scandal in "The Minority Report" is used by Dick to interrogate the "absolute metaphysics" of precrime methodology from the perspective of individual autonomy. The story points out that the commissioner's access to precrime information provided an opportunity for him to choose an alternative course of action. Making precrime information public, it is suggested, will enable would-be criminals to use their autonomy not to commit crimes.

4. PUNISHMENT IN THE NETWORK FORM

1 Peter M. Brien, *Improving Access to and Integrity of Criminal History Records* (Washington, D.C.: U.S. Department of Justice, 2005). Sarah Esther Lageson, "Digital Punishment's Tangled Web," *Contexts* 15, no. 1 (2016): 22–27.

2 Kevin Kelly, *Out of Control: The New Biology of Machines, Social Systems, and the Economic World* (New York: Basic Books, 1994). Galloway and Thacker, *The Exploit.*

3 Castells, *Rise of Network Society.*

4 "National Crime Information Center Celebrates 40th Birthday," *Government Technology,* January 22, 2007.

5 Federal Bureau of Investigation, "NCIC Turns 50: Centralized Database Continues to Prove Its Value in Fighting Crime," https://www.fbi.gov/news/stories/ncic-turns-50.

6 "National Crime Information Center."

7 Gottschalk shows how this populism eventually helped pave the way for the reinstitution of the death penalty in 1976. Marie Gottschalk, *The Prison and the Gallows: The Politics of Mass Incarceration in America* (Cambridge: Cambridge University Press, 2006).

8 Quotation in Office of Technology Assessment, *An Assessment of Alternatives for a National Computerized Criminal History System* (Washington, D.C.: U.S. Government Printing Office, 1982).

9 Office of Technology Assessment.

10 NLETS Inc., *Final Report for National Law Enforcement Telecommunications Systems Upgrade Project* (Phoenix, Ariz.: Office of Justice Programs, 1977).

11 Sal Perri, "Law Enforcement and the Information Highway," *Compiler* 15, no. 1 (1995/1996): 9.

12 U.S. Bureau of Justice Statistics, *National Criminal History Improvement Program: Fiscal Year 1997 Program Announcement* (Washington, D.C.: U.S. Department of Justice, 1997).

13 Brien, *Improving Access.*

14 Brien.

15 "National Crime Information Center Celebrates 40th Birthday."

16 This aspect of the program to make all criminal justice databases interoperable was spearheaded by the Office of Justice Programs and Georgia Technical Research Institute.

17 Edmund F. McGarrell, Joshua D. Freilich, and Steven Chermak, "Intelligence-Led Policing as a Framework for Responding to Terrorism," *Journal of Contemporary Criminal Justice* 23, no. 2 (2007): 142–58. Jerry Ratcliffe, *Intelligence-Led Policing* (New York: Willan, 2008). "Intelligence-Led Policing and the Problems of Turning Rhetoric into Practice," *Policing and Society* 12 (2002): 53–66.

18 See, e.g., Geoffrey Alan Boyce, "The Rugged Border: Surveillance, Policing and the Dynamic Materiality of the US/Mexico Frontier," *Environment and Planning D: Society and Space* 34, no. 2 (2016): 245–62.

19 Joel A. Tarr, Thomas Finholt, and David Goodman, "The City and the Telegraph: Urban Telecommunications in the Pre-Telephone Era," *Urban History* 14, no. 1 (1987): 38–80.

20 James C. McKinley Jr., "Anti-Crime Plan Will Curb Violence, Commissioner Says," *New York Times,* February 9, 1991.

21 Lee Brown, *Policing New York City in the 1990s: The Strategy for Community Policing* (New York: New York Police Department, 1991).

22 Jerome A. Needle and Renée M. Cobb, *Improving Transit Security* (Washington, D.C.: National Academies Press, 1997).

23 New York Police Department, *Developing the NYPD's Information Technology* (New York: New York Police Department, 2015).

24 Criminal Justice Authority, *Annual Report 2014* (New York: Criminal Justice Authority, 2016).

25 New York Police Department, *Developing the NYPD's Information Technology.*

26 "NYPD Technology: Helping the Finest Keep NYC Safe," *NYPD News,* February 20, 2017.

27 Meredith Patten, Erica Bond, Cecilia Low-Weiner, Quinn O. Hood, Olive Lu, Shannon Tomascak, Darren Agboh, and Preeti Chauhan, *Trends in Marijuana Enforcement in New York State, 1990 to 2017* (New York: John Jay College of Criminal Justice, Data Collaborative for Justice, 2019).

28 Illinois Criminal Justice Information Authority, "Illinois Ranks Fourth in Jail Suicides," *Compiler* 9, no. 2 (1988): 3.

29 "Many 'Rap Sheets' Not Automated, Audit Finds," *Compiler* 6, no. 2 (1985): 3, 8.

30 Kevin Morison, "Technology Wave Breaking over Criminal Justice," *Compiler* 7, no. 3 (1986): 1, 13.

31 Paul Fields, "Illinois House Unanimously Approves Authority's Uniform Disposition Reporting Bill," *Compiler* 4, no. 2 (1983): 3.
32 Ben Zajac, "Buffalo Grove Joins PIMS," *Compiler* 4, no. 2 (1983): 1, 6. Kevin Morison, "Using PIMS in Police Management," *Compiler* 8, no. 4 (1988): 11–13.
33 Maureen Hickey and Ed Kennedy, "Mixed News on Backlogs," *Compiler* 11, no. 2 (1991): 5–6.
34 Ed Kennedy and Maureen Hickey, "Computers for Rural Courts," *Compiler* 11, no. 2 (1991): 11–12. Other technological fixes included computer programs that helped police, prosecutors, and victim advocates determine charges and sentences; closed circuit video feeds from jails were also used so inmates could make court appearances without leaving detention, and crime laboratories to hasten criminal processing.
35 Steve Polilli, "The High-Tech Court of the Future," *Compiler* 13, no. 1 (1993): 12–13.
36 Madeleine Hamlin, "In Chicago, Another Public Housing Experiment: Prisoner Reentry," *CITYLAB*, August 10, 2017, https://www.citylab.com /equity/2017/08/in-chicago-another-public-housing-experiement-pris oner-reentry/535947/.
37 Lynne Mock, "The Impact of Employment Restriction Laws on Illinois' Convicted Felons," Illinois Criminal Justice Information Authority, http:// www.icjia.state.il.us/articles/the-impact-of-employment-restriction-laws -on-illinois-convicted-felons.
38 Illinois Criminal Justice Information Authority, *The 1996 Criminal History Records Audit* (Chicago: State of Illinois, 1997).
39 Illinois Criminal Justice Information Authority, *A Comprehensive Examination of the Illinois Criminal History Records Information (CHRI) System* (Chicago: State of Illinois, 1995).
40 Illinois Criminal Justice Information Authority.
41 "Authority's Computer System Helps Counties Manage Jail Populations," *Compiler* 9, no. 4 (1989): 5. To be specific, it processed arrests that involved class B and higher offenses.
42 "New Fingerprint Detection Techniques Boost Police Effectiveness, Says BJS," *Compiler* 8, no. 2 (1987): 2, 14.
43 "Live-Scan: Fingerprints Go Digital," *Compiler* 13, no. 1 (1993): 4–5.
44 Chris Humble, "Advances in Technology Help Boost the Quality of Electronic Criminal History Reporting," *Trends and Issues* 4, no. 1 (2002): 1–4.
45 Castells, *Rise of Network Society*.
46 Illinois Criminal Justice Information Authority, "Authority Endorses Proposed Chri Act," *Compiler* 4, no. 4 (1984): 1, 6.

47 Jamilah Owens, "Law Allows Public to Obtain Records," *Compiler* 14, no. 1 (1994): 15–16.

48 Matt L. Rodriguez, Together We Can (Chicago: City of Chicago, 1993).

49 Skogan et al., *Policing Smarter through It.*

50 Amy Schuck and Dennis P. Rosenbaum, *Building Trust and a Police-Community Website: An Assessment of the CLEARpath Planning ANF Community Engagement Process* (Chicago: University of Illinois, 2008).

51 Michel Foucault, *Discipline and Punish: The Birth of the Prison* (New York: Vintage Books, 1977), 214.

52 Sarah Gonzalez, "The Trouble with NYPD's Crime Dots," *WNYC News,* March 8, 2016.

53 Samuel Lieberman, "Trying Out CompStat 2.0, the NYPD's Yelp for Crime," *New York Magazine,* February 23, 2016.

54 Matthew Fuller, *Behind the Blip* (New York: Autonomedia, 2003).

55 Chandan Reddy, *Freedom with Violence: Race, Sexuality, and the US State* (Durham, N.C.: Duke University Press, 2011).

56 Ed Mullins, *Peek-a-Boo, We See You Too* (New York: Sergeants Benevolent Association, 2015).

57 Neal Stephenson, *The Diamond Age; or, A Young Lady's Illustrated Primer* (New York: Bantam Books, 1995).

58 Stephenson, 56.

59 Paul Wormeli, *Mitigating Risks in the Application of Cloud Computing in Law Enforcement* (Washington, D.C.: IBM Center for the Business of Government, 2012).

60 Reuben Jonathan Miller and Amanda Alexander, "The Price of Carceral Citizenship: Punishment, Surveillance, and Social Welfare Policy in an Age of Carceral Expansion," *Michigan Journal of Law and Race* 21, no. 291 (2016): 291–314.

61 Alexander Galloway and Eugene Thacker, *The Exploit: A Theory of Networks* (Minneapolis: University of Minnesota Press, 2007).

5. HOW TO PROGRAM A CARCERAL CITY

1 Nigel Thrift, "The Promise of Urban Informatics: Some Speculations," *Environment and Planning A* 46 (2014): 1263–66.

2 Quotation from Katherine McKittrick, "Plantation Futures," *Small Axe: A Caribbean Journal of Criticism* 17, no. 3 (2013): 1–15. See also Katherine McKittrick and Clyde Woods, eds., *Black Geographies and the Politics of Place* (Cambridge, Mass.: South End Press, 2007).

3 Transportation infrastructure, including airports, mass transit turnstiles, parking garages, parking meters, skyways, and toll roads, notably came

under private-sector stewardship. See Philip Ashton, Marc Doussard, and Rachel Weber, "The Financial Engineering of Infrastructure Privatization," *Journal of the American Planning Association* 78, no. 3 (2012): 300–312.

4 Gilmore, *Golden Gulag.*

5 For instance, Siemens targets $8.5 billion in annual revenue from its smart grid of energy, high-voltage transmission cables, turbines, and sensors. See Philip Carter, Bill Rojas, and Mayur Sahni, *Delivering Next-Generation Citizen Services: Assessing the Environmental, Social and Economic Impact of Intelligent X on Future Cities and Communities* (Singapore: IDC, 2011). Anthony Townsend, *Smart Cities: Big Data, Civic Hackers, and the Quest for a New Utopia* (New York: W. W. Norton, 2014).

6 Architectural theorist Keller Easterling describes these projects as aspirations to embed infrastructural operating systems into urban space. Easterling, *Extrastatecraft: The Power of Infrastructure Space* (New York: Verso, 2014).

7 Blake Harris, "Chicago Fusion Center Gives Police New Criminal Investigation Tools," Government Technology, 2008, https://www.govtech.com/dc/articles/Chicago-Fusion-Center-Gives-Police-New.html.

8 Joint Chiefs of Staff, *Joint Vision 2020: America's Military—Preparing for Tomorrow* (Washington, D.C.: U.S. Government Printing Office, 2000).

9 Government Accountability Office, *Secure Border Initiative: Technology Delays Persist and the Impact of Border Fencing Has Not Been Assessed* (Washington, D.C.: Government Accountability Office, 2009).

10 The project included an infrastructure of aerial surveillance, border patrol, CCTV cameras, ground sensors, municipal police, and radar towers. The original ambitions of the $3.7 billion initiative were to establish a megastructure consisting of eighteen hundred towers and spanning six thousand miles of the border zones, which relayed data streams to a central control room in the nation's capital.

11 Esri, *GIS for Real-Time Crime Centers* (Redlands, Calif.: Esri, 2013).

12 Motorola Solutions, *Communication Systems Stop Crime in Its Tracks: Real Time Intelligence Takes Police Beyond Responding, to Prediction and Prevention* (Schaumburg, Ill.: Motorola Solutions Inc., 2015).

13 Walter L. Perry, Brian McInnis, Carter C. Price, Susan C. Smith, and John S. Hollywood, *Predictive Policing: The Role of Crime Forecasting in Law Enforcement Operations* (Santa Monica, Calif.: RAND Corporation, 2013).

14 SkyCop, "Stop Watching Crime. Prevent It.," http://www.skycopinc.com/.

15 Maria Cramer, "Watching from a Distance Police Cameras Form a

Wide Net over Boston Area," http://archive.boston.com/news/local/massachusetts/articles/2010/05/03/net_of_surveillance_cameras_expands_over_boston_and_surrounding_communities/.

16 Juliana Reyes, "Real Time Crime Center: 1 Year after Launch, 24-Hour Support Center Will Move to Delaware Valley Intelligence Center This Spring," *Philly*, February 20, 2013.

17 Information Builders, *Houston Police Department Creates Real-Time Crime Center* (New York: Information Builders, 2012).

18 Laurie Johnson, "HPD Tracks Crime in Real Time," Houston Public Media, 2008.

19 GVR, "IoT Security Market Size Worth $9.88 Billion by 2025 | Cagr: 29.7%," Grand View Research, 2018.

20 Rory Appleton, "Fresno Police Unveil State-of-the-Art Crime Tracking System," *Fresno Bee*, July 7, 2015.

21 David Murphy, "Fighting Crime in Real Time," *PC Magazine*, September 28, 2005.

22 New York Police Department (NYPD), "New York City Police Department Releases Draft of the Public Security Privacy Guidelines for Public Comment," press release, February 25, 2009, http://www.nyc.gov/html/nypd/html/pr/pr_2009_005.shtml.

23 New York Police Department, *Best Practice: Real Time Crime Center: Centralized Crime Data System* (New York: NYPD, 2010).

24 IBM, *IBM Crime Information Warehouse: Unlocking Data to Fight Crime* (Somers, N.Y.: IBM Corporation, 2005).

25 George Joseph and Kenneth Lipp, "IBM NYPD Surveillance Footage to Develop Technology That Lets Police Search by Skin Color," *Intercept*, September 6, 2018.

26 NYPD, "Mayor Bloomberg, Police Commisioner Kelly and MTA Chairman Walder Activate Security Cameras inside Times Square, Penn Station and Grand Central Subway Stations as Part of NYPD's Midtown Manhattan Security Initiative," NYC, September 20, 2010, https://www1.nyc.gov/office-of-the-mayor/news/399-10/mayor-bloomberg-police-commissioner-kelly-mta-chairman-walder-activate-security-cameras-inside#/3.

27 New York State Department of Labor, *Employment in New York State* (Albany: New York State Department of Labor, 2010).

28 Michael Hout and Erin Cumberworth, *The Labor Force and the Great Recession* (Stanford, Calif.: Russell Sage Foundation/Stanford Center on Poverty and Inequality, 2012).

29 Hout and Cumberworth.

30 NYPD, *Developing the NYPD's Information Technology* (New York: City of New York, 2015).

31 Dan Verton, "Cybersecurity: NYPD, Microsoft Launch Domain Awareness System," *Homeland Security Today,* August 13, 2012.
32 NYCHA, "New CCTV Cameras Installed at 31 Developments," *NYCHA
Journal* 46, no. 2 (2016).
33 Gary Mason, "NYPD Set to Completely Overhaul Its Data Systems,"
Police Product Insight, February/March 2016.
34 Kevin D. Haggerty and Richard V. Ericson, eds., *The New Politics of
Surveillance and Visibility* (Toronto: University of Toronto Press, 2007).
David Lyon, *The Electronic Eye: The Rise of Surveillance Society* (Minneapolis: University of Minnesota Press, 1994).
35 Haggerty and Ericson, *New Politics.*
36 Simone Browne, *Dark Matters: On the Surveillance of Blackness* (Durham,
N.C.: Duke University Press, 2015).
37 E. S. Levine et al., "The New York City Police Department's Domain
Awareness System," *Interfaces* 47, no. 1 (2017): 1–109.
38 NYPD, "Developing the NYPD's Information Technology."
39 NYPD.
40 This data mining ethos extended to social media surveillance, as DAS
monitored the social media pages of hundreds of youths it designated
as belonging to "proto-gangs." See NYPD.
41 Joseph Goldstein, "Weekly Police Briefing Offers Snapshot of Department and Its Leader," *New York Times,* February 10, 2013.
42 City Council Public Safety Committee, *Marijuana Possession Arrest, Illegal Searches, and the Summons Court System* (New York: City Council
Public Safety Committee, 2012). Levine et al., "New York City Police
Department's Domain Awareness System."
43 Don Babwin, "Cameras Make Chicago Most Closely Watched U.S. City,"
Associated Press, April 6, 2010.
44 ACLU, "Fusion Centers in Illinois," September 2012, https://www.aclu-il
.org/en/publications/fusion-centers-illinois.
45 Anne Chen, "GIS Fights Crime in Chicago," *EWeek,* May 31, 2004.
46 Harris, "Chicago Fusion Center."
47 ACLU, *Chicago's Video Surveillance Cameras: A Pervasive and Unregulated
Threat to Our Privacy* (Chicago: ACLU of Illinois, 2011).
48 ACLU.
49 Matt Stroud, "Did Chicago's Facial Recognition System Catch Its First
Crook?," *Verge,* August 8, 2014.
50 Daniel Schorn, "We're Watching," CBS, September 5, 2006.
51 Chicago Transit Authority, "CTA Security Camera Network," 2017, https://
www.transitchicago.com/security/.
52 U.S. Department of Labor, *Geographic Profile of Employment and Unemployment, 2008* (Washington, D.C.: U.S. Bureau of Labor Statistics,

234 NOTES TO CHAPTER 5

2010). U.S. Bureau of Labor Statistics, "Local Area Unemployment Statistics 2007–2016," in *Databases, Tables and Calculators by Subject* (Washington, D.C.: U.S. Bureau of Labor Statistics, 2016).

53 Kevin Hoffman, "Level of Long-Term Unemployment in Illinois among Highest in US," *Reboot Illinois*, August 5, 2015.

54 U.S. Census, "Poverty Status in the Past 12 Months," in *American Community Survey* (Washington, D.C.: U.S. Census Bureau, 2012).

55 Neeta Fogg, Paul Harrington, and Ishwar Khatiwada, *A Frayed Connection: Joblessness among Teens in Chicago* (Philadelphia: Drexel University Center for Labor Markets and Policy, 2015). Teresa L. Córdova, Matthew D. Wilson, and Jackson C. Morsey, *Lost: The Crisis of Jobless and Out of School Teens and Young Adults in Chicago, Illinois and the U.S.* (Chicago: Great Cities Institute, University of Illinois at Chicago, 2014).

56 Police Accountability Task Force (PATF), *Recommendations for Reform: Restoring Trust between the Chicago Police and the Communities They Serve* (Chicago: PATF, April 2016), https://chicagopatf.org/wp-content /uploads/2016/04/PATF_Final_Report_4_13_16-1.pdf.

57 PATF.

58 Mayor's Press Office, "Police Department Announces Expansion of Predictive Technology in Chatham and Auburn Gresham," press release, July 25, 2017, https://www.chicago.gov/city/en/depts/mayor/press_room /press_releases/2017/july/PolicePredictiveTech.html.

59 Lucius Couloute and Daniel Kopf, *Out of Prison and Out of Work: Unemployment among Formerly Incarcerated People* (Washington, D.C.: Prison Policy Initiative, 2018).

CONCLUSION

1 Huey P. Newton, "Prison, Where Is Thy Victory?," in *The Huey P. Newton Reader*, ed. David Hilliard and Donald Weise (New York: Seven Stories Press, 2002), 154.

2 President's Task Force on 21st Century Policing, *Final Report of the President's Task Force on 21st Century Policing* (Washington, D.C.: Office of Community Oriented Policing Services, 2015).

3 Jean Baudrillard, *The Spirit of Terrorism* (London: Verso, 2003).

4 Ian Ayres and Jonathan Borowsky, *A Study of Racially Disparate Outcomes in the Los Angeles Police Department* (Los Angeles, Calif.: ACLU, 2008).

5 *Amsterdam News*, September 28, 2012.

6 *New York Times*, June 17, 2012.

7 Chris Bilal, *Huffington Post*, June 18, 2012.

8 Djibril Toure, CPR spokesperson.

9 Alison Flowers, Anna Boisseau, Kari Lydersen, Madison Hopkins, and Rajiv Sinclair, "Chicago's 'Skullcap Crew': Band of Police Accused of Brutality Evade Discipline," *Guardian,* August 3, 2016.

10 PCRG, *Regional Gang Intelligence Database,* ed. Policing in Chicago Research Group (Chicago: University of Chicago, 2019).

INDEX

11; spatialization of, 12, 26–31;
standardization of, 19–20, 24–25,
133–34; tagging of, 135; in U.S.
Censuses, 19, 20, 22; uses of,
9–10; visualization of, 12
criminal justice databases:
carceral, 70–71; criminalized
populations in, 66; extent of, 1;
for inmate management, 70, 71;
interoperable, 147, 179, 228n16;
NCIC, 131–32; networked,
131–32, 133; New York City's,
139–42; nonwhite groups in,
11; prisoner surveys, 90; racial
attributes of, 11; social/spatial
patterns in, 31, 54; software of,
1, 2; spatial analysis of, 122;
standardized, 213n9; state-
managed, 1, 11–12; technological
fixes for, 229n34; temporal
dimensions of, 122; topics
covered in, 1; violence indicators
in, 121
criminal justice system:
calculation/computing in, 17,
40–44; decommodifying, 184;
measurement of crime in, 19;
monitoring technology of, 17–18;
racial state and, 7; service to state,
90–91
criminal justice technology, 2;
development of, 16; information
capital in, 2–3, 137; international,
15; origins of, 2, 3–4; political
economy of, 193; profit in, 4–5;
public subsidizing of, 4; of racial
state, 7–9; reasons for explosion
of, 59. See also technology
criminal psychology, risk
assessment in, 90

criminology: corporatized-
bureaucratized, 56; digital,
67–68; digitized publications for,
68; erasure of criminal justice
system from, 56; hot spot, 53;
knowledge industry of, 56;
mathematical abstraction in, 53,
55; microspaces in, 211n76; near-
repeat theory of, 123; as property
of social space, 56; tautological
reasoning in, 124
criminology, computational:
decontextualization of facts, 56;
false equivalences in, 55; and
marginalized populations, 57;
microscales of, 53; positivism in,
55–56; qualitative differences in,
55; social function of, 53
Czolgosz, Leon: assassination of
McKinley, 26

Daley, Richard M.: anticrime
policies of, 97–98; Gang War of,
104, 106
Daniels, et al. v. the City of New
York (1999), 185–86
Dartmouth Summer Research
Project on Artificial Intelligence
(1956), 120
data: classification of, 10; formal
properties of, 10; political
significance of, 10; racialized,
12–13; visualization of, 170. See
also big data; criminal justice data
data, digital, 4; rows and columns
of, 11; social reality and, 11; in
War on Crime, 2
data, spatial, 52; affecting
insurgencies, 61; from Cook
County Juvenile Court, 29;

criminal justice, 12, 26–31;
federal initiatives for, 64; racial
classification of, 123; in War on
Drugs, 64. *See also* carceral space,
digitized
database management systems:
correctional, 70–71; for pretrial
defendants, 87
databases, relational, 47; transit
authority, *48*
databases, state: of British Hong
Kong, 11–12; nonwhite subjects
in, 205n40
data fusion, in Chicago, 177–81
data mining: corporate, 178;
profit in, 61; for social media
surveillance, 233n40
data production: commodity logics
of, 204n35; social figures in,
10–11
data science, justification of
policing, 2
Davis, Angela Y., 215n25; Critical
Resistance of, 82
de Blasio, Bill, 156
decarceration, 83. *See also*
electronic supervision; Global
Positioning System; parole
decision-making: machine, 121;
urban processes of, 60
*Defective, Dependent, and
Delinquent Classes* (1880), 20
defendants: backlogs of, 87;
digital processing of, 46. *See also*
offenders
deindustrialization, 60; black
dispossession in, 35
Delaware Valley Intelligence
Center, 171–72
Deleuze, Gilles: on social control,
6, 120

Denning Mobile Robotics, Inc.:
robotic prison guards of, 73
Department of Defense:
information management system
of, 44; Planning, Programming,
and Budgeting System, 41
Department of Energy Savannah
River Technology Center,
correctional software of, 77
Department of Homeland Security
(DHS): funding of Chicago
datacenter, 177–78; fusion centers
of, 168; Office for Interoperability
and Compatibility, 155; private
sector partners of, 166; Secure
Border Initiative, 169, 231n10;
Silicon Valley Innovation
Program, 4; Silicon Valley office,
172
Department of Justice: criminal
data of, 20; inmate management
database of, 70; technology use
of, 38
deproletarianization: in New York
City, 33, 95; racialized, 59
Destutt de Tracy, Antoine, 202n25
Detroit, crime datacenter of, 172
Diallo, Amadou: murder of, 185
Dick, Philip K.: "The Minority
Report," 127–28, 227n118
digital theory, political, 192
digitization. *See* carceral state,
digitized
Dimension Data, work with NYPD,
173–74
Dinkins, David, 100, 112; mobile
patrol initiative, 140; Safe Streets
program, 101
dissidents, political: incarceration
of, 183
DNA, databases of, 12–13

High Performance Computing Act
(U.S., 1991), 168
Hill, Harland, 49
Hinton, Elizabeth, 36
Hitch, Charles J., 41
Hoffman, Frederick L., 37, 123;
Race Traits, 22, *23*, 24
Hollerith, Herman: Chicago
World's Fair prize, 27;
electromechanical tabulating
machine of, 20, *21*, 22, 26, 29–30,
47
homo economicus, European,
202n24
Hong Kong, British: state databases
of, 11–12
Hoover, John Edgar, 32
hot spot policing, 68; in Chicago,
104; matrices of, 124; NYPD's,
116. *See also* heat lists
Housing Act (U.S., 1949), 34
housing markets, redlining in, 34
Houston Police Department,
surveillance infrastructure of, 172
Hughes Aircraft Company, criminal
justice data of, 44
human dronification, 155–56
Human Rights Watch, on drug
arrests, 87
hypercarceralization, 181–82

IBM Gateway Inc., DNA database
of, 12–13
Ice T, "Cop Killer," 64
I-CLEAR network, 154. *See also*
Citizen and Law Enforcement
Analysis and Reporting (CLEAR)
system
ICON Software Corporation, 87
IIT Research Institute: Law
Enforcement Science and
Technology Center, 40;

semiautomated dispatch system
of, 44–45
Illinois: Automated Disposition
Reporting Users Group,
150–51; Automated Fingerprint
Identification System, 150;
carceral population of, 145, 147;
computerized risk instruments
of, 17; correctional databases
of, 145, 147; court backlog in,
148; Criminal History Record
Improvement Program, 149;
criminal justice networks
in, 145–51; criminal justice
telecommunications systems,
149; fusion centers of, 177–81; jail
suicides, 145; judiciary databases
of, 148–49; parole programs,
161; Sentencing Policy Advisory
Council, 149; teen unemployment
in, 180
Illinois Correctional Institution
Management Information System
(CIMIS), 71, 149–50
Illinois Criminal History Records
Information (CHRI) System, 151;
flowchart, *146*
Illinois Criminal Justice
Information Authority (ICJIA),
103, 145, 147; *Criminal Justice
Internet Applications Online
Handbook*, 150; on felony
callbacks, 149; on judicial
technology, 86, 148
Illinois Information Authority:
Criminal History Records
Information (CHRI) Act, 151; on
police automation, 106
Illinois state government:
Department of Corrections,
161; Department of Housing
and Urban Development, 149;

192; surveillance, 169–70; of War
on Terror, 166
infrastructures, urban: carceral
power in, 13–15; for criminal
justice, 182; public safety,
166; of smart cities, 3; social
management, 116; transportation,
230n3
inmate management: carceral
technology, 70, 71, 73, 75–79;
criminal justice databases, 70,
71; psychological, 76; release
in, 79; standardized, 71; threat
assessment technology, 77;
tracking systems, 74. See also
carceral technology; correctional
apparatus; incarceration
inmate records: racialized, 23; in
U.S. census, 19
inmates: low-risk, 80; sociological
categories of, 78
Institute for Housing Studies,
124–25
Institute for Intergovernmental
Research, federal funding for, 64
insurgencies: black, 35–36;
against correctional facilities,
70; microspaces of, 64; of 1960s,
35–36, 45, 62
Integrated Justice Information
Systems Institute, 137–38, 160
International Association for
Criminal Identification, 33
International Association of Chiefs
of Police (IACP): on cloud
computing, 160–61; Criminal
Intelligence Sharing Summit, 138;
data of, 32; networking of, 135; on
standardized data, 24–25
International Association of
Chiefs of Police/Motorola

Webber Seavey Award in Law
Enforcement, 4
International Association of
Directors of Law Enforcement
Standards and Training, federal
funding for, 64
International Business Machines
(IBM), 3; Center for Exploratory
Studies, 46; companies preceding,
22; crime-forecasting software,
123; police computerization
programs, 45; St. Louis Police
Department's use of, 51–52
International Conference on
Computer Communication (first,
1972), 133
International Data Corporation,
crime reduction claims of, 1
International Data Group, Grand
CIO Enterprise Value Award, 4
International Symposium on
Wearable Computing, 67
internet: applications for
punishment, 129; inclusionist
ideal of, 153; multiple criminal
justice agencies using, 135. See
also networks, criminal justice
Internet of Things (IoT), 159;
biomedical sensors of, 162;
carceral management through,
13–14, 161–62; carceral state
and, 182; infiltration of marginal
communities, 173; infrastructural
logic of, 176; security industry of,
172; in urban society, 166

Jackson, George: Soledad Brother,
70
Jackson, Jesse: National Rainbow
Coalition of, 98
Jacobs, Jane, 211n71

Johnson, Lyndon, 184; War on Crime of, 2, 36, 42
Johnson-Reed Act (U.S., 1924), 31
judicial technology, 46–47, 86–91; algorithms of, 89, 90; artificial intelligence, 86–87; corporations marketing, 89–90; for criminal psychology, 90; digital signing, 89; prisoner survey data, 90; prosecutorial, 87–88; touchscreen, 88; transcript systems, 87; transmission of evidence, 89; trial presentation applications, 89; video, 88, 89. See also technology, digital
judiciary: backlogs of defendants, 87; communication systems use, 46–47; computerization of, 86–91
juvenile delinquency, spatial model of, 29–31
Juvenile Delinquency and Youth Offenses Control Act (U.S., 1961), 36

Kalven v. Chicago (Illinois Court of Appeals), 190
Kelling, George L.: broken windows theory, 112–13, 120
Kelly, Raymond, 169
Kennedy, Edward, 38
Kennedy, John F., 36
Kilgore, James, 85
King, Rodney, 64
knowledge: digitization of, 7–8; discovery in database techniques, 61; human environmental, 67; industries, urban, 61; state, 7–8
knowledge, criminological: microscales of, 56; statistics in, 24
knowledge production: police, 51;

spatial, 62; in War on Crime, 17
Kryder, Mark, 59, 213n1

labor, black male: decrease in, 34. See also unemployment
labor, ethnoracialized divisions of, 28–29
labor forces: downsized, 60; loss of utility, 95
Lambroso, Cesare, 27
landscapes, prisonized, 94
Laney, Doug, 204n35
latinx population: antagonism with police, 156; chronic offenders, 171; gang members, 110; incarceration of, 7, 14, 69; neglect of, 34; unemployment, 124
Law Enforcement Assistance Act (U.S., 1965), 38, 51, 211n72
Law Enforcement Assistance Administration (LEAA), 47; criminal justice network funding, 134; digital computing programs of, 38, 39, 43; fingerprinting system of, 45; systems analysis use, 41, 42–43; technology firms and, 43–50; in War on Crime, 87
Law Enforcement Online: education modules of, 135–36; Virtual Command Center, 136
LEA Data Technologies and Target Solutions, 135
Lefebvre, Henri, 65
Lessig, Lawrence, 201n17
Linnaeus, Carl: biological tables of, 22
Lockheed Missiles and Space Company, 44
long-term evolution (LTE) wireless networks, 155, 170

in UCR system, 27. *See also* infrastructures, urban; space, urban
Urobuchi, Gen: *Psycho-Pass*, 84
U.S. Attorney's Office: geographical informational technology, 88; mapping database, 90
U.S. Defense Mapping Agency, 64

Van Dyke, Jason, 180
videoconferencing, 88
Vietnam War, digital mapping in, 64
Violent Crime Control and Law Enforcement Act (U.S., 1994), 67, 97, 100–101
Vitale, Alex S., 97
Voekler, Carl, 46
Vollmer, August, 26

War on Crime: in Chicago, 125; correctional apparatus of, 49; cost of, 42; digital computing in, 37–43, 51, 193; digital data in, 2; geographically concentrated, 53; incarceration in, 215n25; knowledge production in, 17; LEAA in, 87; NYPD in, 95, 114; political prisoners of, 87; positivist science in, 42; and Posse Comitatus Act, 202n27; racialized criminality of, 50; Reagan's, 53, 87; spatial representations in, *54*; technological innovation in, 8, 16
War on Drugs: carceral state in, 87; in Chicago, 103, 110, 126; computer use in, 41; digital data

in, 2; judicial computerization in, 88; judicial inefficiency during, 86; knowledge production in, 17; mobile computing during, 66; under Nixon, 36, 211n76; politics of punishment in, 133; racialized, 126; Reagan's, 64, 103
War on Terror: digital infrastructure of, 166; law enforcement databases and, 138; protection of economy, 168; surveillance network of, 168, 169–70
warrants, computerized systems for, 49
wealth, urban: securitized centers of, 60
Web 3.0, natural language in, 161
Weiner, Norbert, 203n33
welfare rights movement, data analytics and, 202n23
Wilson, James Q.: broken windows theory of, 112–13
Wilson, O. W., 37
Wilson, William Julius, 60
women, incarceration of, 69
Woodley Company: car locator devices, 44; dispatch system, 45
Woods, Clyde, 166
World Economic Forum, 2
World War II, technological advancement in, 33–34

Young, Malcolm C., 82

Zimbardo, Philip, 113

Brian Jefferson is associate professor of geography and geographic information science and O'Connell Scholar in the College of Liberal Arts and Sciences at the University of Illinois Urbana–Champaign.